Memory Management

Algorithms and Implementation in C/C++

by
Bill Blunden

Wordware Publishing, Inc.

Library of Congress Cataloging-in-Publication Data

Blunden, Bill, 1969-
    Memory management: algorithms and implementation in C/C++ / by Bill Blunden.
       p. cm.
    Includes bibliographical references and index.
    ISBN 1-55622-347-1
    1. Memory management (Computer science)   2. Computer algorithms.
    3. C (Computer program language)   4. C++ (Computer program
    language)   I. Title.
    QA76.9.M45 .B558 2002
    005.4'35--dc21   2002012447
                                        CIP

© 2003, Wordware Publishing, Inc.

All Rights Reserved

2320 Los Rios Boulevard
Plano, Texas 75074

No part of this book may be reproduced in any form or by
any means without permission in writing from
Wordware Publishing, Inc.

Printed in the United States of America

ISBN 1-55622-347-1
10 9 8 7 6 5 4 3 2 1
0208

Product names mentioned are used for identification purposes only and may be trademarks of their respective companies.

All inquiries for volume purchases of this book should be addressed to Wordware Publishing, Inc., at the above address. Telephone inquiries may be made by calling:

(972) 423-0090

This book is dedicated to Rob, Julie, and Theo.

And also to David M. Lee
"I came to learn physics, and I got Jimmy Stewart"

Table of Contents

Acknowledgments xi
Introduction xiii

Chapter 1   **Memory Management Mechanisms. 1**
     Mechanism Versus Policy 1
     Memory Hierarchy 3
     Address Lines and Buses. 9
     Intel Pentium Architecture 11
         Real Mode Operation. 14
         Protected Mode Operation. 18
             Protected Mode Segmentation 19
             Protected Mode Paging 26
             Paging as Protection. 31
             Addresses: Logical, Linear, and Physical. 33
             Page Frames and Pages 34
         Case Study: Switching to Protected Mode 35
     Closing Thoughts 42
     References. 43

Chapter 2   **Memory Management Policies. 45**
     Case Study: MS-DOS 46
         DOS Segmentation and Paging 46
         DOS Memory Map 47
         Memory Usage 49
         Example: A Simple Video Driver 50
         Example: Usurping DOS 52
         Jumping the 640KB Hurdle 56
     Case Study: MMURTL 59
         Background and Design Goals. 60
         MMURTL and Segmentation 61
         Paging Variations 63
         MMURTL and Paging 64

Table of Contents

Memory Allocation 66
Case Study: Linux 67
   History and MINIX 67
   Design Goals and Features 68
   Linux and Segmentation 69
   Linux and Paging 72
      Three-Level Paging 72
      Page Fault Handling 76
   Memory Allocation 76
   Memory Usage 81
   Example: Siege Warfare 82
   Example: Siege Warfare, More Treachery 87
Case Study: Windows 92
   Historical Forces 92
   Memory Map Overview 96
   Windows and Segmentation 99
      Special Weapons and Tactics 99
      Crashing Windows with a Keystroke 102
      Reverse Engineering the GDT 102
   Windows and Paging 105
      Linear Address Space Taxonomy 105
      Musical Chairs for Pages 106
      Memory Protection 108
      Demand Paging 109
   Memory Allocation 110
   Memory Usage 114
   Turning Off Paging 117
   Example: Things That Go Thunk in the Night 118
Closing Thoughts 122
References 123
   Books and Articles 123
   Web Sites 125

Chapter 3   **High-Level Services 127**
View from 10,000 Feet 127
Compiler-Based Allocation 129
   Data Section 132
   Code Section 134
   Stack 136
      Activation Records 138
      Scope 144

Table of Contents

    Static or Dynamic? 150
  Heap Allocation 151
    System Call Interface 151
    The Heap 156
      Manual Memory Management 157
      Example: C Standard Library Calls 158
      Automatic Memory Management 160
      Example: The BDW Conservative Garbage Collector
      161
      Manual Versus Automatic? 164
  The Evolution of Languages 168
    Case Study: COBOL 171
    Case Study: FORTRAN 177
    Case Study: Pascal 181
    Case Study: C 184
    Case Study: Java 192
      Language Features 192
      Virtual Machine Architecture 194
      Java Memory Management 196
  Memory Management: The Three-layer Cake 202
  References 204

Chapter 4 — Manual Memory Management 207

  Replacements for `malloc()` and `free()` 207
  System Call Interface and Porting Issues 208
  Keep It Simple…Stupid! 211
  Measuring Performance 212
    The Ultimate Measure: Time 212
      ANSI and Native Time Routines 213
      The Data Distribution: Creating Random Variates . 215
    Testing Methodology 219
  Indexing: The General Approach 224
  `malloc()` Version 1: Bitmapped Allocation 224
    Theory 224
    Implementation 226
      tree.cpp 227
      bitmap.cpp 232
      memmgr.cpp 236
      mallocV1.cpp 239
      perform.cpp 241
      driver.cpp 241

Table of Contents

Tests 242
Trade-Offs 247
`malloc()` Version 2: Sequential Fit 248
Theory 249
Implementation 251
   memmgr.cpp 251
   mallocV2.cpp 260
   driver.cpp 261
Tests 262
Trade-Offs 264
`malloc()` Version 3: Segregated Lists 265
Theory 265
Implementation 266
   memmgr.cpp 267
   mallocV3.cpp 274
Tests 275
Trade-Offs 279
Performance Comparison 279

Chapter 5 **Automatic Memory Management** **281**
Garbage Collection Taxonomy 281
`malloc()` Version 4: Reference Counting 283
Theory 283
Implementation 284
   driver.cpp 285
   mallocV4.cpp 287
   perform.cpp 288
   memmgr.cpp 289
Tests 299
Trade-Offs 302
`malloc()` Version 5: Mark-Sweep 304
Theory 304
Implementation 307
   driver.cpp 307
   mallocV5.cpp 309
   perform.cpp 311
   memmgr.cpp 312
Tests 325
Trade-Offs 330
Performance Comparison 332
Potential Additions 332

Table of Contents

   Object Format Assumptions 333
   Variable Heap Size 335
   Indirect Addressing 335
   Real-Time Behavior 337
   Life Span Characteristics 338
   Multithreaded Support 339

Chapter 6 **Miscellaneous Topics** **343**
   Suballocators 343
   Monolithic Versus Microkernel Architectures 348
   Closing Thoughts 351

   Index 355

Acknowledgments

Publishing a book is an extended process that involves a number of people. Writing the final manuscript is just a small part of the big picture. This section is dedicated to all the people who directly, and indirectly, lent me their help.

First and foremost, I would like to thank Jim Hill of Wordware Publishing for giving me the opportunity to write a book and believing in me. I would also like to extend thanks to Wes Beckwith and Beth Kohler. Wes, in addition to offering constant encouragement, does a great job of putting up with my e-mails and handling the various packages that I send. Beth Kohler, who performed the incredible task of reading my first book for Wordware in a matter of days, has also been invaluable.

I first spoke with Barry Brey back in the mid-1990s when I became interested in protected mode programming. He has always taken the time to answer my questions and offer his insight. Barry wrote *the* first book on the Intel chip set back in 1984. Since then, he has written well over 20 books. His current textbook on Intel's IA32 processors is in its sixth edition. This is why I knew I had to ask Barry to be the technical editor for this book. Thanks, Barry.

> "Look, our middleware even runs on that little Windows NT piece of crap."
> — George Matkovitz

> "Hey, who was the %& ^ $ son of a &*$# who wrote this optimized load of . . . oh, it was me."
> — Mike Adler

Mike Adler and George Matkovitz are two old fogeys who worked at Control Data back when Seymour Cray kicked the tar out of IBM. George helped to implement the world's first message-passing operating system at Control Data. Mike also worked on a number of groundbreaking system software projects. I met these two codgers while performing R&D for an ERP vendor in the Midwest. I hadn't noticed how much these engineers had influenced me until I left

Acknowledgments

Minnesota for California. It was almost as though I had learned through osmosis. A lot of my core understanding of software and the computer industry in general is based on the bits of hard-won advice and lore that these gentlemen passed on to me. I distinctly remember walking into Mike's office and asking him, "Hey Mike, how do you build an operating system?"

I would also like to thank Frank Merat, a senior professor at Case Western Reserve University. Frank has consistently shown interest in my work and has offered his support whenever he could. There is no better proving ground for a book than an established research university.

Finally, I would like to thank SonicWALL, Inc. for laying me off and giving me the opportunity to sit around and think. The days I spent huddled with my computers were very productive.

Introduction

"Pay no attention to the man behind the curtain."
— *The Wizard of Oz*

There are a multitude of academic computer science texts that discuss memory management. They typically devote a chapter or less to the subject and then move on. Rarely are concrete, machine-level details provided, and actual source code is even scarcer. When the author is done with his whirlwind tour, the reader tends to have a very limited idea about what is happening behind the curtain. This is no surprise, given that the nature of the discussion is rampantly ambiguous. Imagine trying to appreciate Beethoven by having someone read the sheet music to you or experience the Mona Lisa by reading a description in a guidebook.

This book is different. Very different.

In this book, I am going to pull the curtain back and let you see the little man operating the switches and pulleys. You may be excited by what you see, or you may feel sorry that you decided to look. But as Enrico Fermi would agree, knowledge is always better than ignorance.

This book provides an in-depth look at memory subsystems and offers extensive source code examples. In cases where I do not have access to source code (i.e., Windows), I offer advice on how to gather forensic evidence, which will nurture insight. While some books only give readers a peak under the hood, this book will give readers a power drill and allow them to rip out the transmission. The idea behind this is to allow readers to step into the garage and get their hands dirty.

My own experience with memory managers began back in the late 1980s when Borland's nifty Turbo C 1.0 compiler was released. This was my first taste of the C language. I can remember using a disassembler to reverse engineer library code in an attempt to see how the `malloc()` and `free()` standard library functions

Introduction

operated. I don't know how many school nights I spent staring at an 80x25 monochrome screen, deciphering hex dumps. It was tough going and not horribly rewarding (but I was curious, and I couldn't help myself). Fortunately, I have done most of the dirty work for you. You will conveniently be able to sidestep all of the hurdles and tedious manual labor that confronted me.

If you were like me and enjoyed taking your toys apart when you were a child to see how they worked, then this is the book for you. So lay your computer on a tarpaulin, break out your compilers, and grab an oil rag. We're going to take apart memory management subsystems and put them back together. Let the dust fly where it may!

Historical Setting

In the late 1930s, a group of scholars arrived at Bletchley Park in an attempt to break the Nazis' famous Enigma cipher. This group of codebreakers included a number of notable thinkers, like Tommy Flowers and Alan Turing. As a result of the effort to crack Enigma, the first electronic computer was constructed in 1943. It was named *Colossus* and used thermionic valves (known today as *vacuum tubes*) for storing data. Other vacuum tube computers followed. For example, *ENIAC* (electronic numerical integrator and computer) was built by the U.S. Army in 1945 to compute ballistic firing tables.

NOTE Science fiction aficionados might enjoy a movie called *Colossus: The Forbin Project*. It was made in 1969 and centers around Colossus, a supercomputer designed by a scientist named Charles Forbin. Forbin convinces the military that they should give control of the U.S. nuclear arsenal to Colossus in order to eliminate the potential of human error accidentally starting World War III. The movie is similar in spirit to Stanley Kubrick's *2001: A Space Odyssey*, but without the happy ending: Robot is built, robot becomes sentient, robot runs amok. I was told that everyone who has ever worked at Control Data has seen this movie.

The next earth-shaking development arrived in 1949 when ferrite (iron) core memory was invented. Each bit of memory was made of a small, circular iron magnet. The value of the bit switched from "1" to "0" by using electrical wires to magnetize the circular loops in one of two possible directions. The first computer to utilize ferrite core memory was IBM's 705, which was put into production in 1955. Back in those days, 8KB of memory was considered a huge piece of real estate.

Everything changed once transistors became the standard way to store bits. The transistor was presented to the world in 1948 when Bell Labs decided to go public with its new device. In 1954, Bell Labs constructed the first transistor-based computer. It was named *TRADIC* (TRAnsistorized DIgital Computer). TRADIC was much smaller and more efficient than vacuum tube computers. For example, ENIAC required 1,000 square feet and caused power outages in Philadelphia when it was turned on. TRADIC, on the other hand, was roughly three cubic feet in size and ran on 100 watts of electricity.

NOTE Before electronic computers became a feasible alternative, heavy mathematical computation relied on *human computers*. Large groups of people would be assembled to carry out massive numerical algorithms. Each person would do a part of a computation and pass it on to someone else. This accounts for the prevalence of logarithm tables in mathematical references like the one published by the Chemical Rubber Company (CRC). Slide rules and math tables were standard fare before the rise of the digital calculator.

ASIDE

"After 45 minutes or so, we'll see that the results are obvious."

— David M. Lee

I have heard Nobel laureates in physics, like Dave Lee, complain that students who rely too heavily on calculators lose their mathematical intuition. To an extent, Dave is correct. Before the dawn of calculators, errors were more common, and developing a feel for numeric techniques was a useful way to help catch errors when they occurred.

During the Los Alamos project, a scientist named Dick Feynman ran a massive human computer. He once mentioned that the performance and accuracy of his group's computations were often more a function of his ability to motivate people. He would sometimes assemble people into teams and have them compete against each other. Not only was this a good idea from the standpoint of making things more interesting, but it was also an effective technique for catching discrepancies.

Introduction

In 1958, the first integrated circuit was invented. The inventor was a fellow named Jack Kilby, who was hanging out in the basement of Texas Instruments one summer while everyone else was on vacation. A little over a decade later, in 1969, Intel came out with a 1 kilobit memory chip. After that, things really took off. By 1999, I was working on a Windows NT 4.0 workstation (service pack 3) that had 2GB of SDRAM memory.

The general trend you should be able to glean from the previous discussion is that memory components have solved performance requirements by getting smaller, faster, and cheaper. The hardware people have been able to have their cake and eat it too. However, the laws of physics place a limit on how small and how fast we can actually make electronic components. Eventually, nature itself will stand in the way of advancement. Heisenberg's Uncertainty Principle, shown below, is what prevents us from building infinitely small components.

$$\Delta x \Delta p \geq (h/4\pi)$$

For those who are math-phobic, I will use Heinsenberg's own words to describe what this equation means:

> "The more precisely the position is determined, the less precisely the momentum is known in this instant, and vice versa."

In other words, if you know exactly where a particle is, then you will not be able to contain it because its momentum will be huge. Think of this like trying to catch a tomato seed. Every time you try to squeeze down and catch it, the seed shoots out of your hands and flies across the dinner table into Uncle Don's face.

Einstein's General Theory of Relativity is what keeps us from building infinitely fast components. With the exception of black holes, the speed limit in this universe is 3×10^8 meters per second. Eventually, these two physical limits are going to creep up on us.

When this happens, the hardware industry will have to either make larger chips (in an effort to fit more transistors in a given area) or use more efficient algorithms so that they can make better use of existing space. My guess is that relying on better algorithms will be the cheaper option. This is particularly true with regard to memory management. Memory manipulation is so frequent and crucial to performance that designing better memory management subsystems will take center stage in the future. This will make the time spent reading this book a good investment.

Impartial Analysis

In this book, I try very hard to offer memory management solutions without taking sides. I have gone to great lengths to present an unbiased discussion. This is important because it is extremely tempting to champion a certain memory management algorithm (especially if you invented it). There are some journal authors who would have you believe that their new algorithm is a panacea to cure the ills of the world. I do not have the ulterior motives of a college professor. I am here to offer you a set of tools and then let you decide how best to use them. In this book, I will present you with different techniques and try to point out the circumstances in which they perform well.

The question "Which is the best memory management algorithm?" is very similar in spirit to any of the following questions:

"Which operating system is the best?"
"Which programming language is the best?"
"Which data structure is the best?"
"Which type of screwdriver is the best?"

I can recall asking a program manager at Eaton Corp., John Schindler, what the best operating system was. John was managing at least a dozen different high-end platforms for Eaton, and I thought he would know. I was expecting him to come right back with a quick answer like: "Oh, OpenBSD is the best." What actually happened was something that surprised me. He looked at me for a minute, as if the question was absurd. Then he smiled and said, "Well, it really depends on what you're going to use the machine for. I use Solaris for networking, HP-UX for app servers, AIX to talk to our mainframe, NT for mail, ... "

The truth is there is no "best" solution. Most solutions merely offer certain trade-offs. In the end, the best tool to use will depend upon the peculiarities of the problem you are trying to solve.

This is a central theme that appears throughout the domain of computer science. Keep it in the back of your mind, like some sort of Buddhist mantra:

"There is no best solution, Grasshopper, only trade-offs."

For example, linked lists and arrays can both represent a linear set of items. With a linked list, you get easy manipulation at the expense of speed. Adding an element to a linked list is as easy as modifying a couple of pointers. However, to find a given list element, you may have to traverse the entire list manually until you find it. Conversely, with an array, you get access speed at the expense of flexibility. Accessing an array element is as easy as adding an integer to a base address, but adding and deleting array elements requires a lot of costly shifting. If your code is not going to do a lot of list modification, an array is the best choice. If your code will routinely add and delete list members, a linked list is the better choice. It all depends upon the context of the problem.

Audience

This book is directed toward professional developers and students who are interested in discovering how memory is managed on production systems. Specifically, engineers working on PC or embedded operating systems may want to refresh their memory or take a look at alternative approaches. If this is the case, then this book will serve as a repository of algorithms and software components that you can apply to your day-to-day issues.

Professionals who design and construct development tools will also find this book useful. In general, development tools fall into the class of online transaction processing (OLTP) programs. When it comes to OLTP apps, pure speed is the name of the game. As such, programming language tools, like compilers, often make use of suballocators to speed up the performance of the code that manipulates their symbol table.

With regard to compiling large software programs consisting of millions of lines of code, this type of suballocator-based optimization can mean the difference between waiting for a few minutes and waiting for a few hours. Anyone who mucks around with suballocators will find this book indispensable.

Software engineers who work with virtual machines will also be interested in the topics that I cover. The Java virtual machine is famous for its garbage collection facilities. In this book I explore several automatic memory management techniques and also provide a couple of concrete garbage collection implementations in C++.

Finally, this book also targets the curious. There is absolutely nothing wrong with being curious. In fact, I would encourage it. You may be an application developer who has used memory management facilities countless times in the past without taking the time to determine how they really work. You may also have nurtured an interest that you have had to repress due to deadlines and other priorities. This book will offer such engineers an opportunity to indulge their desire to see what is going on under the hood.

Organization

This book is divided into six chapters. I will start from the ground up and try to provide a comprehensive, but detailed, view of memory management fundamentals. Because of this, each chapter builds on what has been presented in the previous one. Unless you are a memory management expert, the best way to read this book is straight through.

Chapter 1 – Memory Management Mechanisms

The first chapter presents a detailed look at the machinery that allows memory management to take place. Almost every operating system in production takes advantage of facilities that are provided by the native processor. This is done primarily for speed, since pushing repetitive bookkeeping down to the hardware benefits overall performance. There have been attempts by some engineers to track and protect memory strictly outside of the hardware. But speed is key to the hardware realm, and this fact always forces such attempts off of the playing field. The end result is that understanding how memory management is performed means taking a good look at how memory hardware functions.

Chapter 2 – Memory Management Policies

Computer hardware provides the mechanism for managing memory, but the policy decisions that control how this mechanism is applied are dictated by the operating system and its system call interface to user programs. In this chapter, the memory management components provided by the operating system are analyzed and dissected. This will necessarily involve taking a good, hard look at the internals of production operating systems like Linux and Windows.

In general, hardware always provides features that are ahead of the software that uses it. For example, Intel's Pentium provides four distinct layers of memory protection. Yet, I could not find a single

Introduction

operating system that took advantage of all four layers. All the systems that I examined use a vastly simplified two-layer scheme.

 NOTE The relationship between hardware and software is analogous to the relationship between mathematics and engineering. Mathematics tends to be about 50 years ahead of engineering, which means that it usually takes about 50 years for people to find ways to apply the theorems and relationships that the mathematicians uncover.

Chapter 3 – High-Level Services

Above the hardware and the cocoon of code that is the operating system are the user applications. Because they are insulated from the inner workings of the operating system, applications have an entirely different way to request, use, and free memory. The manner in which a program utilizes memory is often dependent on the language in which the program was written. This chapter looks at memory management from the perspective of different programming languages. This chapter also serves as a launch pad for the next two chapters by presenting an overview of memory management at the application level.

Chapter 4 – Manual Memory Management

In Chapter 4, a number of manual memory management algorithms are presented in explicit detail. The algorithms are presented in theory, implemented in C++, and then critiqued in terms of their strengths and weaknesses. The chapter ends with suggestions for improvements and a look at certain hybrid approaches.

Chapter 5 – Automatic Memory Management

In Chapter 5, a number of automatic memory management algorithms are examined. The algorithms are presented in theory, implemented in C++, and then critiqued in terms of their strengths and weaknesses. A significant amount of effort is invested in making this discussion easy to follow and keeping the reader focused on key points. Two basic garbage collectors are provided and compared to other, more advanced collection schemes.

Chapter 6 – Miscellaneous Topics

This chapter covers a few special-purpose subjects that were difficult to fit into the previous five chapters. For example, I describe how to effectively implement a suballocator in a compiler. I also take a look at how memory management subsystems can be made to provide dynamic algorithm support at run time via a microkernel architecture.

Approach

When it comes to learning something complicated, like memory management, I believe that the most effective way is to examine a working subsystem. On the other hand, it is easy to become lost in the details of a production memory manager. Contemporary memory managers, like the one in Linux, are responsible for keeping track of literally hundreds of run-time quantities. Merely tracking the subsystem's execution path can make one dizzy. Hence, a balance has to be struck between offering example source code that is high quality and also easy to understand. I think I have done a sufficient job of keeping the learning threshold low without sacrificing utility.

NOTE I am more than aware of several books where the author is more interested in showing you how clever he is instead of actually trying to teach a concept. When at all possible, I try to keep my examples relatively simple and avoid confusing syntax. My goal is to instruct, not to impress you so much that you stop reading.

In this book, I will follow a fairly standard three-step approach:

1. Theory
2. Practice
3. Analysis

I will start each topic by presenting a related background theory. Afterwards, I will offer one or more source code illustrations and then end each discussion with an analysis of trade-offs and alternatives. I follow this methodology throughout the entire book.

Introduction

Typographical Conventions

Words and phrases will appear in *italics* in this book for two reasons:
- To place emphasis
- When defining a term

The `courier` font will be used to indicate that text is one of the following:
- Source code
- An address in memory
- Console input/output
- A filename or extension

Numeric values appear throughout this book in a couple of different formats. Hexadecimal values are indicated by either prefixing them with "`0x`" or appending "`H`" to the end.

For example:

```
0xFF02
0FF02H
```

The C code that I include will use the former notation, and the assembler code that I include will use the latter format.

Binary values are indicated by appending the letter "`B`" to the end. For example:

```
0110111B
```

Prerequisites

"C makes it easy to shoot yourself in the foot; C++ makes it harder, but when you do, it blows away your whole leg."
— Bjarne Stroustrup

In this book, I have primarily used three different development languages:
- 80x86 assembler
- C
- C++

For some examples, I had no other choice but to rely on assembly language. There are some things, like handling processor interrupts, that can only be fleshed out using assembler. This is one reason why mid-level languages, like C, provide syntactic facilities for inline assembly code. If you look at the Linux source code, you will see a variety of inline assembly code snippets. If at all possible, I wrapped my assembly code in C. However, you can't always do this.

Learning assembly language may seem like an odious task, but there are several tangible and significant rewards. Assembly language is just a mnemonic representation of machine instructions. When you have a complete understanding of a processor's assembly language, including its special "privileged" instructions, you will also have a fairly solid understanding of how the machine functions and what its limitations are. In addition, given that compilers generate assembly code, or at least spit it out in a listing file, you will also be privy to the inner workings of development tools.

In short, knowing assembly language is like learning Latin. It may not seem immediately useful, but it is...just give it time.

I use C early in the book for small applications when I felt like I could get away with it. Most of the larger source code examples in this book, however, are written in C++. If you don't know C or C++, you should pick up one of the books mentioned in the "References" section at the end of the Introduction. After a few weeks of cramming, you should be able to follow my source code examples.

I think C++ is an effective language for implementing memory management algorithms because it offers a mixture of tools. With C++, you can manipulate memory at a very low, bit-wise level and invoke inline assembly code when needed. You can also create high-level constructs using the object-oriented language features in C++. Encapsulation, in particular, is a compiler-enforced language feature that is crucial for maintaining large software projects.

NOTE At times, you may notice that I mix C libraries and conventions into my C++ source code. I do this, most often, for reasons related to performance. For example, I think that C's printf() is much more efficient than cout.

C++ is often viewed by engineers, including myself, as C with a few object-oriented bells and whistles added on. Bjarne Stroustrup, the inventor of C++, likes to think of it as a "better form of C." According to Stroustrup, the original C++ compiler (named *Cfront*, as in "C front end") started off as an elaborate preprocessor that produced C code as output. This C code was then passed on to a

Introduction

full-fledged C compiler. As time progressed, C++ went from being a front end to a C compiler to having its own dedicated compiler. Today, most software vendors sell C++ compilers with the implicit understanding that you can also use them to write C code.

In general, C is about as close to assembly language as you can get without losing the basic flow-control and stack-frame niceties that accompany high-level languages. C was because Ken Thompson got tired of writing assembly code. The first version of UNIX, which ran on a DEC PDP-7 in the late 1960s, was written entirely in assembler (and you thought that Mike Podanoffsky had it tough). Ken solved his assembly language problems by creating a variation of BCPL, which he called B. The name of the programming language was then changed to "C" by Dennis Ritchie, after some overhauling. Two Bell Labs researchers, Brian Kernighan and Dennis Ritchie, ended up playing vital roles in the evolution of the language. In fact, the older form of C's syntax is known as Kernighan and Ritchie C (or just *K&R C*).

C and C++ are both used to implement operating systems. Linux, for example, is written entirely in C. Although C is still the dominant system language for historical reasons, C++ is slowly beginning to creep into the source code bases of at least a couple commercial operating systems. Microsoft's Windows operating system has chunks of its kernel written in C++. One might speculate that this trend can be directly linked to the rapidly increasing complexity of operating systems.

Companion Files

Software engineering is like baseball. The only way you will ever acquire any degree of skill is to practice and scrimmage whenever you get the chance. To this end, I have included the source code for most of the examples in this book in a downloadable file available at www.wordware.com/memory.

Dick Feynman, who was awarded the Nobel Prize in physics in 1965, believed that the key to discovery and insight was playful experimentation. Dick was the kind of guy who followed his own advice. In his biography, *Surely You're Joking, Mr. Feynman*, Dick recounts how spinning plates in a dining hall at Cornell led to historic work in quantum mechanics. By testing a variety of new ideas and comparing the results to your predictions, you force yourself to gain a better understanding of how things work. This approach also gives you the hands-on experience necessary to nurture a sense of intuition.

It is in this spirit that I provide this book's source code in the downloadable files. By all means, modify it, hack it, and play with it. Try new things and see where they lead you. Make predictions and see if empirical results support your predictions. If the results don't, then try to determine why and construct alternative explanations. Test those explanations. Add new functionality and see how it affects things. Take away components and see what happens. Bet a large sum of money with a friend to see who can implement the best improvement. But above all, have fun.

References

Brey, Barry. *The Intel Microprocessors: 8086/8088, 80186, 80286, 80386, 80486, Pentium, Pentium Pro, and Pentium II*. 2000, Prentice Hall, ISBN: 0-13-995408-2.

    This is a fairly recent book and should take care of any questions you may have. Barry has been writing about Intel chips since the first one came out.

Kernighan, Brian and Dennis Ritchie. *The C Programming Language*. 1988, Prentice Hall, ISBN: 0131103628.

    This is a terse, but well-read introduction to C by the founding fathers of the language.

Reid, T. R. *The Chip: How Two Americans Invented the Microchip and Launched a Revolution*. 2001, Random House, ISBN: 0375758283.

Schildt, Herbert. *C++ From the Ground Up*. 1998, Osborne McGraw-Hill, ISBN: 0078824052.

    If you have never programmed in C/C++, read this book. It is a gentle introduction written by an author who knows how to explain complicated material. Herb starts by teaching you C and then slowly introducing the object-oriented features of C++.

Stroustrup, Bjarne and Margaret Ellis. *The Annotated C++ Reference*. 1990, Addison-Wesley, ISBN: 0201514591.

    Once you have read Schildt's book, you can use this text to fill in the gaps. This book is exactly what it says it is — a reference — and it is a good one.

Introduction

Stroustrup, Bjarne. *The Design and Evolution of C++*. 1994, Addison-Wesley Pub. Co., ISBN: 0201543303.

This is an historical recount of C++'s creation by the man who invented the language. The discussion is naturally very technical and compiler writers will probably be able to appreciate this book the most. This is not for the beginner.

Warning

In this book I provide some rather intricate, and potentially dangerous, source code examples. This is what happens when you go where you are not particularly supposed to be. I recommend that you use an expendable test machine to serve as a laboratory. Also, you might want to consider closing all unnecessary applications before experimenting. If an application dies in the middle of an access to disk, you could be faced with a corrupt file system.

If you keep valuable data on the machine you are going to use, I suggest you implement a disaster recovery plan. During the writing of this book's manuscript, I made a point to perform daily incremental backups and complete weekly backups of my hard drive. I also had a secondary machine that mirrored by primary box. Large corporations, like banks and insurance companies, have truly extensive emergency plans. I toured a production site in Cleveland that had two diesel fuel generators and a thousand gallons of gas to provide backup power.

Neither the publisher nor author accept any responsibility for any damage that may occur as a result of the information contained within this book. As Stan Lee might say, "With great power comes great responsibility."

Author Information

Bill Blunden has been obsessed with systems software since his first exposure to the DOS `debug` utility in 1983. His single-minded pursuit to discover what actually goes on under the hood led him to program the 8259 interrupt controller and become an honorable member of the triple-fault club. After obtaining a BA in mathematical physics and an MS in operations research, Bill was unleashed upon the workplace. It was at an insurance company in the beautiful city of Cleveland, plying his skills as an actuary, that Bill got into his first fist fight with a cranky IBM mainframe. Bloody but not beaten, Bill decided that groking software beat crunching numbers. This led him to a major ERP player in the midwest, where he developed CASE tools in Java, wrestled with COBOL middleware, and was assailed by various Control Data veterans. Having a quad-processor machine with 2GB of RAM at his disposal, Bill was hard pressed to find any sort of reason to abandon his ivory tower. Nevertheless, the birth of his nephew forced him to make a pilgrimage out west to Silicon Valley. Currently on the peninsula, Bill survives rolling power blackouts and earthquakes, and is slowly recovering from his initial bout with COBOL.

Chapter 1

Memory Management Mechanisms

"Everyone has a photographic memory. Some people just don't have film."
— Mel Brooks

NOTE In the text of this book, *italics* are used to define or emphasize a term. The `Courier` font is used to denote code, memory addresses, input/output, and filenames. For more information, see the section titled "Typographical Conventions" in the Introduction.

Mechanism Versus Policy

Accessing and manipulating memory involves a lot of accounting work. Measures have to be taken to ensure that memory being accessed is valid and that it corresponds to actual physical storage. If *memory protection* mechanisms are in place, checks will also need to be performed by the processor to ensure that an executing task does not access memory locations that it should not. Memory protection is the type of service that multiuser operating systems are built upon. If *virtual memory* is being used, a significant amount of bookkeeping will need to be maintained in order to track which disk sectors belong to which task. It is more effort than you think, and all the steps must be completed flawlessly.

NOTE On the Intel platform, if the memory subsystem's data structures are set up incorrectly, the processor will perform what is known as a *triple fault*. A *double fault* occurs on Intel hardware when an exception occurs while the processor is already trying to handle an exception. A triple fault occurs when the double-fault handler fails and the machine is placed into the SHUTDOWN cycle. Typically, an Intel machine will reset when it encounters this type of problem.

For the sake of execution speed, processor manufacturers give their chips the capacity to carry out advanced memory management chores. This allows operating system vendors to effectively push most of the tedious, repetitive work down to the processor where the various error checks can be performed relatively quickly. This also has the side effect of anchoring the operating system vendor to the hardware platform, to an extent.

The performance gains, however, are well worth the lost portability. If an operating system were completely responsible for implementing features like paging and segmentation, it would be noticeably slower than one that took advantage of the processor's built-in functionality. Imagine trying to play a graphics-intensive, real-time game like Quake 3 on an operating system that manually protected memory; the game would just not be playable.

NOTE You might be asking if I can offer a quantitative measure of how much slower an operating system would be. I will admit I have been doing a little arm waving. According to a 1993 paper by Wahbe, Lucco, et al. (see the "References" section), they were able to isolate modules of code in an application using a technique they labeled as *sandboxing*. This technique incurred a 4% increase in execution speed. You can imagine what would happen if virtual memory and access privilege schemes were added to such a mechanism.

ASIDE

An *arm-waving* explanation is a proposition that has not been established using precise mathematical statements. Mathematical statements have the benefit of being completely unambiguous: They are either true or false. An arm-waving explanation tends to eschew logical rigor entirely in favor of arguments that appeal to intuition. Such reasoning is at best dubious, not only because intuition can often be incorrect, but also because intuitive arguments are ambiguous. For example, people who argue that the world is flat tend to rely on arm-waving explanations.

NOTE Back when Dave Cutler's brainchild, Windows NT, came out, there was a lot of attention given to the operating system's Hardware Abstraction Layer (HAL). The idea was that the majority of the operating system could be insulated from the hardware that it ran on by a layer of code located in the basement. This was instituted to help counter the hardware dependency issue that I mentioned a minute ago. To Dave's credit, NT actually did run on a couple of traditionally UNIX-oriented hardware platforms. This included Digital's Alpha processor and the MIPS RISC processor. The problem was that Microsoft couldn't get a number of its higher-level technologies, like DCOM, to run on anything but Intel. So much for an object technology based on a binary standard!

The solution that favors speed always wins. I was told by a former Control Data engineer that when Seymour Cray was designing the 6600, he happened upon a new chip that was quicker than the one he was currently using. The problem was that it made occasional computational errors. Seymour implemented a few slick workarounds and went with the new chip. The execs wanted to stay out of Seymour's way and not disturb the maestro, as Seymour was probably the most valuable employee Control Data had. Unfortunately, they also had warehouses full of the original chips. They couldn't just throw out the old chips; they had to find a use for them. This problem gave birth to the CDC 3300, a slower and less expensive version of the 6600.

My point: Seymour went for the faster chip, even though it was less reliable.

Speed rules.

The result of this tendency is that every commercial operating system in existence has its memory management services firmly rooted in data structures and protocols dictated by the hardware. Processors provide a collection of primitives for manipulating memory. They constitute the *mechanism* side of the equation. It is up to the operating system to decide if it will even use a processor's memory management mechanisms and, if so, how it will use them. Operating systems constitute the *policy* side of the equation.

In this chapter, I will examine computer hardware in terms of how it offers a mechanism to access and manipulate memory.

Memory Hierarchy

When someone uses the term "memory," they are typically referring to the data storage provided by dedicated chips located on the motherboard. The storage these chips provide is often referred to as *Random Access Memory* (RAM), *main memory*, and *primary storage*. Back in the iron age, when mainframes walked the earth, it was called the *core*. The storage provided by these chips is *volatile*, which is to say that data in the chips is lost when the power is switched off.

There are various types of RAM:

- DRAM
- SDRAM
- SRAM

- VRAM

Dynamic RAM (DRAM) has to be recharged thousands of times each second. *Synchronous DRAM* (SDRAM) is refreshed at the clock speed at which the processor runs the most efficiently. *Static RAM* (SRAM) does not need to be refreshed like DRAM, and this makes it much faster. Unfortunately, SRAM is also much more expensive than DRAM and is used sparingly. SRAM tends to be used in processor caches and DRAM tends to be used for wholesale memory. Finally, there's Video RAM (VRAM), which is a region of memory used by video hardware. In the next chapter, there is an example that demonstrates how to produce screen messages by manipulating VRAM.

Recent advances in technology and special optimizations implemented by certain manufacturers have led to a number of additional acronyms. Here are a couple of them:

- DDR SDRAM
- RDRAM
- ESDRAM

DDR SDRAM stands for Double Data Rate Synchronous Dynamic Random Access Memory. With DDR SDRAM, data is read on both the rising and the falling of the system clock tick, basically doubling the bandwidth normally available. RDRAM is short for Rambus DRAM, a high-performance version of DRAM sold by Rambus that can transfer data at 800 MHz. Enhanced Synchronous DRAM (ESDRAM), manufactured by Enhanced Memory Systems, provides a way to replace SRAM with cheaper SDRAM.

A *bit* is a single binary digit (i.e., a 1 or a 0). A bit in a RAM chip is basically a cell structure that is made up of, depending on the type of RAM, a certain configuration of transistors and capacitors. Each cell is a digital switch that can either be on or off (i.e., 1 or 0). These cells are grouped into 8-bit units call *bytes*. The byte is the fundamental unit for measuring the amount of memory provided by a storage device. In the early years, hardware vendors used to implement different byte sizes. One vendor would use a 6-bit byte and another would use a 16-bit byte. The de facto standard that everyone seems to abide by today, however, is the 8-bit byte.

There is a whole set of byte-based metrics to specify the size of a memory region:

1 byte   = 8 bits
1 word   = 2 bytes
1 double word = 4 bytes

1 quad word	= 8 bytes	
1 octal word	= 8 bytes	
1 paragraph	= 16 bytes	
1 kilobyte (KB)	= 1,024 bytes	
1 megabyte (MB)	= 1,024KB	= 1,048,576 bytes
1 gigabyte (GB)	= 1,024MB	= 1,073,741,824 bytes
1 terabyte (TB)	= 1,024GB	= 1,099,511,627,776 bytes
1 petabyte (PB)	= 1,024TB	= 1,125,899,906,842,624 bytes

NOTE In the 1980s, having a megabyte of DRAM was a big deal. Kids used to bug their parents for 16KB memory upgrades so their Atari 400s could play larger games. At the time, having only a megabyte wasn't a significant problem because engineers tended to program in assembly code and build very small programs. In fact, this 1981 quote is often attributed to Bill Gates: "640K ought to be enough for anybody."

Today, most development machines have at least 128MB of DRAM. In 2002, having 256MB seems to be the norm. Ten years from now, a gigabyte might be the standard amount of DRAM (if we are still using DRAM). Hopefully, someone will not quote me.

RAM is not the only place to store data, and this is what leads us to the memory hierarchy. The range of different places that can be used to store information can be ordered according to their proximity to the processor. This ordering produces the following hierarchy:

1. Registers
2. Cache
3. RAM
4. Disk storage

The primary distinction between these storage areas is their *memory latency*, or lag time. Storage closer to the processor takes less time to access than storage that is further away. The latency experienced in accessing data on a hard drive is much greater than the latency that occurs when the processor accesses memory in its cache. For example, DRAM latency tends to be measured in nanoseconds. Disk drive latency, however, tends to be measured in milliseconds! (See Figure 1.1 on the following page.)

Registers are small storage spaces that are located within the processor itself. Registers are a processor's favorite workspace. Most of the processor's day-to-day work is performed on data in the registers. Moving data from one register to another is the single most expedient way to move data.

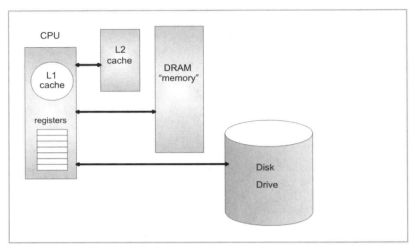

Figure 1.1

Software engineers designing compilers will jump through all sorts of hoops just to keep variables and constants in the registers. Having a large number of registers allows more of a program's state to be stored within the processor itself and cut down on memory latency. The MIPS64 processor has 32, 64-bit, general-purpose registers for this very reason. The Itanium, Intel's next generation 64-bit chip, goes a step further and has literally hundreds of registers.

The Intel Pentium processor has a varied set of registers (see Figure 1.2). There are six, 16-bit, segment registers (CS, DS, ES, FS, GS, SS). There are eight, 32-bit, general-purpose registers (EAX, EBX, ECX, EDX, ESI, EDI, EBP, ESP). There is also a 32-bit error flag register (EFLAGS) to signal problems and a 32-bit instruction pointer (EIP).

Advanced memory management functions are facilitated by four system registers (GDTR, LDTR, IDTR, TR) and five mode control registers (CR0, CR1, CR2, CR3, CR4). The usage of these registers will be explained in the next few sections.

NOTE It is interesting to note how the Pentium's collection of registers has been constrained by historical forces. The design requirement demanding backward compatibility has resulted in the Pentium having only a few more registers than the 8086.

A cache provides temporary storage that can be accessed quicker than DRAM. By placing computationally intensive portions of a program in the cache, the processor can avoid the overhead of having

Memory Management Mechanisms

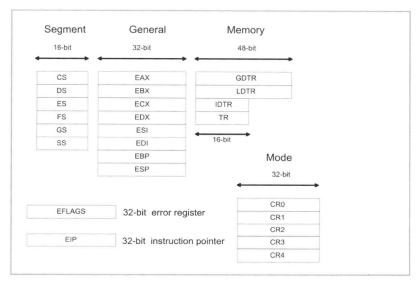

Figure 1.2

to continually access DRAM. The savings can be dramatic. There are different types of caches. An *L1 cache* is a storage space that is located on the processor itself. An *L2 cache* is typically an SRAM chip outside of the processor (for example, the Intel Pentium 4 ships with a 256 or 512KB L2 Advanced Transfer Cache).

NOTE If you are attempting to optimize code that executes in the cache, you should avoid unnecessary function calls. A call to a distant function requires the processor to execute code that lies outside the cache. This causes the cache to reload. This is one reason why certain C compilers offer you the option of generating inline functions. The other side of the coin is that a program that uses inline functions will be much larger than one that does not. The size-versus-speed trade-off is a balancing act that rears its head all over computer science.

Disk storage is the option of last resort. Traditionally, disk space has been used to create *virtual memory*. Virtual memory is memory that is simulated by using disk space. In other words, portions of memory, normally stored in DRAM, are written to disk so that the amount of memory the processor can access is greater than the actual amount of physical memory. For example, if you have 10MB of DRAM and you use 2MB of disk space to simulate memory, the processor can then access 12MB of virtual memory.

NOTE A recurring point that I will make throughout this book is the high cost of disk input/output. As I mentioned previously, the latency for accessing disk storage is on the order of milliseconds. This is a long time from the perspective of a processor. The situation is analogous to making a pizza run from a remote cabin in North Dakota. If you are lucky, you have a frozen pizza in your freezer/cache and it will only take 30 minutes to heat up. If you are not lucky, you will have to call the pizza delivery guy (i.e., access the data from disk storage) and wait for five hours as he makes the 150-mile trek to your cabin.

Using virtual memory is like making a deal with the devil. Sure, you will get lots of extra memory, but you will pay an awful cost in terms of performance. Disk I/O involves a whole series of mandatory actions, some of which are mechanical. It is estimated that paging on Windows accounts for roughly 10% of execution time. Managing virtual memory requires a lot of bookkeeping on the part of the processor. I will discuss the precise nature of this bookkeeping in a later section.

ASIDE

I worked at an ERP company where one of the VPs used to fine engineers for performing superfluous disk I/O. During code reviews, he would `grep` through source code looking for the `fopen()` and `fread()` standard library functions. We were taught the basic lesson that you cached everything you possibly could in memory and only moved to disk storage when you absolutely had no other alternative (and even then you needed permission). To the VP's credit, the company's three-tier middleware suite was the fastest in the industry.

Disk storage has always been cheaper than RAM. Back in the 1960s when 8KB of RAM was a big investment, using the disk to create virtual memory probably made sense. Today, however, the cost discrepancy between DRAM and disk drives is not as significant as it was back then. Buying a machine with 512MB of SDRAM is not unheard of. It could be that virtual memory will become a complete relic or implemented as some sort of emergency safeguard.

Address Lines and Buses

Each byte in DRAM is assigned a unique numeric identifier called an *address*, just like houses on a street. An address is an integer value. The first byte in memory is assigned an address of zero. The region of memory near address zero is known as the *bottom of memory*, or *low memory*. The region of memory near the final byte is known as *high memory*. The number of physical (i.e., DRAM) bytes that a processor is capable of addressing is known as the processor's *physical address space*. (See Figure 1.3.)

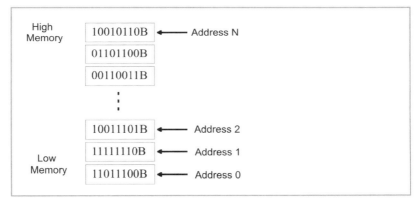

Figure 1.3

The physical address space of a processor specifies the *potential* number of bytes that can be addressed, *not* the actual number of physical bytes present. People normally don't want to spend the money necessary to populate the entire physical address space with DRAM chips. Buying 4GB of DRAM is still usually reserved for high-end enterprise servers.

The physical address space of a processor is determined by the number of address lines that it has. Address lines are a set of wires connecting the processor to its DRAM chips. Each address line specifies a single bit in the address of a given byte. For example, the Intel Pentium has 32 address lines. This means that each byte is assigned a 32-bit address so that its address space consists of 2^{32} addressable bytes (4GB). The 8088 had 20 address lines, so it was capable of addressing 2^{20}, or 1,048,576, bytes.

NOTE If virtual memory is enabled on the Pentium 4, there is a way to enable four additional address lines using what is known as Physical Address Extension (PAE). This allows the Pentium processor's physical address space to be defined by 36 address lines, which translates into an address space of 2^{36} bytes (64GB).

To access and update physical memory, the processor uses a control bus and a data bus. A *bus* is a collection of related wires that connect the processor to a hardware subsystem. The control bus is used to indicate if the processor wants to read from memory or write to memory. The data bus is used to ferry data back and forth between the processor and memory. (See Figure 1.4.)

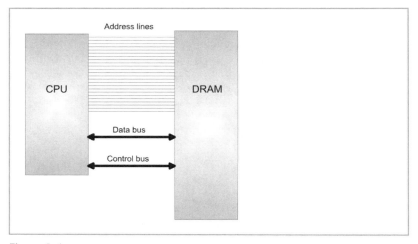

Figure 1.4

When the processor reads from memory, the following steps are performed:

1. The processor places the address of the byte to be read on the address lines.
2. The processor sends the read signal on the control bus.
3. The DRAM chip(s) return the byte specified on the data bus.

When the processor writes to memory, the following steps are performed:

1. The processor places the address of the byte to be written on the address lines.
2. The processor sends the write signal on the control bus.
3. The processor sends the byte to be written to memory on the data bus.

This description is somewhat of an oversimplification. For example, the Pentium processor reads and writes data 4 bytes at a time. This is one reason why the Pentium is called a 32-bit chip. The processor will refer to its 32-bit payload using the address of the first byte (i.e., the byte with the lowest address). Nevertheless, I think the general operation is clear.

Intel Pentium Architecture

You have seen how a processor reads and writes bytes to memory. However, most processors also support two advanced memory management mechanisms: segmentation and paging.

Segmentation is instituted by breaking up a computer's address space into specific regions, known as *segments*. Using segmentation is a way to isolate areas of memory so that programs cannot interfere with one another. Segmentation affords what is known as *memory protection*. It is possible to institute memory segmentation without protection, but there are really no advantages to such a scheme.

Under a segmentation scheme that enforces memory protection, each application is assigned at least one segment. Large applications often have several segments. In addition, the operating system will also have its own custom set of segments. Segments are assigned a specific set of access writes so that policies can be created with regard to who can update what. Typically, the operating system code segments will execute with the highest privilege and applications will be loaded into segments with less authority.

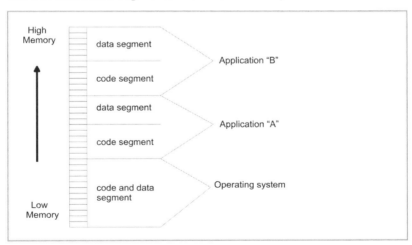

Figure 1.5

Paging is a way to implement virtual memory. The physical memory provided by DRAM and disk storage, which is allocated to simulate DRAM, are merged together into one big amorphous collection of bytes. The total number of bytes that a processor is capable of addressing, if paging is enabled, is known as its *virtual address space*.

The catch to all this is that the address of a byte in this artificial/virtual address space is no longer the same as the address that the processor places on the address bus. This means that translation data structures and code will have to be established in order to map a byte in the virtual address space to a physical byte (regardless of whether that byte happens to be in DRAM or on disk).

When the necessary paging constructs have been activated, the virtual memory space is divided into smaller regions called *pages*. If the operating system decides that it is running low on physical memory, it will take pages that are currently stored in physical memory and write them to disk. If segmentation is being used, bookkeeping will have to be performed in order to match a given page of memory with the segment that owns it. All of the accounting work is done in close conjunction with the processor so that the performance hit associated with disk I/O can be kept to a minimum.

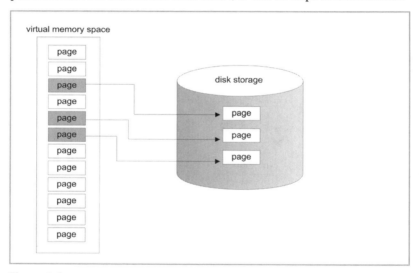

Figure 1.6

NOTE When pages of data are stored in physical memory (i.e., DRAM), they are placed in page-sized slots that are known as *page frames*. In addition to keeping track of individual pages, most operating systems also monitor page frame usage. The number of page frames is usually much smaller than the number of pages, so it is in the best interest of the operating system to carefully manage this precious commodity.

NOTE It is possible to use paging without using disk space. But in this case, paging transforms into a hybrid form of segmentation that deals with 4KB regions of memory.

Memory Management Mechanisms

Because Intel's Pentium class of processors is easily accessible, I decided to use the Pentium to help illustrate segmentation and paging. I would love to demonstrate theory with a MIPS64 processor, but I can't afford an SGI server (sigh). Being inexpensive is one of the primary reasons for Intel's continued success. Hackers, like me, who couldn't afford an Apple IIe back in the 1980s were left scrounging for second-hand Intel boxes. There were thousands of people who had to make this kind of financial decision. So, in a sense, the proliferation of Intel into the workplace was somewhat of a grass roots movement.

The Pentium class of processors is descended from a long line of popular CPUs:

CPU	Release Date	Physical Address Space
8086	1978	1MB
8088	1979	1MB
80286	1982	16MB
80386	1985	4GB
80486	1989	4GB
Pentium	1993	4GB
Pentium Pro	1995	64GB
Pentium II	1997	64GB
Pentium III	1999	64GB
Pentium 4	2000	64GB

NOTE When the IBM PC came out in 1981, it shipped with a 4.77 MHz 8088. Without a doubt, mainframe developers were overjoyed. This was because the PC gave them a place of their own. In those days, the standard dummy terminals didn't do anything more than shuttle a data buffer back and forth to a mainframe. In addition, an engineer had little or no control over when, or how, his code would be run. The waiting could be agonizing. Tom Petty was right. Bribing a sysop with pizza could occasionally speed things up, but the full court grovel got tiring after a while. With an IBM PC, an engineer finally had a build machine that was open all night with no waiting.

ASIDE

I know one CDC engineer, in particular, who ported a FORTRAN '77 compiler to a PC in 1982 for this very reason. His supervisor would walk over and say: "Why do you want to run on that little three-wheeler instead of the production machine?" His answer: "Because it is mine, damn it." This one statement probably summarizes the mindset that made PCs wildly successful.

In an attempt to keep their old customers, Intel has gone to great lengths to make their 32-bit processors backward compatible with the previous 16-bit models. As testimony to Intel's success, I can boot my laptop with a DOS 6.22 boot disk and run most of my old DOS applications (including Doom and Duke Nukem).

A product of the requirement for backward compatibility is that the Pentium chip operates in a number of different modes. Each mode dictates how the processor will interpret machine instructions and how it can access memory. Specifically, the Pentium is capable of operating in four modes:

- Real mode
- Protected mode
- System management mode (SMM)
- Virtual 8086 mode

System management mode and virtual 8086 mode are both special-purpose modes of operation that are only used under special circumstances. I will focus primarily on the first two modes of operation: real mode and protected mode. In addition, I will investigate how each of these modes support segmentation and paging.

Having the processor operate in different modes is not a feature limited to the Intel platform. The MIPS64 processor, for example, also operates in four modes:

- Kernel mode
- User mode
- Debug mode
- Supervisor mode

Real Mode Operation

The first IBM PC ran strictly in real mode. Furthermore, all 32-bit Intel computers also start in real mode when they are booted. This sort of provides a least common denominator behavior that backward compatibility depends upon.

Real mode operating systems tend to be very small (i.e., less than 128KB) because they rely on the BIOS to provide an interface to the hardware. This allows them to easily fit on a 1.44MB floppy diskette. Virus protection rescue disks rely on this fact, as do system repair disks. I have also bought drive partitioning software that can be run from a boot disk.

In real mode, the general-purpose registers we saw earlier in Figure 1.2 are truncated into 16-bit registers, as are the error flag and instruction pointer registers. The real mode register setup is displayed in Figure 1.7.

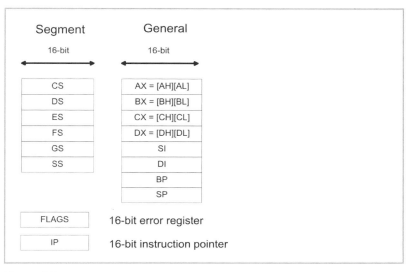

Figure 1.7

As you can see, the "E" prefix has been removed from the register names. In addition, each of the 16-bit general registers, AX, CX, DX, and EX, can be manipulated in terms of two 8-bit registers. For example, the AX register can be seen as the combination of the AH and AL registers. The AH register refers to the high byte in AX, and the AL register refers to the low byte in AX.

NOTE The memory and mode registers shown in Figure 1.2 are still visible in real mode. They still exist if the processor is a 32-bit class CPU but they have no significance or use in real mode. The only exception to this rule is if you are trying to switch to protected mode.

A machine in real mode can address 1MB of DRAM. This implies that only 20 address lines are used in real mode. The address of a byte in memory, for a processor real mode, is formed by adding an offset address to a segment address. The result of the sum is always a 20-bit value (remember this fact; it is important), which confirms our suspicion that there are 20 address lines.

The address formed by the sum of the segment and offset addresses corresponds directly to the value that is placed on the processor's address lines. Now you can get a better idea of why they call it "real" mode. The address of a byte in real mode maps directly to a "real" byte in physical memory.

An address is denoted, in Intel assembly language, by a `segment:offset` pair. For example, if a byte is located in segment `0x8200` and is situated at an offset of `0x0100`, the address of this byte is specified as:

`0x8200:0x0100`

Sometimes, for reasons that I will explain later, this is also written as:

`0x8200[0]:0x0100`

The real mode address resolution process is displayed in Figure 1.8.

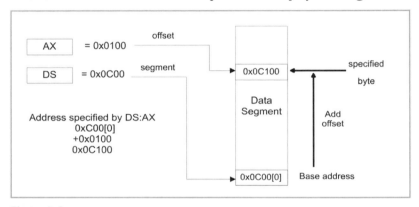

Figure 1.8

Segment addresses denote a particular memory segment and are always stored in one of the 16-bit segment registers. Specifically, a segment address specifies the *base address*, the lowest address, of a memory segment. Each segment register has a particular use:

Register	Use
CS	Segment address of code currently being executed
SS	Segment address of stack
DS	Data segment address
ES	Extra segment address (usually data)
FS	Extra segment address (usually data)
GS	Extra segment address (usually data)

NOTE The fact that there are six segment registers means that at any time, only six segments of memory can be manipulated. A program can have more than six segments, but only six can be accessible at any one point in time.

Offset addresses can be stored in the general registers and are 16 bits in size. Given that an offset address is 16 bits, this limits each segment to 64KB in size.

QUESTION
If the segment address and offset address are both stored in 16-bit registers, how can the sum of two 16-bit values form a 20-bit value?

ANSWER
The trick is that the segment address has an implicit zero added to the end. For example, a segment address of 0x0C00 is treated as 0x0C000 by the processor. This is denoted, in practice, by placing the implied zero in brackets (i.e., 0x0C00[0]). This is where the processor comes up with a 20-bit value.

As you can see, the real mode segment/offset approach does provide a crude sort of segmentation. However, at no point did I mention that the boundaries between segments are protected. The ugly truth is that there is no memory protection in real mode. When you run a program in real mode, it owns everything and can run amok if it wants.

Running an application in real mode is like letting a den of Cub Scouts into your home. They're young, spirited, and all hopped-up on sugar. If you're not careful, they will start tearing the house down. Crashing a real mode machine is simple, and there is little you can do to prevent it (other than back up your work constantly).

In case you are wondering, and I'm sure some of you are, here is an example of a C program that can crash a computer running in real mode:

```
/* --crashdos.c-- */

void main()
{
    unsigned char *ptr;
    int i;

    ptr = (unsigned char *)0x0;
    for(i=0;i<1024;i++)
    {
        ptr[i]=0x0;
    }
    return;
}
```

See how little effort it takes? There is nothing special or secret about this attack. I just overwrite the interrupt vector table that is located at the bottom of memory. If you wanted to hide this type of code in a large executable, you could probably cut down the program to less than five lines of assembly code.

If you really wanted to be malicious, you could disable the keyboard and then start reformatting the hard drive. The only defense a person would have is to yank the power cord, and even then, by the time they realize what is going on, it would probably be too late. My point, however, is not to tell you how to immobilize a DOS machine. Nobody uses them anymore, anyway. My motive is to demonstrate that real mode is anything but a secure environment.

To make matters worse, real mode does not support paging. All you have to play with is 1MB of DRAM. In reality, you actually have less than 1MB because the BIOS and video hardware consume sizeable portions of memory. Remember the Bill Gates quote?

NOTE No memory protection? No paging? Now you understand how the first version of PC-DOS was less than 5,000 lines of assembler. Perhaps "real" mode is called such because it is really minimal.

Intel's processors would never have made inroads into the enterprise with this kind of Mickey Mouse memory management. In an attempt to support more robust operating systems and larger address spaces, Intel came out with the 80386. The 80386 had a physical address space of 4GB and supported a new mode of operation: protected mode.

Protected Mode Operation

Protected mode supplies all the bells and whistles that are missing in real mode. The Pentium processor was specifically designed to run in protected mode. Its internal plumbing executes 32-bit instructions more efficiently than it executes 16-bit instructions. Having the Pentium start in real mode during a machine's power-up was sort of a courtesy that the Intel engineers have extended to help operating systems bootstrap.

An Intel processor running in protected mode supports protected segmentation, and it also can support paging. This means that address resolution will be much more complicated. In real mode, we just added an offset address to a segment address to produce a value that corresponded directly to physical memory address. In protected mode, the processor expects a whole load of special data structures to be in place. In addition, the segment and offset pair may no longer correspond directly to a physical address. So hang on, here we go...

Protected Mode Segmentation

The best way to understand segmentation on Intel is to take a visual look at how it is implemented. A picture is worth 1,024 words, and that is particularly true in this case. So take a good, hard look at Figure 1.9 and compare it to Figure 1.8. You might also want to bookmark Figure 1.9 so that you can return to it when needed.

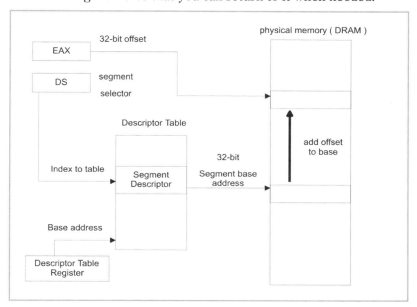

Figure 1.9

The first thing to note is that protected mode uses the full-blown set of Pentium registers displayed in Figure 1.2. Back to 32-bit registers we go. Also, the segment registers no longer store 16-bit segment address values. Instead, it holds what is known as a *segment selector*.

A segment selector is a 16-bit data structure containing three fields. Its composition is displayed in Figure 1.10. The really important field is the index field. The index field stores an index to a descriptor table. Index values start at zero.

 NOTE The index field in the segment selector is *not* an address. It is an index like the kind of index you would use to access an array element in C. The processor will take the index and internally do the necessary math to match the index to the linear address corresponding to that index. Note that I said *linear* address, not physical address. For the time being, linear and physical addresses are the same, but when paging is enabled, they are not. Keep this in mind.

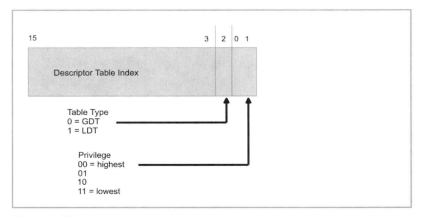

Figure 1.10

A *descriptor table* is an array of entries in which each entry (known as a *segment descriptor*) describes the attributes of a specific memory segment. Included in a descriptor is the base address of the memory segment that it describes. The 32-bit offset address is added to the segment descriptor's base address in order to specify the address of a byte in memory.

There are two types of descriptor tables: the *Global Descriptor Table* (GDT) and the *Local Descriptor Table* (LDT). Every operating system must have a GDT, but having one or more LDT structures is optional. Usually, if an LDT is to be used, it will be utilized to represent the memory segments belonging to a specific process. The base address of the GDT is stored in the GDTR system register. Likewise, the base address of the LDT is stored in the LDTR register. Naturally, there are special system instructions to load these registers (i.e., the LGDT and LLDT instructions).

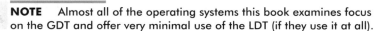

NOTE Almost all of the operating systems this book examines focus on the GDT and offer very minimal use of the LDT (if they use it at all).

The GDTR is 48 bits in size. One unusual characteristic of the GDTR is that it stores two distinct values. The first 16 bits contain the size limit, in bytes, of the GDT. The next 32 bits store the base linear address of the GDT in physical memory. This is illustrated in Figure 1.11.

Figure 1.11

QUESTION
How does the processor map a segment selector's index to a descriptor?

ANSWER
The processor takes the index, specified by the segment selector, multiplies the index by eight (as in 8 bytes because descriptors are 64 bits in length), and then adds this product to the base address specified by GTDR or LDTR.

> **NOTE** In case you are looking at Figure 1.2 and wondering about the other two memory management registers, IDTR and TR, I did not forget them. They are not as crucial to this discussion as GDTR and LDTR. The IDTR and TR registers are used to manage hardware interrupts and multitasking. This book is focused on pure memory management, so I will not discuss these registers in any detail. If you happen to be interested, I recommend that you pick up the Intel manual referenced at the end of this chapter.

Earlier I mentioned that segment descriptors store the base linear address of the memory segment they describe. However, they also hold a whole lot of other metadata. Figure 1.12 should give you a better idea of what lies within a segment descriptor. In this figure, I have broken the 64-bit descriptor into two 32-bit sections. The higher-order section is on top of the lower-order section.

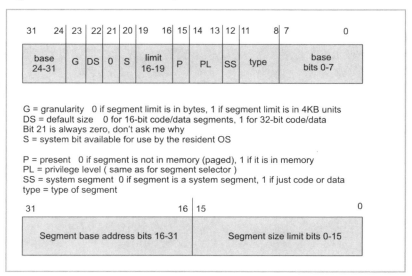

Figure 1.12

There is a lot of information packed into those 64 bits. As you can see, several fields are broken up and stored in different parts of the descriptor. There are two fields that might not be obvious just from looking at Figure 1.11. First is the SS flag, which indicates whether the segment is a *system segment* or just a normal code/data segment. A system segment, in case you are scratching your head, is a segment that is used to provide interrupt handling and multitasking services. I will not investigate either of those subjects.

NOTE You will see a number of 1-bit flags in the following few sections. For future reference, a bit is *set* when it is one. A bit is *cleared* when it is zero. Low-level operating system code is rife with bit-based manipulation. There is no way around it. Engineers who work with high-level languages tend to look down on engineers who write this type of low-level code. They are called *bit-bashers* or *bit-twiddlers*. Programmers can be cruel.

Assuming that the SS flag is set, the 4-bit type field in the descriptor describes the specific properties of the segment:

Table 1.1

Bit					
11	10	9	8	Type	Description
0	0	0	0	data	read-only
0	0	0	1	data	read-only, accessed
0	0	1	0	data	read-write
0	0	1	1	data	read-write, accessed
0	1	0	0	data	read-only, expand down
0	1	0	1	data	read-only, expand down, accessed
0	1	1	0	data	read-write, expand down
0	1	1	1	data	read-write, expand down, accessed
1	0	0	0	code	execute-only
1	0	0	1	code	execute-only, accessed
1	0	1	0	code	execute-read
1	0	1	1	code	execute-read, accessed
1	1	0	0	code	execute-only, conforming
1	1	0	1	code	execute-only, conforming, accessed
1	1	1	0	code	execute-read, conforming
1	1	1	1	code	execute-read, conforming, accessed

Accessed memory segments are segments that have been recently accessed so that bit 8 is set. *Expand down* segments are useful for creating stacks because they support memory constructs, which grow from high memory down toward low memory. *Conforming* code segments allows less privileged code segments to jump to them and execute their code at the lower privilege level.

Security-conscious system engineers would be wise to exercise caution with regard to the circumstances in which they allow operating system segments to be conforming.

QUESTION

OK, so we understand how the segments are referenced and what kind of metadata the segment descriptors store. How are these memory segments protected?

ANSWER

As it turns out, the segment selector and segment descriptor contain most of the information needed to implement a protection scheme. The processor makes ample use of this metadata to track down memory access violations.

For example, the limit field in the segment descriptor is used to help keep memory from being referenced beyond the designated last byte of a memory segment. Also, the type field in the segment descriptor ensures that a segment that is specified as read-only is not written to. The privilege fields in the segment selector and segment descriptor are used by the processor to prevent a program from illegally executing code or data that has a higher privilege.

NOTE It is easy to get confused. 0x00 is the *highest* privilege even though it is the *lowest* number.

Privilege levels are how the operating system prevents user applications from manipulating the kernel image and compromising security. In the real mode discussion, you saw how easy it was to cause havoc and crash the system. I merely waltzed over to the interrupt vector table and erased it. In protected mode, this threat can be dealt with. Vital data structures and operating system code can be safeguarded at the hardware level.

Intel supports four different privilege levels (0-3). Another way to say this is that Intel supports four *rings of protection*. These rings are illustrated in Figure 1.13 on the following page. This is actually a pretty simple scheme as far as memory protection is concerned. Decades ago when Control Data was building the NOSVE operating system, the architects wanted to have 15 rings of protection! The odd thing about contemporary operating systems like Linux and Windows is that they only implement two rings of protection (one for the kernel and another for everything else). They don't take full advantage of the facilities offered by the Pentium.

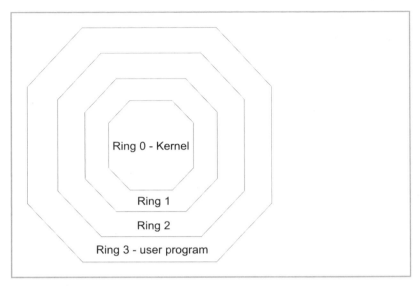

Figure 1.13

When a memory location is referenced, the processor performs a series of checks. These checks occur at the same time that the memory address is resolved to its physical location. Because these checks are performed concurrently with the address resolution cycle, there is no performance hit. This is the true beauty of pushing memory management down to the hardware.

If one of the processor's various checks discovers a protection violation, the processor will generate an *exception*. An exception is a signal produced by the processor. Exceptions are caught and processed using a variation of the processor's interrupt handling features. The exact steps taken are beyond the scope of this discussion. In very general terms, the processor will use special data structures, like the Interrupt Descriptor Table (IDT), to hand off exceptions to the operating system, which can then decide what to do. The operating system is actually responsible for establishing and setting up things like the IDT on behalf of the processor when it bootstraps. This allows the operating system the freedom to register special handlers with the IDT so that the appropriate routines can be invoked when a memory violation occurs.

When a memory exception occurs in Windows, a dialog box will typically appear to announce an access violation and Windows will terminate your program. To see what I mean, compile and run the following program under Windows:

Memory Management Mechanisms

```
/* --overflow.c-- */

#include<stdio.h>

void main()
{
    int array[4];
    int i;
    for(i=0;i<100;i++)
    {
        array[i]=i;
        printf("set array[%d]=%d\n",i);
    }
    return;
}
```

There is a blatant array overflow in the code above. When you run this application, it will crash and Windows will present you with a dialog box like the one shown in Figure 1.14. If you've never seen a dialog box like this before, take a good look. If you do any sort of pointer-intensive development on Windows, you are bound to see it sooner or later.

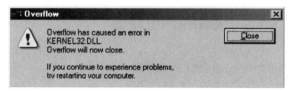

Figure 1.14

I have not said much about the control registers. The only control register relevant to this current section is the CR0 control register. We'll see a couple of the other control registers in the next section. The CR0 register's first bit (the lowest-order bit) is known as the PE flag (as in Protected Enable). By setting the PE flag to 1, we switch the processor into protected mode and enable all of the segment protection features discussed earlier. Here is a snippet of assembly code that performs this crucial task:

```
MOV EAX,CR0
OR AL,1
MOV CR0,EAX
```

Another equivalent way to do this is to use the special-purpose SMSW and LMSW system instructions:

```
SMSW AX
OR AL,1
LMSW AX
```

You've heard a lot of terms bandied about here: selector, descriptor, etc. If this is your first time reading about protected mode, you may still be confused about what is what. Here is a short summary to help you keep all the cast members of this sitcom organized:

Cast Member	Purpose
Segment selector	Selects a descriptor in a descriptor table
Segment descriptor	Describes a memory segment (metadata)
Descriptor table	Holds an array of segment descriptors
Descriptor table register	Stores the base address of the descriptor table

If paging has not been enabled, the final address produced by the scheme in Figure 1.9 is also a physical address, which is to say that it is the same 32-bit value that the processor places on its 32 address lines.

If paging is enabled, this is not the case; this leads us to the next section.

Protected Mode Paging

When paging is enabled, the address resolution scheme in Figure 1.9 becomes a bit more complicated. Take a look at Figure 1.15. Take a deep breath, and try not to panic.

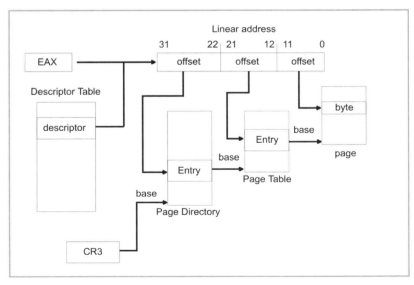

Figure 1.15

Basically, we have taken the address resolution process in Figure 1.9 and appended it with several steps so that we can accommodate all of the extra bookkeeping needed for paging. The address formed by the segment descriptor and the offset address in Figure 1.9 is no longer the address of a byte in physical memory. Instead, a 32-bit quantity is formed that is composed of three distinct offset addresses. Two of these offset addresses are 10 bits in size and the remaining offset address is 12 bits in size.

> **NOTE**   I will refer to this three-part, 32-bit quantity as a *linear address* to help distinguish it from the physical address of a byte in memory. The GDTR register holds the linear address of the base of the GDT data structure. Now you know why I emphasized this distinction earlier.
>
> Code that runs in protected mode with paging enabled lives in the alternate reality of linear addresses. Such code deals with "fake" 32-bit addresses that seem real enough to the code. Behind the scenes, the processor resolves fake/linear addresses to addresses that specify actual physical storage.

> **NOTE**   Paging facilities on the Intel platform were first introduced so that the processor could backfill unused areas of system memory (`0xB0000` to `0xFFFFF`) with the `EMM386.EXE` program.

The last 10 bytes of the linear address are an offset address of an entry in the *page directory*. The page directory is just an array of 32-bit entries whose base address is stored in the CR3 control register. A page directory's entry contains, among other things, the base address of a *page table*.

Given that a page directory entry has referenced the base address of a certain page table, the middle 10 bytes of the linear address serve as an offset address into that page table. This offset address references a 32-bit page table entry. The 32-bit page table entry contains, among other things, the base address of an actual 4KB *page* of memory.

This is where the first 12 bytes of the linear address come into play. These 12 bytes form an offset address that is added to the base address in the page table entry. The sum of these values forms an actual physical address of a byte in virtual memory. This byte is either in DRAM or has been paged to disk. You might also notice that a 12-bit offset limits the size of the memory page, in this case, to 4,096 bytes (4KB).

> **NOTE**   The base address stored in the page table entry is 20 bits in size. The processor assumes that these are the 20 most significant bits in a 32-bit base address, which is another way to say that the extra 12 bits are implied and all zero.

For example, a base address of: 0xCAFEB
is really: 0xCAFEB[0][0][0].

This is similar to real mode, where the segment address, expressed in hexadecimal, has a single implied zero at the end. This convention guarantees that the base address of a page always occurs in multiples of 4KB.

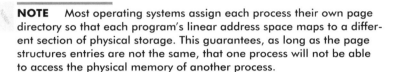

NOTE Most operating systems assign each process their own page directory so that each program's linear address space maps to a different section of physical storage. This guarantees, as long as the page structures entries are not the same, that one process will not be able to access the physical memory of another process.

If the byte referenced in the page is in physical memory, then we are done. If the byte is not in memory, then a *page fault* is generated. When this happens, the processor will produce a page fault and hand it off to the local operating system using the exception handling data structures. The operating system is expected to set these data structures up. The operating system, once it has received the fault signal, will then load the page containing this byte into DRAM so that it can be manipulated. Page faults are the backbone of virtual memory on the Intel hardware.

Now you know why your computer's hard drive goes crazy when you have too many applications running. The computer is busy moving programs, or parts of programs, on and off the hard drive. *Thrashing* occurs when you have so many applications loaded that the computer is too busy managing them and has no time to actually run them.

NOTE For the sake of simplicity (and sanity) I am going to stick to a 4KB paging scheme that uses only 32 address lines. This is shown in Figure 1.15. Intel has paging schemes where the page size is 4MB or 2MB. However, I don't see much use for a 4MB or 2MB paging scheme. Perhaps these larger paging settings were introduced to help kernels save their own images. There are high-availability operating systems, like EROS, that periodically save an image of the entire operating system. The only thing that would make these two larger paging schemes valuable, in the traditional sense, would be dramatic advances in disk I/O hardware.

Let's take a closer look at what the page directory and page table entries look like. (See Figure 1.16.)

A page directory entry has a number of special-purpose flags related to caching that I am not going to go into. The really important fields of the entry are the base address of the page table and the page size (PS) flag. The present flag (P) is maintained by the local operating system and is used to indicate if the page table is present in memory. If it is not, the page table will need to be loaded via a

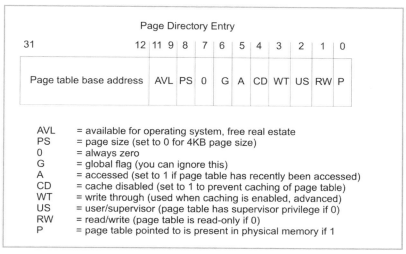

Figure 1.16

page fault so that the address resolution cycle can continue. Most operating systems, however, are wise enough to leave their crucial data structures in memory.

The layout of a page table entry is displayed in Figure 1.17. As you can see, it is very similar to the setup of the page directory entry. The difference is that the fields in a page directory entry are concerned with a page table. The fields in the page table entry are concerned with a 4KB page of memory.

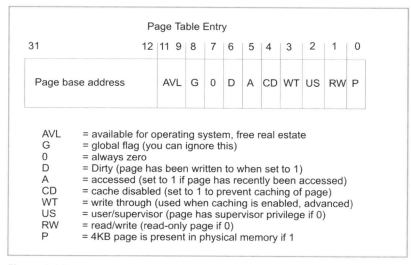

Figure 1.17

One new thing you might notice is the *dirty bit*. The dirty bit indicates that the page being referenced has been written to recently. The present (P) flag and the dirty (D) flag are both used by the operating system to help manage the process of paging. The operating system will usually clear the dirty flag when a page is loaded into DRAM for the first time. The processor will then set the dirty bit the first time that the page is updated.

You've already seen how the PE bit in CR0 is used to switch the processor into protected mode. Using the paging facilities of the processor requires even more participation of the control registers. Figure 1.18 displays a summary of important control registers. Reserved areas that should not be modified are shaded gray.

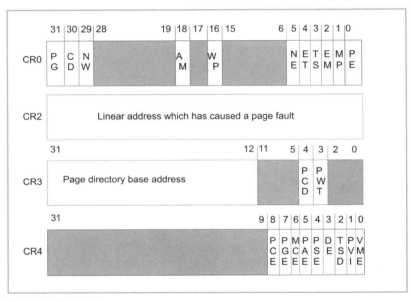

Figure 1.18

The CR0 is used to control the processor mode and state of the processor. In the last section, we took a look at the PE flag, which is responsible for placing the processor in protected mode. The other really important flag in CR0, as far as paging is concerned, is the PG flag at the other end of the register. When the PG flag is set, the processor is enabled for paging. When the PG flag is cleared, linear addresses are treated like physical addresses.

The CR1 is reserved, which is a nice way to say that it isn't used for anything. This is why I didn't include it in Figure 1.18. For the remainder of this section, you can ignore CR1. My guess is that CR1 may have been created for the sake of some future use.

> **NOTE** Digging a well before you are thirsty is not a bad idea. Any software architects worth their salt will make accommodations for future modification and extension. If you have ever worked with the Win32 API, you will, no doubt, have noticed a number of ambiguous `void*` function parameters reserved for future use.

The CR2 register is used to store the linear address that has caused a page fault. Mercifully, this value takes up the entire register.

The CR3 plays a central role in the resolution of physical addresses when paging has been enabled. Specifically, this register holds the base address of the page directory. If you look at Figure 1.15, you will see that CR3 plays a vital role in the address resolution process. If CR3 is corrupt, you can kiss your memory manager goodbye. The other two flags (PCD and PWT) in this register are related to caching and are not directly relevant to the immediate discussion.

The CR4 register is used to enable a couple of advanced mechanisms. For example, the PAE flag enables four extra address lines when it is set. This would bring the number of address lines to 36. Note that the PG flag must be set in CR0 in order for PAE to be effective. Another flag of interest is the PSE bit. If PSE is cleared to zero, the page size is 4KB. If PSE is set, the page size is 4MB. If both PAE and PSE are set, the page size is 2MB.

Paging as Protection

Traditionally, paging has been used to artificially expand the amount of memory to which a processor has access. Nevertheless, the Intel architecture has embedded enough functionality into its paging scheme that it is possible to use only paging facilities to implement memory protection. In fact, if you wanted to push the envelope, you could turn off segmentation-based protection and rely completely on paging to provide memory protection. Naturally, this kind of scenario is a little unusual, and there are a few conditions that need to be satisfied.

The first condition is that a *flat memory model* is implemented. In a flat memory model, there is one big segment. It is the simplest possible memory model that can be used in protected mode. Everything shares the same memory segment, and all the protective services provided by segmentation are thrown to the wind. A flat memory model is implemented by creating a GDT with three entries. The first entry to the GDT is never used for some reason, so in a sense it is just a placeholder. The second and third descriptors are used to represent code and data segments. The trick is to have both descriptors point to the same segment. The segment these descriptors point to has base address 0x00000000 and a size limit of 4GB. The size limit is set to the maximum possible value (0xFFFFFFFF) in order to prevent "outside of limit" exceptions from being thrown.

If you use a segment register in an assembly code instruction, like DS, ES, or CS, it must contain a segment selector that indexes one of the two valid descriptors in the GDT. Keep in mind that there are three possible selectors. Two of the three possible segment selectors point to the code and data segment descriptors. There is also a segment selector that points to the vacant segment descriptor, called a *null selector*. Assuming a privilege of zero is used, these three selectors will look like this:

Segment Descriptor	Segment Selector
0	0 (a.k.a. null selector)
1	0x08
2	0x10

The flat memory model setup is displayed in Figure 1.19.

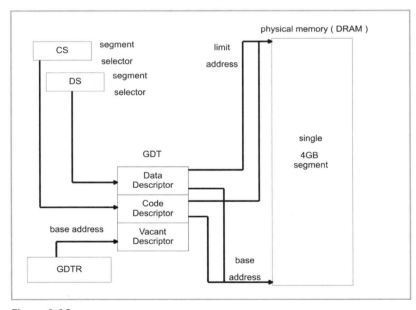

Figure 1.19

NOTE Don't forget about the first segment descriptor (index = 0) in the GDT being vacant. This is a tricky point, and the Intel docs seem to mention it only in passing.

Given that a flat memory model is implemented, none of the traditional segmentation checks can be performed. This leaves us with two ways to protect areas of memory, assuming that paging has been enabled. Both of these paging-based mechanisms rely on the information in page table entries.

If you look back at Figure 1.17, you will see that there is a read-write flag (bit 1) and also a user-supervisor flag (bit 2). The user-supervisor flag can be used to institute a two-ring security scheme. For example, by placing pages that constitute the operating system in supervisor mode and application pages in user mode, the kernel can be protected from malicious programs. If a user application attempts to access pages that are in supervisor mode, the processor will generate a page fault.

The read-write flag can be used to help enforce the user-supervisor division. Specifically, when the processor is executing code in a supervisor page, it can read and write anything. In other words, the read-only flag for other memory pages is ignored. However, if the processor is executing code in a user page, it can only read and write to other user-level pages. If it tries to access a page marked with supervisor status, the processor generates a page fault. A user page's ability to access other user pages depends on the status of their read-write flags, which is to say that user-level code must obey the read/write permissions of all the other pages.

Addresses: Logical, Linear, and Physical

I have made certain distinctions between types of addresses in this chapter. It is easy to get them confused. I am going to try to reinforce this distinction by devoting an entire section to the topic. On Intel hardware, there are three types of addresses:

- Physical
- Logical
- Linear

Take a look at Figure 1.20 on the following page, which shows the entire address resolution cycle when both segmentation and paging are used.

A *physical address* is the address of a byte in DRAM. It is the value that the processor places on its address lines in order to access a value in chip-based memory.

The *logical address* is the address that is specified by the segment register and the general register. Only in real mode does the logical address correspond to a physical address. This is because real mode

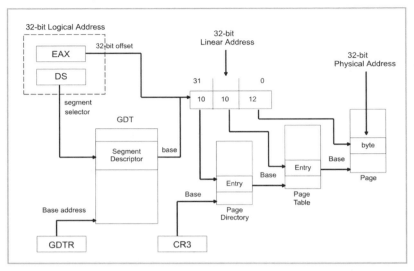

Figure 1.20

doesn't use segmentation or paging and Figure 1.19 does not apply at all. You might also want to keep in mind that the offset portion of a logical address does not necessarily have to be stored in a general register; I am just using a general register for the sake of illustration.

The *linear address* is the 32-bit value that is formed using the base address value in the segment descriptor and the offset value in the general register. If paging is not being used, the linear address corresponds to an actual physical address.

If paging facilities are being used, the linear address will be decomposed into three parts and the whole page directory/page table cycle will need to be performed in order to arrive at a physical address.

Page Frames and Pages

This is another area where confusion can creep in. I can remember confusing pages and page frames when I first started looking at memory management. A page frame is not the same as a page. When paging is enabled, physical memory (i.e., DRAM) is divided into 4KB units called page frames. This is analogous to a picture frame, which is empty until you place a photograph in it. A *page frame* specifies a particular plot of real estate in physical memory. A *page*, on the other hand, is just a chunk of 4,096 bytes that can either reside on disk or be loaded into a page frame in physical memory. If a page of data is stored on disk, and a program attempts to access that page, a page fault is generated. The native operating system is responsible for catching the fault and loading the page into an available page frame. The operating system will also set the present flag (P) in the page's corresponding page table entry.

The relationship between pages and page frames is illustrated in Figure 1.21.

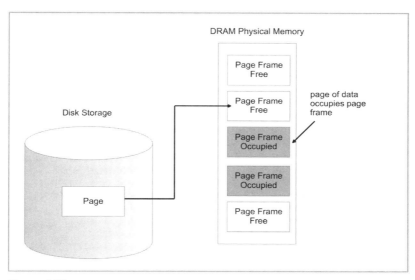

Figure 1.21

Case Study: Switching to Protected Mode

You've just waded through a mountain of theory. It's time to take a look at protected mode in practice. In this section, I am going to walk you through jumping from real mode to protected mode. To save myself from being labeled a sadist, I am going to stick to pure segmentation without enabling paging.

NOTE The following program was written in Intel 80x86 assembler. If you are not familiar with Intel assembly code, you should pick up Barry Brey's book, mentioned in the "References" section of this chapter.

Switching to protected mode is a dance that has six steps:
1. Build the GDT
2. Disable interrupts

3. Enable the A20 address line
4. Load the GDTR register
5. Set the PE flag in CR0
6. Perform a long jump

Switching to protected mode is perilous enough that you'll want to disable interrupts so that you have the undivided attention of the processor. Otherwise, you'll run the risk that an interrupt will occur and the processor will have to drop everything and service it. While the processor runs the interrupt handler, instructions could be executed that change the state of your machine enough to foil your attempt to switch modes.

NOTE Disabling interrupts is how many processors implement the atomic operations needed to maintain semaphores. By disabling interrupts, you can halt any extraneous activity (like a task switch), and this is what allows a snippet of code to run "atomically." I must have trudged through seven or eight books on operating systems before I stumbled upon this fact in Tanenbaum's MINIX book.

The third step may be foreign, even to those who know Intel assembler — ah yes, the dreaded A20 address line. When the 8086 was released, it had 20 address lines (A0 through A19). This allowed the 8086 to manage a 1MB address space. Any attempt to access memory beyond 1MB would wrap around to address 0. The Pentium normally uses 32 address lines. However, the Pentium starts in real mode at boot time and will try to mimic the 8086 by leaving the A20 address line disabled as the power-on default.

It just so happens that there is a logical AND gate called the A20 gate, which the A20 address line must pass through on its way to the outside world. Just like a bit-wise AND operator in C, an AND gate requires two inputs. The other input is derived from an output pin on the 8042 keyboard controller. Most peripheral attachments to the PC have their own dedicated microcontroller. The 8042 can be programmed via the OUT assembly command so that it sends a 1 to the A20 gate and enables the A20 address line.

NOTE More than anything else, the A20 line workaround was basically a kludge to allow compatibility between the 8086 and the 80286. Using an available pin on a keyboard controller to address memory issues is not exactly what I would call an elegant solution. It is not exactly a fast solution either. Yikes!

Once the GDTR register has been loaded via the LDTR instruction and the PE flag has been set in CR0, a FAR jump must be performed. In Intel assembler, a FAR jump instruction is used to make inter-segment jumps. This causes both the code segment register (CS) and the instruction pointer register (IP) to be loaded with new values. The motivation behind performing a FAR jump is that it serves as a way to load CS with a segment selector.

The tricky part of the FAR jump is that it must be coded in binary. Before we make the jump to protected mode, we are in real mode. That means that the assembler will be treating instructions using the traditional 16-bit interpretations. If we tried to code the 32-bit FAR jump in assembly language, the assembler (which is chugging along in 16-bit mode) would either signal an error or encode the jump instructions incorrectly. Thus, we are left with doing things the hard way.

Here is the assembly source code in all its glory:

```
.486P

; -- pmode.asm --

; create a single 16-bit segment containing real-mode
        instructions
CSEG SEGMENT BYTE USE16 PUBLIC 'CODE'
ASSUME CS:CSEG, DS:CSEG, SS:CSEG
ORG 100H

;start here-------------------------------------------------
here:
JMP _main

;make the jump to protected mode----------------------------
PUBLIC _makeTheJump
_makeTheJump:

; disable interrupts
CLI

; enable A20 address line via keyboard controller
; 60H = status port, 64H = control port on 8042
MOV AL,0D1H
OUT 64H,AL
MOV AL,0DFH
OUT 60H,AL

; contents which we will load into the GDTR via LGDTR need
; to jump over the data to keep it from being executed as code
JMP overRdata
gdtr_stuff:
gdt_limit   DW   0C0H
gdt_base    DD   0H
```

```
; copy GDT to 0000[0]:0000 ( linear address is 00000000H )
; makes life easier, so don't have to modify gdt_base
; but it also destroys the real-mode interrupt table (doh!)
; REP MOVSB moves DS:[SI] to ES:[DI] until CX=0
overRdata:
MOV AX,OFFSET CS:nullDescriptor
MOV SI,AX
MOV AX,0
MOV ES,AX
MOV DI,0H
MOV CX,0C0H
REP MOVSB

; load the GDTR
LGDT FWORD PTR gdtr_stuff

; set the PE flag in CR0
smsw    ax      ; get machine status word
or      al,1    ; enable protected mode bit
lmsw    ax      ; now in protected mode

; perform manual far jump
DB 66H
DB 67H
DB 0EAH                 ; FAR JMP opcode
DW OFFSET _loadshell
DW 8H                   ; 16-bit selector to GDT

;end of line, infinte loop
_loadshell:
NOP
JMP _loadshell
RET

; Global Descriptor Table (GDT)--------------------------------
PUBLIC _GDT
_GDT:
nullDescriptor:
NDlimit0_15      dw  0     ; low 16 bits of segment limit
NDbaseAddr0_15   dw  0     ; low 16 bits of base address
NDbaseAddr16_23  db  0     ; next 8 bits of base address
NDflags          db  0     ; segment type and flags
NDlimit_flags    db  0     ; top 4 bits of limit, more flags
NDbaseAddr24_31  db  0     ; final 8 bits of base address

codeDescriptor:
CDlimit0_15      dw  0FFFFH  ; low 16 bits of segment limit
CDbaseAddr0_15   dw  0       ; low 16 bits of base address
CDbaseAddr16_23  db  0       ; next 8 bits of base address
CDflags          db  9AH     ; segment type and flags
CDlimit_flags    db  0CFH    ; top 4 bits of limit, more flags
```

```
CDbaseAddr24_31    db   0       ; final 8 bits of base address

dataDescriptor:
DDlimit0_15        dw   0FFFFH  ; low 16 bits of segment limit
DDbaseAddr0_15     dw   0       ; low 16 bits of base address
DDbaseAddr16_23    db   0       ; next 8 bits of base address
DDflags            db   92H     ; segment type and flags
DDlimit_flags      db   0CFH    ; top 4 bits of limit, more flags
DDbaseAddr24_31    db   0       ; final 8 bits of base address

;main-------------------------------------------------------
PUBLIC _main
_main:

PUSH BP
MOV BP,SP

; set up temporary stack
MOV AX,CS
MOV SS,AX
MOV AX, OFFSET CSEG:_tstack
ADD AX,80H
MOV SP,AX

CALL _makeTheJump

POP BP
RET

;temp stack-------------------------------------------------
PUBLIC _tstack
_tstack DB 128 DUP(?)

CSEG ENDS
END here
```

You might notice that I intersperse data with code. Given that everything has to lie in a single segment, I really don't have a choice. It is, however, legal to mix data in with your code, as long as the region of memory storing the data is not treated like code and executed. This is a trick they don't always teach you in the books.

I built the previous program as a .COM executable using Microsoft's MASM. The command line to build the binary is:

```
C:\myfiles>ml /AT /FlpmodeList.txt pmode.asm
```

The /AT option causes the assembler to construct a .COM file (i.e., /AT means assemble with tiny memory model), which is really nothing more than a raw binary. There are no address relocations or fix-ups to be performed. The /Fl option causes a listing file to be generated. Listing files are a handy way to see what binary encoding your assembler generates.

There is a little bit of a catch. Unfortunately, once the switch to protected mode is made, I can't do that much because the processor expects (and wants) 32-bit machine code. Because the assembler that created the program is running in 16-bit mode, I am plain out of luck.

There is a way around this dilemma: The various snippets of operating system bootstrap code that I have read typically load the kernel into memory before the actual switch to protected mode is performed. This allows the FAR jump to transfer processor control to something that the processor can digest once it has switched modes. The kernel is exclusively 32-bit code, so the processor will have no problem following directions.

The side effect of all this is that you'll need two different compilers to write an OS on Intel. You need a 16-bit compiler to create the boot code and a 32-bit compiler to write the operating system proper. This whole process is illustrated in Figure 1.22.

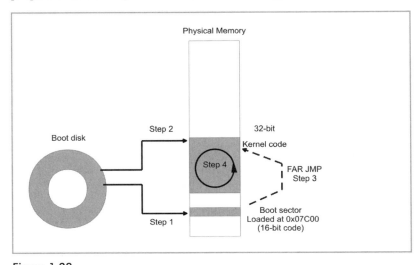

Figure 1.22

 NOTE Borland still sells a 16-bit DOS compiler with its TurboC++ suite. Microsoft sells Visual C++ 1.52, which can also generate 16-bit code. There are also a number of freebie compilers on the Internet that create 16-bit executables. I like Dave Dunfield's MICRO-C compiler.

You can also get Microsoft's 16-bit CL.EXE compiler and MASM assembler for free as part of the Windows Device Driver Kit. MASM consists of two files: ML.EXE and ML.ERR. The only downside is that they do not come with documentation.

Typically, when a computer is powered on, the BIOS (which is burnt into ROM) will spring into action and look for a bootable device. Remember that PCs start off in real mode. For the sake of simplicity, let us assume that the BIOS locates a bootable diskette in drive A. The BIOS will load the diskette's boot sector into DRAM at address `0000[0]:7C00` (i.e., physical address `0x07C00`). This is step number one.

Once the BIOS has loaded the boot sector, it hands over control of the machine to whichever machine instructions now reside at `0000[0]:7C00`. However, there are still a number of BIOS services that can be accessed using interrupts. This is where the BIOS plays a crucial role because there is a set of primitive disk I/O interrupts that can be used to load the kernel.

Diskette sectors are 512 bytes in size, so there is really only enough code to load the kernel from disk into memory (step 2) and then switch to protected mode. At the end of the transition to protected mode, the 16-bit boot sector code will perform a manually coded FAR jump to the kernel's entry point (step 3). The kernel code takes matters from there and the system is now in protected mode and executing 32-bit instructions (step 4).

NOTE You will have to run this program under the auspices of DOS. When I say this, I mean something like DOS 6.22. Do *not* try to run this program in a virtual DOS console running on Windows 2000. You will also have to make sure that no other memory management software (i.e., HIMEM.SYS, EMM386.EXE) has been installed.
Unfortunately, you will need to reboot your machine, seeing as how I overwrite the real mode interrupt vector table that lies at the bottom of memory.

If you are interested in taking this discussion to the next level by actually building such a boot sector, I can make a few recommendations. First, you should write the boot sector in assembly code to save space. Next, your boot code should only make use of BIOS interrupts to interact with the hardware. You should not try to invoke a DOS interrupt. DOS will not be there.

Also, you should assemble and link the boot sector program as a 16-bit `.COM` file binary. PCs boot into real mode and thus only understand the 16-bit instruction set. The boot sector must also be 100% code, which means that you need to avoid extra formatting in the finished executable. This is why you will want to build a `.COM` file. They are raw binaries.

To place this code on a diskette's boot sector, you will need to use Microsoft's `debug` utility. The following set of `debug` commands can be used to perform this task:

```
C:\code\boot>debug boot.com
-l
-w cs:0100 0 0 1
-q
C:\code\boot>
```

The `-l` command loads the `boot.com` file into memory. By default, the `boot.com` file will be loaded by debug to address `CS:0x0100`. The next command takes the instructions starting at this address and writes them to drive A (i.e., drive 0) starting at logical sector 0. A single, 512-byte sector is written. This may be easier to understand by looking at the general format of the `-w` command.

```
w    startAddr    driveLetter    startSector    nSectors
```

Once this has been done, the only thing left to do is to write the kernel and place it on the diskette. You will need a 32-bit compiler to write the kernel, and you should be aware that the compiler will package your kernel code within some executable file format (i.e., the Windows Portable Executable (PE) file format), although I have heard that `gcc` has a switch that will allow you to build a raw 32-bit binary.

The best way to deal with this extra baggage is to jump over it, which is to say that the boot sector code should take the formatting headers into account and merely sidestep them. You might want to disassemble your kernel file to determine where the header data stops and where your kernel code begins.

You can use `debug` to write your kernel to the diskette, the same way you as the boot sector.

Closing Thoughts

By now you should understand why memory management requires the operating system and the processor to work closely together. Nevertheless, the roles that the hardware and operating system assume are, without a doubt, complementary.

The processor defines a *mechanism* for accessing, protecting, and emulating memory. The hardware does, indeed, expect a special set of data structures to be in place, like the GDT and the Page Directory. But these are merely extensions of the mechanism that the processor provides.

It is the responsibility of the operating system to make use of the processor's services and mandate *policy* for using them. In the next chapter, we will see how different operating systems tackle the issue of implementing memory management policies.

References

Blunden, Bill. "Methodology for OS Construction," *Phrack* Issue 59. www.phrack.com.

Brey, Barry. *Intel Microprocessors 8086/8088, 80186/80188, 80286, 80386, 80486 Pentium, and Pentium Pro Processor, Pentium II, Pentium III, and Pentium IV: Architecture, Programming, and Interfacing*. 2002, Prentice Hall, 6th Edition, ISBN: 0130607142.

This is a fairly recent book and should take care of any questions you may have. Barry has been writing about Intel chips since the first one came out.

Intel Corporation. *Intel Architecture Software Developer's Manual, Volume 3: System Programming Guide*. 1997, order number 243192.

MIPS Technologies. *MIPS64 Architecture For Programmers, Volume III: The MIPS64 Privileged Resource Architecture*. 2001, document number: MD00091.

Podanoffsky, Michael. *Dissecting DOS*. 1995, Addison-Wesley, ISBN: 020162687X.

This book has a useful summary of the boot process on Intel hardware. It also details the design and operation of RxDOS, an enhanced clone of MS-DOS. In the spirit of the original DOS implementation, Podanoffsky has written the entire OS in assembly code. I'm not sure whether to admire his programming fortitude or be disheartened by the lack of portability.

Wahbe, Lucco, Anderson, Graham. *Efficient Software-Based Fault Isolation*. 1993, Proceedings of the Symposium on Operating System Principles.

Chapter 2

Memory Management Policies

"If I could remember the names of all these particles, I'd be a botanist."
— Enrico Fermi

In the previous chapter, I discussed the basic mechanisms that processors provide to allow memory regions to be read, modified, isolated, and simulated. Now you are ready to examine the ways in which operating systems construct policies that make use of these mechanisms. The processor presents the means to do things with memory through a series of dedicated data structures, system instructions, and special registers. It offers a set of primitives that can be combined to form a number of different protocols. It is entirely up to the operating system to decide how to use the processor's fundamental constructs, or even to use them at all.

There are dozens of operating systems in production. Each one has its own design goals and its own way of deciding how to use memory resources. In this chapter I will take an in-depth look at the memory subsystems of several kernels, ranging from the simple to the sophisticated. I will scrutinize source code when I can and hopefully give you a better feel for what is going on inside the LeMarchand cube.

In this chapter, I am going to gradually ramp up the level of complexity. I will start with DOS, which is possibly the most straightforward and simple operating system that runs on a PC. DOS is really nothing more than a thin layer of code between you and the hardware. Next, I will kick the difficulty up a notch with MMURTL. MMURTL, unlike DOS, is a 32-bit operating system that runs in protected mode. Finally, this chapter will culminate with a discussion of two production-quality systems: Linux and Windows.

After having looked at all four operating systems, I think that Windows is the most complicated system. Anyone who disagrees with me should compare implementing a loadable kernel module for Linux with writing a kernel mode PnP driver for Windows. There are people who make a living off of telling people how to write Windows kernel mode drivers. Don't get me wrong, the documentation for writing kernel mode drivers is accessible and copious; it is just that the process is so involved. After literally wading through Windows, I gained an appreciation for the relatively straightforward nature of the Linux kernel.

Case Study: MS-DOS

DOS Segmentation and Paging

Microsoft's disk operating system (DOS) is a study in minimalism. The operating system's conspicuous lack of advanced features, however, was not completely intentional. Rather, the nature of DOS was a result of the context in which it was constructed. Back in 1980, when Bill Gates offered to provide an operating system for IBM's first PC, the hardware (i.e., the 8088) didn't support anything other than strict real mode addressing. To compound matters, Microsoft was under such strict time-to-market constraints that they outsourced everything by purchasing a CP/M clone written for the 8088 by a man named Tim Paterson.

Suffice it to say, talking about memory segmentation and paging on DOS is of limited use, primarily because neither of these features exist. DOS operates strictly in real mode, where it is very easy for a program in execution to pillage memory.

NOTE It is interesting to see how being at the right place at the right time can change history. IBM had originally intended to use the CP/M operating system sold by Digital Research. For whatever reason, the deal fell through and Microsoft was there to catch the ball. Had Bill Gates decided to complete his degree at Harvard, or had Digital Research not bungled its deal with IBM, we would all probably be using Apple computers.

DOS Memory Map

The DOS operating system consists of three files:
- IO.SYS
- MSDOS.SYS
- COMMAND.COM

IO.SYS interfaces directly to the computer's hardware. It is written, or at least modified, by the Original Equipment Manufacturer (OEM). All requests for hardware services from user programs must travel through MSDOS.SYS, a device-neutral I/O manager, which translates the request into a format that can then be passed to IO.SYS. MSDOS.SYS can be thought of as the kernel of DOS (although your definition of "kernel" would have to be pretty loose). COMMAND.COM is a command interpreter.

IO.SYS and MSDOS.SYS are both core system files. Without these files, there is no DOS. The command interpreter, on the other hand, can be replaced. There were several companies in the 1980s that offered their own, enhanced version of COMMAND.COM. How many readers remember Norton Commander?

Before DOS is loaded, the real mode address space of a bare computer resembles that displayed in Figure 2.1. A bare-bones DOS bootstrap will load all of its components into the region between the BIOS data and video RAM.

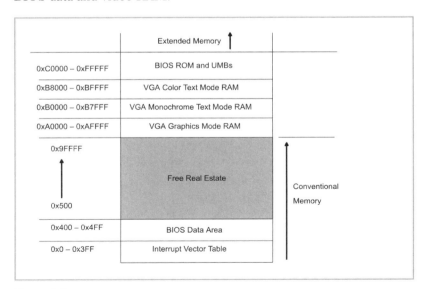

Figure 2.1

Low memory is populated by BIOS code and the interrupt vector table (IVT). The first 640KB of memory is known as *conventional memory*. This is where DOS will load itself and run its user programs. There are also several small regions of memory not used by the video hardware or the BIOS. These are called *Upper Memory Blocks* (UMBs). The region of memory above the 1MB limit is known as *extended memory*. In the next section, I will discuss extended memory in more depth. For now, you can assume that DOS is confined to a 1MB space.

NOTE *Expanded memory is extra storage space that was created by swapping memory below the 1MB mark to special memory chips. Expanded memory is strictly an historical artifact and its use was replaced by extended memory.*

When a DOS machine boots, the BIOS locates a bootable disk and loads its boot sector to 0000[0]:7C00. The boot sector then inspects its disk for IO.SYS. How do I know this? One quick way to verify this without performing a gruesome disassembly is to dump the boot sector and look for character data that is hard coded.

This is how the debug utility could be used to perform this type of investigation:

```
C:\WINDOWS>debug
-l cs:0100 0 0 1
-d cs:0280
158E:0280  C3 B4 02 8B 16 4D 7C B1-06 D2 E6 0A 36 4F 7C 8B   .....M|.....6O|.
158E:0290  CA 86 E9 8A 16 24 7C 8A-36 25 7C CD 13 C3 0D 0A   .....$|.6%|.....
158E:02A0  4E 6F 6E 2D 53 79 73 74-65 6D 20 64 69 73 6B 20   Non-System disk
158E:02B0  6F 72 20 64 69 73 6B 20-65 72 72 6F 72 0D 0A 52   or disk error..R
158E:02C0  65 70 6C 61 63 65 20 61-6E 64 20 70 72 65 73 73   eplace and press
158E:02D0  20 61 6E 79 20 6B 65 79-20 77 68 65 6E 20 72 65    any key when re
158E:02E0  61 64 79 0D 0A 00 49 4F-20 20 20 20 20 53 59 53   ady...IO     SY
158E:02F0  53 4D 53 44 4F 53 20 20-20 53 59 53 00 00 55 AA   SMSDOS   SYS..U.
-q
```

The first thing I do is load the boot sector into memory at CS:0100. Then I just start perusing the memory image until I hit pay dirt. As you can see, the string "IO.SYS" is there. This doesn't necessarily prove that DOS looks for IO.SYS and loads it (to prove this, you would have to disassemble), but it provides evidence.

Once IO.SYS has been loaded, it locates MSDOS.SYS and loads it into memory. The operating system, whose core files now exist in memory, then loads COMMAND.COM. After this, the CONFIG.SYS configuration file will be processed to load device drivers and set system parameters. Finally, COMMAND.COM will automatically process a batch file of commands named AUTOEXEC.BAT. The AUTOEXEC.BAT file is used to set up the operating system's environment (i.e., PATH and TEMP variables) and load Terminate and Stay Resident (TSR) programs.

NOTE TSR programs are loaded into memory and remain there even after they terminate so that they can be reactivated quickly. The `doskey` program, which supports command line history services, is a good example of a TSR as is the DOS mouse driver. Because TSRs are usually small, they are typically stuck into a UMB if possible.

Memory Usage

The `mem` command can be used to obtain a snapshot of the operating system's memory usage:

```
Memory Type          Total   =   Used    +   Free
----------------    -------     -------     -------
Conventional          638K          97K        541K
Upper                   0K           0K          0K
Reserved                0K           0K          0K
Extended (XMS)     65,532K      65,532K          0K
----------------    -------     -------     -------
Total memory       66,170K      65,629K        541K

Total under 1 MB      638K          97K        541K

Largest executable program size    541K  (553,664 bytes)
Largest free upper memory block      0K      (0 bytes)
```

The `mem /D` command can also be utilized to get a precise look at where, in conventional memory, DOS has placed its core components:

```
Conventional Memory Detail:

Segment       Total            Name         Type
-------     ---------------   ----------    --------
 00000       1,039    (1K)                  Interrupt Vector
 00040         271    (0K)                  ROM Communication Area
 00050         527    (1K)                  DOS Communication Area
 00070       2,560    (3K)    IO            System Data
                              CON           System Device Driver
                              AUX           System Device Driver
                              PRN           System Device Driver
                              CLOCK$        System Device Driver
                              A: - B:       System Device Driver
                              COM1          System Device Driver
                              LPT1          System Device Driver
                              LPT2          System Device Driver
                              LPT3          System Device Driver
                              COM2          System Device Driver
                              COM3          System Device Driver
                              COM4          System Device Driver
 00110      42,784   (42K)    MSDOS         System Data
```

```
00B82       10,832    (11K)   IO          System Data
              192     (0K)                FILES=8
              256     (0K)                FCBS=4
            7,984     (8K)                BUFFERS=15
              448     (0K)                LASTDRIVE=E
            1,856     (2K)                STACKS=9,128
00E27       4,720     (5K)    COMMAND     Program
00F4E          80     (0K)    MSDOS       -- Free --
00F53         272     (0K)    COMMAND     Environment
00F64         112     (0K)    MEM         Environment
00F6B      88,992    (87K)    MEM         Program
02525     501,168   (489K)    MSDOS       -- Free --
```

As you can see, most of the system binaries are loaded into low memory, where they share space with vital system data structures. The segment addresses provided in the previous listing will need to be multiplied by 16 (i.e., append the implied zero) in order to specify an actual segment.

Example: A Simple Video Driver

Because DOS offers no memory protection, it is possible to sidestep DOS and the BIOS and write your own video driver.

It so happens that text characters can be sent to the screen by modifying VRAM. For example, VGA color text mode video RAM starts at 0xB8000. A VGA text screen consists of 80 columns and 25 rows. Each character requires a word of memory, so 4,000 bytes of VRAM are consumed. The low byte of each word stores an ASCII character, and the high byte of each character is an attribute byte. I am going to keep things simple and use a monochrome scheme so the attribute byte is 0xF.

The following program takes advantage of this fact by clearing the screen and displaying a small message.

```
/* --crtio.c-- */

int offset;

/*
    Have 80x25 screen
    Each screen character in VRAM is described by two bytes:

                [ASCII char][attribute]
                  lo byte    hi byte

    80x25 = 2000 screen characters = 4000 bytes of VRAM
*/
void putCRT(ch)
char ch;
{
```

Memory Management Policies

```c
    /*
    ch = BP + savedBP + retaddress
       = BP + 4 bytes
    display attribute = BP+5
    ( 0FH = white foreground, black background )
    */
    asm "MOV SI,BP";
    asm "ADD SI,4H";
    asm "MOV BYTE PTR +5[BP],BYTE PTR 0FH";

    /* set destination ES:DI pair */
    asm "MOV DX,0B800H";
    asm "MOV ES,DX";
    asm "MOV DI,_offset";

    /* place [char][attr] word in memory */
    asm "MOV CX,2H";
    asm "REP MOVSB";
    return;
}/*end putCRT-----------------------------------------------*/

/*
    puts string at text position 'pos'
    note: 2 bytes for each screen character,
          so mult. offset by 2
*/

void putCRTStr(str,pos)
char *str;
int pos;
{
    int i;
    i=0;
    offset=pos*2;
    while(str[i]!=0)
    {
        putCRT(str[i]);
        offset = offset+2;
        i++;
    }
    return;
}/*end putCRTStr--------------------------------------------*/

/* clears the screen and places cursor to [0,0]*/

void clearCRT()
{
    int i;
    offset=0;
    for(i=0;i<=(80*25);i++){ putCRT(' '); offset=offset+2; }
    offset=0;
    return;
}/*end clearCRT--------------------------------------------*/
```

```
/*
test driver
*/

void main()
{
    clearCRT();
    putCRTStr("DOS is dead, Use Linux!",240);
    return;
}/*end main---------------------------------------------------*/
```

You might notice that I am using rather old K&R syntax and unusual inline statements. This is due to the fact that the compiler I am using is Dave Dunfield's handy MICRO-C PC86 C compiler. It's one of the only freebies on the Internet that I could find that would generate MASM friendly 16-bit assembler. In case you are interested, here is my build script:

```
del crtio.obj
del crtio.exe
del crtio.asm
mcp crtio.c | mcc > crtio.asm
ML /Zm -c crtio.asm
LINK crtio.obj PC86RL_S.OBJ
```

NOTE You can also get Microsoft's 16-bit `CL.EXE` compiler and MASM assembler for free as part of the Windows Device Driver Kit. MASM consists of two files: `ML.EXE` and `ML.ERR`. The only downside is that they do not come with documentation.

Example: Usurping DOS

Another unfortunate result of the lack of memory protection in DOS is that vital system data structures can be modified by ordinary programs. The interrupt vector table (IVT) is particularly susceptible to being hacked.

Each IVT entry is 4 bytes in size and consists of a 16-bit offset address in the lower word, followed by a 16-bit segment address. This segment and offset address specify the address of the Interrupt Service Routine (ISR). If you want to take control of an interrupt, you can easily overwrite an IVT entry with your own segment and offset address.

An ISR is just a function that implements an interrupt. DOS ISRs are all accessed through interrupt 0x21 in conjunction with a function specifier in the 8-bit AH register. The DOS API, in fact, is nothing more than a series of interrupts and their specifications.

Memory Management Policies

The DOS operating system itself is merely the implementation of this API.

There is no need to write your own routine to hijack interrupts. DOS makes life easy for you by providing services for replacing IVT entries (i.e., functions AH=0x25 and AH=0x35 of DOS interrupt 0x21). In the following program, I seize control of the keyboard and only surrender control after the user types eight keys in a row.

```
/* --usurp.c-- */

int oldseg;
int oldoff;
char kbd_buffer;
int delay;

void saveOldISR()
{
    asm "MOV AH,35H";
    asm "MOV AL,09H";
    asm "INT 21H";
    asm "MOV _oldseg,ES";
    asm "MOV _oldoff,BX";
    return;
}/*end saveOldISR----------------------------------------------*/

void setUpISR()
{
    asm "PUSH   DS";
        asm "MOV    CX,CS";
        asm "MOV    DS,CX";
        asm "MOV    DX,OFFSET newISR";
        asm "MOV    AH,25H";
        asm "MOV    AL,09H";
        asm "INT    21H";
        asm "POP    DS";
    return;
}/*end setUpISR-----------------------------------------------*/

void restoreOldISR()
{
    asm "STI";
    asm "PUSH DS";
    asm "MOV CX,_oldseg";
    asm "MOV DS,CX";
    asm "MOV DX,_oldoff";
    asm "MOV AH,25H";
    asm "MOV AL,09H";
    asm "INT 21H";
    asm "POP DS";

    asm "MOV AX,4C00H";
    asm "INT 21H";
```

```c
    return;
}/*end restoreOldISR----------------------------------------*/

void readKBD()
{
    while(kbd_buffer==-1){}
    kbd_buffer=-1;
    return;
}/*end readKBD----------------------------------------------*/

void ISR()
{
    asm "newISR:";
    asm "STI";
    asm "PUSH AX";
    asm "PUSH BX";
    asm "IN AL,60H ;get [scan code][status] from port 60H";
    asm "MOV BL,AL";

    asm "IN    AL,61H ;tell KBD have received (twiddle bit)";
    asm "MOV   AH,AL";
    asm "OR    AL,80H";
    asm "OUT   61H,AL";
    asm "XCHG AL,AH";
    asm "OUT   61H,AL";

    asm "mov AL,BL";
    asm "and BL,7FH  ; get [scan code]";
    asm "test AL,80H ; check for key release";
    asm "jnz exitInterrupt";

    asm "mov _kbd_buffer,BL";

    asm "exitInterrupt:";
        asm "mov    AL,20H";
    asm "out    20H,AL";
    asm "pop    BX";
    asm "pop    AX";
    asm "iret";
    return;
}/*end ISR--------------------------------------------------*/

void printBiosCh(ch)
char ch;
{
    /*
    ch = BP + savedBP + retaddress
       = BP + 4 bytes
    */
    asm "MOV AH,0EH";
    asm "MOV AL,+4[BP]";
    asm "INT 10H";
    return;
```

```c
}/*end printBiosCh-----------------------------------------------*/

void printBiosStr(cptr,n)
char* cptr;
int n;
{
    int i;
    for(i=0;i<n;i++){ printBiosCh(cptr[i]); }
    return;
}/*end printBiosStr----------------------------------------------*/

/* wrestle control from DOS and go on a joy ride */

void main()
{
    kbd_buffer = -1;
    delay=0;

    printBiosStr("save-",5);
    saveOldISR();

    printBiosStr("setUp-",6);
    setUpISR();

    readKBD();
    while(delay<=7)
    {
        printBiosCh('1'+delay);
        delay++;
        readKBD();
    }

    printBiosStr("-restore",8);
    restoreOldISR();

    return;
}/*end main------------------------------------------------------*/
```

As with the previous example, I am using MICRO-C and MASM to build the executable. The steps necessary to build this program are:

```
del usurp.obj
del usurp.exe
del usurp.asm
mcp usurp.c | mcc > usurp.asm
ML /Zm -c usurp.asm
LINK usurp.obj PC86RL_S.OBJ
```

Also, I use a trick in this example that might not be completely obvious. In C, labels are limited to the scope of the function that they are defined in. This prevents a nefarious programmer like me from making arbitrary random jumps from function to function.

Naturally, there are exceptions to the rule. For example, `longjmp()` and `setjmp()` are ANSI C functions that allow nonlocal transfers of control. In addition, anyone who has abused exception handling knows that throwing an exception can be subverted to do an abrupt hop between procedures. The technique that I use is just not as conventional, or as obvious, as the previous two. I take advantage of the fact that assembly language labels tend to be global in scope.

So instead of being limited to a function with ANSI C labels:

```
mylabel:
    Printf("local function jump\n");
    Goto mylabel;
```

I surreptitiously hide the label definition inside of an inline assembly code snippet:

```
asm "my_global_label:";
```

This effectively camouflages the label from the compiler's syntax checker. The only caveat is that you can only reference the label in other inline assembly statements.

In the example above, I needed to specify an address without being constrained by C's structured programming paradigm. I needed this address to create a new entry in the IVT. Using the inline assembler tactic that I just explained, it worked fine.

Jumping the 640KB Hurdle

In the beginning, DOS programs lived in a 1MB jail cell. Escaping the conventional memory barrier was a lot like the sound barrier; it was just a matter of time before it was broken. In the later half of the 1980s, a number of products emerged that allowed extended memory to be accessed. These products may be referred to, in general, as *DOS extenders*. DOS extenders allowed the 640KB jail cell to grow into a 4GB prison.

"I am not a number; I am a free man."
— Prisoner number 6, *The Prisoner*

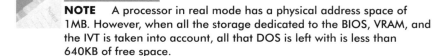
NOTE A processor in real mode has a physical address space of 1MB. However, when all the storage dedicated to the BIOS, VRAM, and the IVT is taken into account, all that DOS is left with is less than 640KB of free space.

A DOS extender is a collection of library calls and software components that allow programs to manipulate extended memory but still access the DOS file system, system calls, and BIOS. Because support must be compiled into a program, DOS extenders tended to be shipped with compilers as a sort of add-on third-party tool. For example, Visual C++ version 1.0 Professional was sold with Phar Lap's 286|DOS Extender. Watcom's C compiler also came with Rational System's DOS/4G extender. DOS/4G is also still being sold by Tenberry Software. It may also be of interest to the reader that Phar Lap still sells a DOS extender. DOS may never die.

NOTE If you are interested in looking at a free DOS extender, take a look at DJGPP's cwsdpmi.exe DPMI host.

Because DOS is not designed to access extended memory, there was no established protocol for managing extended memory. Vendors selling DOS extenders were free to design their own unique bridge over the 1MB moat. Eventually, groups of companies got together and developed a number of standard ways to manage extended memory. A few of the more notable standards are:

- DOS Protected Mode Interface (DPMI)
- Virtual Control Program Interface (VCPI)
- eXtensible Memory Specification (XMS)

Each standard has a specification. The DPMI spec is available at Tenberry's site (see the reference section at the end of the chapter). The XMS standard was implemented by Microsoft, Lotus, and AST Research. The VCPI standard was an attempt to allow other DOS extenders to cohabitate with Expanded Memory Specification (EMS) services.

The role of a DOS extender in the execution of a user application is displayed in Figure 2.2.

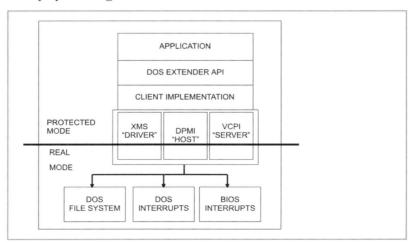

Figure 2.2

The application itself runs in protected mode. The extender exposes an API to the application, which may look and smell like a normal 16-bit API. Beneath the API is a set of libraries that will manage the application's switch to protected mode and transmit its requests for real mode services. The client transmits these requests to a component that will do the necessary dirty work in real mode. According to the standard you are looking at, these worker components are called "drivers," "servers," or "hosts."

The relationships between these different pieces remind me of a restaurant. The customer (i.e., the application) requests a specific entrée from the waiter (i.e., the extender client). The waiter writes up the order and gives it to a cook (i.e., an XMS driver) in the back room. When the cook has completed the entrée, he gives it to the waiter, who then passes it back to the customer. The kitchen, where the food is cooked, is real mode. The dining area, with its fancy linen, is protected mode.

Most commercial DOS extenders will have client layers that are capable of interacting with a number of different extended memory environments. In fact, the first thing the client code usually does is check to see which environments exist. For example, the following code can be used by DOS extender clients to see if an XMS driver exists:

```
; Is an XMS driver installed?
mov ax,4300h
int 2Fh
cmp al,80h
jne NoXMSDriver
```

NOTE Vendors who sell DOS extenders often required the developer to embed all the memory management components in the application itself. The motivation behind this was to guarantee that the application could run on any DOS machine without having to impose a set of prerequisites. This tended to make applications using DOS extenders relatively large. Some DOS extenders were almost entire operating systems by themselves, especially when you compare them to DOS. It is rumored that DOS extender technology, at Microsoft, was first implemented in 1988 for a monster DOS application called Windows.

DOS 6.22 was released with two memory management drivers: `HIMEM.SYS` and `EMM386.EXE`.

`HIMEM.SYS` is an XMS driver. It is mentioned in the XMS specification. `EMM386.EXE` simulates expanded memory with extended memory for old dinosaur applications that need expanded memory. `EMM386.EXE` provides services conforming to both the XMS and VCPI specifications.

`HIMEM.SYS` and `EMM386.EXE` are loaded into memory as device drivers when the operating system boots. The following entries in `CONFIG.SYS` perform this task:

```
DEVICE=A:\DRIVER\HIMEM.SYS /VERBOSE
DEVICE=A:\DRIVER\EMM386.EXE VERBOSE
```

Like DOS itself, DOS extenders have faded into obscurity. However, they serve as interesting, if not curious, artifacts that demonstrate just how far system software engineers are willing to go to solve a memory problem. They also show how problems related to backward compatibility can be extremely unpleasant.

Case Study: MMURTL

"There are two types of people in this world, good and bad. The good sleep better, but the bad seem to enjoy the waking hours much more."
— Woody Allen

Richard Burgess is a one-man army. He is the sole creator of the MMURTL operating system. Not only did he build his own protected mode multitasking operating system, but he also wrote a 32-bit compiler, assembler, and debugger to go with it. I guess this is what happens when you retire. Like Ken Thompson, Burgess was bitten by the operating system bug. It is just one of those things. Even if you try to resist, you find yourself compelled to design and implement an operating system. You pace, you rant, and you lose sleep over all sorts of tiny hardware idiosyncrasies.

I can only guess that Burgess spent a lot of his time munching on chocolate-covered coffee beans and washing them down with Jolt. I bought a copy of Richard's book on MMURTL back in 1995, and I am glad to see that it has been brought back from the dead. After a stint of being out-of-print, Sensory Publishing came out with a new release in 2000.

Like DOS, MMURTL is an operating system that runs on Intel hardware. Compared to DOS, MMURTL is a huge step forward. Nevertheless, on the complexity spectrum, MMURTL lies somewhere between DOS and Linux. This explains why I have decided to present MMURTL before Linux. You will get a better understanding of exactly how MMURTL is "simple" in the next few sections.

Background and Design Goals

Burgess was careful to invest effort in deciding on a set of design goals. It is actually possible to understand what some of these goals are just by dissecting the operating system's name (Message-based, MUltitasking Real-Time kerneL). To get a better idea of what Richard wanted to build, here is a complete list:

- Single-user environment
- Message-passing kernel
- Priority-based, pre-emptive, multitasking
- Real-time operation
- 32-bit protected mode memory management

MMURTL is not meant to be a multiuser machine, like a UNIX box or mainframe. Instead, it is meant to interact with other users via the client-server model. This is in the same vein as Microsoft's Distributed Network Architecture (DNA), where the computing workload is spread out among users.

NOTE When Windows NT 4.0 was released in 1996, Microsoft really marketed DNA. DNA, however, was built around the limitations of the NT system more than anything else. It was not an independent movement with its own agenda. In other words, rather than point out the fact that NT was hobbled by its lack of multiuser support, the DNA campaign seemed to say, "yes, of course NT is not a multiuser system — we meant to do that."

The Intel Pentium of 1996 was not capable of handling the kind of massive transaction load that high-end RISC hardware did. Again, the marketing people piped up, "oh, of course Windows machines can't handle 10 million transactions a day ... that's because Windows machines are meant to be clustered."

I imagine that when some poor sysadmin pointed out NT's propensity to bluescreen back in 1996, years before the advent of service pack 5, a Microsoft marketing guy jumped onto a table and said, "hey, that's not a bluescreen. That's a nifty screen saver you can watch while the memory image dumps."

The primary IPC and synchronization mechanism in MMURTL is message passing. MMURTL's message-passing code is buried deep in the bowels of the kernel so that it is an integral part of the kernel's normal operation. For example, the task-switch mechanism in MMURTL is firmly rooted in the message-passing API.

Instituting real-time response features also shaped MMURTL to a greater extent. With real-time systems, certain outside events must be acknowledged and processed in a specific amount of time. A good example of this would be patient monitoring equipment in a hospital. The primary impact that this had on MMURTL was to allow outside events (i.e., the user) to force a task switch. Some multiuser operating systems implement their own strict policies and individual users have little or no control. With MMURTL, however, the user has much more control over what gets the processor's attention. Given that MMURTL is a single-user operating system, this makes sense.

Unlike DOS, MMURTL was originally designed to use Intel's protected mode memory management. Surprisingly, MMURTL uses only minimal segmentation and does not bother to implement memory protection on the segment level. Instead, MMURTL makes use of paging to provide both memory allocation features and protection. These architectural idiosyncrasies are what make this operating system a good place to start.

MMURTL and Segmentation

MMURTL has only three memory segments. That is it. They are described in the operating system's GDT. MMURTL constructs a segment for the operating system, a segment for application code, and a segment for application data. The best way to see this is to look at MMURTL's GDT definitions:

```
NullDesc     DQ  0000000000000000h  ;The first desc is always null

OSCodeDesc   DW  0FFFFh              ; Limit 15-0 (4Gb)
             DW  0000h               ; Base  15-0
             DB  00h                 ; Base  23-16 ;10000h
             DB  10011010b           ; P(1) DPL(00) 1 1 C(0) R(1) A(0)
             DB  11001111b           ; G(1) D(1) 0 0 Limit[19-16]
             DB  00h                 ; Base  31-24

DataDesc     DW  0FFFFh              ; Limit (bits 0:15) at linear 00K
             DW  0000h               ; base (bits 15:0)
             DB  00h                 ; base (bits 23:16)
             DB  10010010b           ; P(1) DPL(00) 1 0 E(0) W(1) A(0)
             DB  11001111b           ; G(1), B(1) 0 0 limit[19-16]
             DB  00h                 ; Base at 0 (bits 31:24)

CodeDesc     DW  0FFFFh              ; Limit 15-0 (0FFFFh)
             DW  0000h               ; Base  15-0
             DB  00h                 ; Base  23-16
             DB  10011010b           ; P(1)-DPL(00)-1-1-C(0)-R(1)-A(0)
             DB  11001111b           ; G(1) D(1) 0 0 Limit[19-16]
             DB  00h                 ; Base  31-24
```

It might be easier to see what this means if we decode the fields in each descriptor and construct a matrix. This is what I have done in Table 2.1. I have always had a hard time reading descriptor tables myself:

Table 2.1

	OsCodeDesc	DataDesc	CodeDesc
Base address	0x00000000	0x00000000	0x00000000
Size limit	0xFFFFF	0xFFFFF	0xFFFFF
Limit units	4KB increments	4KB increments	4KB increments
32-bit code/data	Yes	Yes	Yes
Present in memory	Yes	Yes	Yes
Privilege	0x0	0x0	0x0
Type	Execute/Read	Read/Write	Execute/Read

Obviously, Intel is using what I would call a *Flat Segment Model*. There is really only a single segment (according to the descriptors) that spans the address space of the processor.

NOTE MMURTL never uses an LDT, only a single GDT and a single IDT (for interrupt handling). During the boot phase, the MMURTL 16-bit boot sector code loads the 32-bit kernel code from the disk to memory at 0x6000. The kernel is loaded at 0x6000 to avoid wiping out the BIOS data area, which is still needed. The boot code then points the GDTR and IDTR registers to the GDT and IDT. The GDT and IDT were loaded into memory as a part of the kernel image. The boot sector code then switches the processor to protected mode and jumps to the kernel entry point. Once this has transpired, the kernel will reload itself to address 0x0. The BIOS code and data, which are overwritten in the process, are no longer needed.

Because there are only three segment descriptors to index, there are only three segment selectors possible (0x8, 0x10, and 0x18). Each one indexes a specific descriptor. These three selectors are presented and decomposed in Figure 2.3:

	GDT Index	GDT?	Privilege	
OS Code Selector	0000000000001	0	00	= 0x8
User Code Selector	0000000000011	0	00	= 0x18
User Data Selector	0000000000010	0	00	= 0x10

Figure 2.3

From looking at the descriptors and the selectors, it is easy to see that the entire memory address space has been set to privilege level zero. In addition, the segment limits have all been set to the maximum value (0xFFFFF in 4KB increments). This means that no memory protection scheme is used at the segment level. MMURTL uses the simplest protected mode segment model possible and avoids using any other segment-related features.

Paging Variations

I have been using the terms "paging" and "virtual memory" synonymously. The historical motivation for paging was to make use of disk storage to simulate core memory. This traditional use is why I have emphasized the employment of paging as a way to artificially expand a computer's address space. Those tiny little magnets were expensive, and 8KB of core memory could only take you so far.

There are, however, other ways to use paging. If you recall from Chapter 1, the Pentium's paging facilities take a linear address and map it to a byte in physical memory. This address resolution mechanism allows physical memory to be mapped to an artificial/linear address space. A program running in a linear memory space uses pointers holding linear addresses, which to the program appear to correspond to actual physical memory locations. However, the actual physical location of the program and its data have addresses that are usually much different from the linear values. The nature of the Pentium's paging hardware allows for two distinct uses for virtual memory:

- Virtual-paged memory
- Demand-paged virtual memory

In the case of *virtual-paged memory*, physical memory is broken up into a series of pages. A linear address space is implemented, and the hardware takes care of translating the linear addresses to the physical addresses. The linear address space can be much larger than the physical address space, but *you will only be able to manage an amount of memory equal in size to the physical address space*. Virtual-paged memory is "virtual" because the addresses being used (i.e., the linear addresses) do not correspond to physical addresses.

NOTE Virtual-paged memory is virtual memory without disk I/O. Page faults are used in virtual-paged memory to indicate memory access violations. Disk storage is not used to expand a processor's address space.

Demand-paged virtual memory is where we bring disk storage into the fray. In this case, not only are the addresses fake (i.e., linear), but they might also resolve to physical bytes that are stored on a disk instead of in physical memory. This method is called demand paging because an operating system that uses demand paging will load pages from disk storage "on demand" when they are needed. In addition to reporting access violations, this form of paging also makes use of page faults in order to determine when pages should be loaded from disk storage.

MMURTL and Paging

One important characteristic of MMURTL's paging subsystem is that it does not provide disk-based virtual memory. Specifically, MMURTL does not use a disk drive to artificially expand its address space. Instead, MMURTL merely uses the Intel processor's paging hardware to provide memory protection and memory allocation. In other words, MMURTL implements a virtual-paged memory model. Burgess speculates in his book that support for demand-paged virtual memory might be added in the future.

MMURTL uses paging facilities to map each application to the same linear address region, while having them reside in different physical memory regions. This creates the illusion that all the applications exist in the same region of physical memory. However, it is an illusion. The user applications only share the same linear address region. Their page directories and page tables are distinctly different. This bookkeeping technique allows processes to appear to be in the same place simultaneously, when they are really not.

MMURTL uses a 2GB *linear* address space. Be careful! I am not talking about physical memory; you don't have to go out and buy 2GB of SDRAM to run MMURTL. The OS owns the bottom 1GB of the fake/linear address space and each application thinks that it owns everything above 1GB. In addition, each user application also thinks that it is the only program running above 1GB.

Figure 2.4 displays the memory map, as seen by a MMURTL user application.

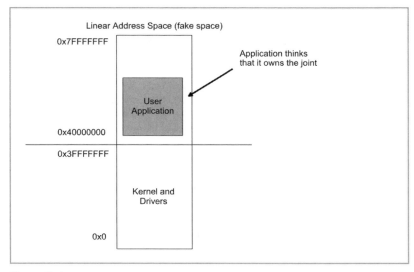

Figure 2.4

In reality, what is actually happening is illustrated in Figure 2.5.

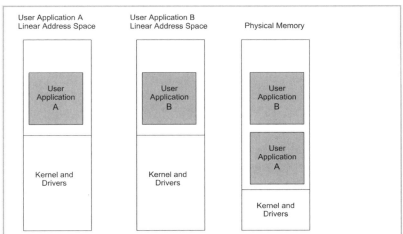

Figure 2.5

QUESTION

How can this be done? How can applications share the same linear address memory but still reside in separate regions of physical memory?

ANSWER

The key is in the page tables and page directories. It is possible for a linear address to correspond to two different physical addresses because it is nothing but a series of offsets. The base addresses of items can differ, and this is what results in different locations in DRAM. This is illustrated in Figure 2.6.

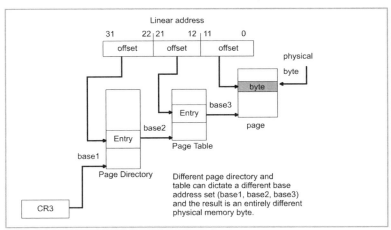

Figure 2.6

For example, two applications could exist: A and B. In MMURTL, each application has its own page directory. This means that applications A and B will have different sets of paging data structures. Application A will have base addresses set (base1A, base2A, and base3A) and application B will have base addresses set (base1B, base2B, and base3B). The byte that these two sets reference will be completely different, but the linear address is the same because the linear address is nothing but a set of offsets.

Now let's look at how MMURTL implements memory protection. If you recall the page directory and page table entries that were described in the previous chapter, you should remember that the Intel processor supports two different privilege levels: supervisor and user. Page table entries have a field, consisting of a single bit, to specify the privilege level of the memory page that the entry references. If the field is clear, the page of memory possesses supervisor rights. If the field is set, the page possesses only user privileges.

In MMURTL, the kernel and all the device drivers exist at the supervisor level, and the user applications exist at the user level. If a user application attempts to access the kernel, a page fault is thrown and MMURTL responds via the IDT. This two-ring privilege scheme based on paging is a compromise between the single-ring scheme of DOS (where there is no distinction between the operating system and user applications) and the elaborate four-ring privilege hierarchy supported by the Pentium's segmentation hardware.

Memory Allocation

MMURTL provides memory to user applications in 4KB pages. If your application only needs 24 bytes, it will be up to the user space libraries (i.e., `malloc()`) to take a 4KB page and break it into smaller pieces. MMURTL exposes the following memory allocation system calls to user applications:

- `extern far U32 AllocPage(U32 nPages, U8 **ppMemRet);`
- `extern far U32 DeAllocPage(U8 *pOrigMem, U32 nPages);`
- `extern far U32 QueryPages(U32 *pdPagesLeft);`

Let's look at each function individually:

- AllocPage
  nPages — The number of 4KB pages to allocate

- ppMemRet — A pointer to a pointer that stores the address of the memory allocated
- DeAllocPage
  pOrigMem — A pointer to address of the page to free
  nPages — The number of 4KB pages to free (assume pages are contiguous)
- QueryPages
  pdPagesLeft — A pointer to a variable that will hold the number of free pages left

The `AllocPage()` function allocates memory in contiguous pages. In addition, the memory address returned is the address of the lowest byte in memory (i.e., the first byte of the first page).

All of these functions return a number of possible error codes. There are dozens of error codes defined in MMURTL's header files. It is important to realize that an error code of zero means that there are no problems.

```
#define ErcOK        0    /* Alls Well */
```

NOTE As far as protected mode operating systems are concerned, MMURTL is about as spartan as you can get. There is no demand paging, and the page-based allocation scheme is uncomplicated. In the next two case studies, you will see how much more involved memory management can become.

Case Study: Linux

"The memory management on the PowerPC can be used to frighten small children."
— Linus Torvalds

Now we arrive at the production operating systems. Linux has a sophisticated and fairly mature kernel, one that IBM is willing to sell on its mainframes. This additional, but necessary, complexity will make our discussion a little more interesting.

History and MINIX

In the beginning, there was a professor in Amsterdam named Andrew S. Tanenbaum. He wanted his students to be able to get their hands dirty with operating system internals without having to spend months dissecting a large production system. In 1987 Tanenbaum wrote MINIX, a small UNIX clone that originally ran on the 8086/88. He wrote it from scratch and did an impressive job of making its source code easy to read and follow. I can attest to this fact, as I have read portions of the source myself. The code that programs the 8259 PIC is particularly well done. MINIX was also designed as a microkernel-based system so that the file system and memory manager could be switched with new ones at run time.

Tanenbaum received megabytes of e-mail from people who wanted to add features to MINIX. Tanenbaum's goal, however, was to present his students with something that they could explore as a learning tool. Adding extra functionality, like demand paging, was out of the question.

Into the picture came Linus Torvalds, a computer science student in Finland who decided that he was going to hack MINIX into a production-quality operating system. In 1991, Linus made an announcement of his intentions on the MINIX users newsgroup. By December of 1991, version 0.1 was released and Linux began its ascendance to worldwide popularity.

NOTE It may seem a bit odd, but one of the original detractors of Linux was Tanenbaum! In January of 1992, Tanenbaum left a posting on comp.os.minix titled "Linux is obsolete." Needless to say, he was wrong.

Design Goals and Features

According to Linus' first posting on comp.os.minix, Linux started off as "just a hobby." Over the years, it has morphed into a powerful system that easily holds its own against proprietary flavors of UNIX. According to the README file in the kernel's base source code directory, "Linux is a Unix clone written from scratch by Linus Torvalds with assistance from a loosely-knit team of hackers across the Net. It aims towards POSIX compliance."

POSIX, the Portable Operating System Interface, is a specification that establishes a standard set of operating system calls. It was introduced as an effort to help unify the UNIX operating system. Different vendors, like IBM, HP, Sun, and SGI, all sell their own version of UNIX. I should not have to tell you that these vendors have a vested interest in locking customers in to their own special blend. The POSIX standard is an effort to at least give the appearance that there is a least common denominator, even if the different vendors would be more than happy to stab each other in the back.

The POSIX standard is maintained by the IEEE (Institute of Electrical and Electronics Engineers) and is also known as IEEE 1003.1-2001. The full title is:

Memory Management Policies

```
1003.1-2001 IEEE Std 1003.1-2001
(Open Group Technical Standard, Issue 6),
Portable Operating System Interface (POSIX®) 2001
```

The last time I looked, the price of this standard was around $176. This is why a search for "POSIX" on Google or Yahoo will not prove very fruitful. Trust me on this. Fortunately, someone in the Linux development effort bought a copy. It was a good investment. Any operating system worth its salt will be POSIX compliant.

The following sample list of features supported by Linux reads like a Christmas list to Santa:

- Multiuser
- Symmetric multiprocessing (SMP)
- Protected mode memory protection
- Demand-paged virtual memory
- Dynamically and statically linked libraries
- Multiple file system support
- Loadable kernel modules (LKMs)
- High-performance TCP/IP stack

If you compare this feature list to MMURTL's, you will see why I discussed MMURTL first.

NOTE It would be very easy to fill an entire book with an explanation of the inner workings of Linux. In fact, I reference a couple of such books at the end of this chapter. I am going to stick to somewhat of a tourist's view in the following discussion; this will allow me to highlight the principal architectural features, which illustrate various memory management policies, without getting too weighed down.

Linux and Segmentation

Like MMURTL, Linux makes only minimal use of the Pentium's segmentation facilities. I must say, I was a little surprised by this. I was expecting Linux to implement a full-blown, four-ring segmentation scheme. The Linux kernel does not make use of an LDT. The GDT, which the kernel does use, is fairly small:

```
ENTRY(gdt_table)
    .quad 0x0000000000000000    /* NULL descriptor */
    .quad 0x0000000000000000    /* not used */
    .quad 0x00cf9a000000ffff    /* 0x10 kernel 4GB code at
                                   0x00000000 */
    .quad 0x00cf92000000ffff    /* 0x18 kernel 4GB data at
                                   0x00000000 */
    .quad 0x00cffa000000ffff    /* 0x23 user   4GB code at
                                   0x00000000 */
```

```
        .quad 0x00cff2000000ffff    /* 0x2b user    4GB data at
                                              0x00000000 */
        .quad 0x0000000000000000    /* not used */
        .quad 0x0000000000000000    /* not used */
        /*
         * The APM segments have byte granularity and their bases
         * and limits are set at run time.
         */
        .quad 0x0040920000000000    /* 0x40 APM set up for bad
                                              BIOSs */
        .quad 0x00409a0000000000    /* 0x48 APM CS    code */
        .quad 0x00009a0000000000    /* 0x50 APM CS 16 code (16 bit) */
        .quad 0x0040920000000000    /* 0x58 APM DS    data */
        .fill NR_CPUS*4,8,0         /* space for TSSs and LDTs */
```

These structures are defined in /usr/src/linux/arch/i386/kernel/head.S. The previous assembly code does not use MASM-compatible directives. Instead, it follows AT&T syntax. Linux only uses one more kernel segment than MMURTL, and it is used to accommodate kernel data. Let's dissect the GDT and place the results in a table for easy reading (see Table 2.2).

Table 2.2

	Kernel Code	Kernel Data	User Code	User Data
Base address	0x0	0x0	0x0	0x0
Size limit	0xFFFFF	0xFFFFF	0xFFFFF	0xFFFFF
Limit units	4KB units	4KB units	4KB units	4KB units
32-bit code/data	Yes	Yes	Yes	Yes
Present in memory	Yes	Yes	Yes	Yes
Privilege	0x0	0x0	0x3	0x3
Type	Execute/Read	Read/Write	Execute/Read	Read/Write

The segment selectors corresponding to these descriptors are displayed in Figure 2.7.

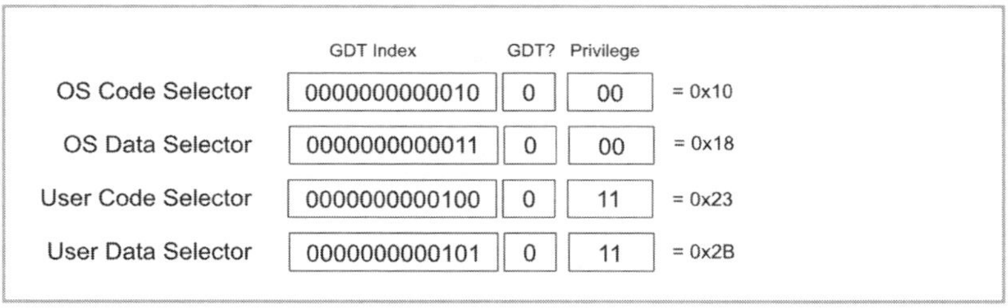

```
                        GDT Index       GDT?  Privilege
    OS Code Selector   0000000000010    0     00        = 0x10
    OS Data Selector   0000000000011    0     00        = 0x18
  User Code Selector   0000000000100    0     11        = 0x23
  User Data Selector   0000000000101    0     11        = 0x2B
```

Figure 2.7

There are 12 descriptors defined in the source code snippet. Four are not used and four are dedicated to advanced power management (APM). The GDT, however, is not guaranteed to be a fixed size. As of kernel version 2.4, every CPU on the motherboard gets two segment descriptors in the GDT. Each CPU gets a descriptor specifying a Task State Segment (TSS) and a descriptor specifying a segment that stores a Local Descriptor Table (LDT). This is illustrated in Figure 2.8.

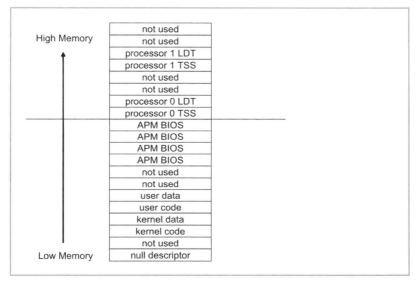

Figure 2.8

Notice how each processor's TSS and LDT segment descriptor is delimited by two unused segment descriptors.

The segment descriptor pointing to an LDT in Linux typically stores the address of the default_ldt variable. The default_ldt variable is basically an LDT with a single NULL descriptor. It is declared in /usr/src/linux/include/asm-i386/desc.h.

```
struct desc_struct
{
    unsigned long a,b;
};
```

The default_ldt variable is defined in /usr/src/linux/arch/i386/kernel/traps.c.

```
struct desc_struct default_ldt[] =
{ { 0, 0 }, { 0, 0 }, { 0, 0 },{ 0, 0 }, { 0, 0 }};
```

The reason that Linux can get away with its minimal GDT is that all processes use the same linear address space but are stored in different regions of physical memory. This is very similar in spirit to MMURTL's memory management approach.

Notice the privilege difference between the kernel segments and the user segments. Unlike MMURTL, which gave every segment a privilege of zero, Linux institutes two rings of protection. The kernel executes with privilege level 0x0, and user code executes with privilege level 0x3.

Linux and Paging

The techniques of segmentation and paging are both used to divide up an address space into distinct regions. So in a way, perhaps the lack of an elaborate segmentation scheme in Linux is merely an effort to avoid being redundant. To implement demand paging and protection, Linux uses Intel's paging facilities.

Three-Level Paging

In the previous chapter, I examined what is known as a two-level paging model that uses two bookkeeping data structures: page directories and page tables. Linux adds another data structure and extends the linear address that it uses so that it has a *three-level paging model*. I assume that this has been implemented to allow Linux to seamlessly extend itself to 64-bit architectures. The three-level paging model is displayed in Figure 2.9

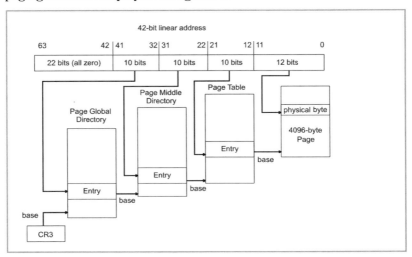

Figure 2.9

The CR3 control register holds the base address of the page global directory. The highest-order 10-bit section of the linear address stores an offset address into the page global directory and is added to the base address in CR3 to specify a page global directory entry.

This entry stores the base address to a page middle directory structure.

The middle 10-bit section of the linear address is added to the base address in the global page directory entry to specify an entry in the page middle directory. The entry in the page middle directory stores the base address of a page table.

The lowest-order 10-bit portion of the linear address is added to the base address in the page middle directory to specify an entry in the page table. This page table entry will specify the base address of a physical 4KB page of memory. The 12-bit portion of the linear address is an offset into the physical page and specifies an actual physical byte of memory.

QUESTION

Wait! Hold on a minute! (At least, I hope this is what you are thinking.) The Pentium is a 32-bit processor that deals with 32-bit linear addresses. How does Linux resolve this fact?

ANSWER

As it turns out, Linux assumes that the portion of the linear address that serves as an offset into the page middle directory consists of zero bits. However, the page middle directory is kept in the address resolution cycle for the sake of forward compatibility. It is just that Linux fixes the page middle directory so that it has a single entry. In the case of the 32-bit Pentium, the page global directory reverts to the page directory we know from earlier. These adjustments are illustrated in Figure 2.10.

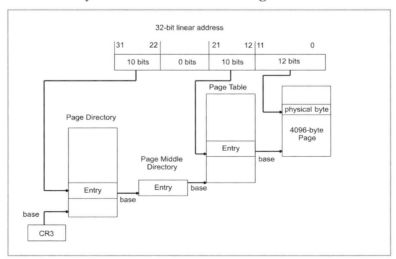

Figure 2.10

To get a ground-zero look at how the engineers saw their own solution, here is how the Linux source documentation explains the workaround in /usr/src/linux/include/asm-i386/pgtable.h:

```
/*The Linux memory management assumes a three-level page
 * table setup. On the i386, we use that, but "fold" the
 * mid level into the top-level page table, so that we
 * physically have the same two-level page table as the
 * i386 mmu expects.
 */
```

NOTE When Linux runs on a 64-bit processor, the 42-bit linear address in the three-level model will represent the 42 least significant bits in a 64-bit linear address. The other, higher-order bits would be assumed to be zero.

Linux uses a number of C structures to represent table entries. The page directory and the page table themselves are just arrays of these 32-bit entries. These structures are defined in /usr/src/linux/include/asm-i386/page.h:

```
typedef struct { unsigned long pte_low; } pte_t;
typedef struct { unsigned long pmd; } pmd_t;
typedef struct { unsigned long pgd; } pgd_t;
```

These structures will change for special cases, like when the address bus has been extended to 36 bits or when a 64-bit processor is being used. I am sticking to the run-of-the-mill 32-bit Pentium scenario for the sake of simplicity.

Remember from the previous chapter that it is the duty of the operating system to maintain the state of the present flag (P) in the page table. It is also the duty of the operating system to clear the dirty bit (D) when a page is loaded into memory. The processor will set the dirty bit the first time that the page is accessed. This entails accounting work on the part of the operating system. To this end, Linux uses a set of macros to perform its accounting. For example, the following macros are used to query the P flag in the page table entry, set the page table entry, and clear the page table entry:

```
#define _PAGE_PRESENT      0x001
#define _PAGE_PROTNONE     0x080    /* If not present */
#define pte_present(x)     ((x).pte_low & (_PAGE_PRESENT | \
                                          _PAGE_PROTNONE))
#define set_pte(pteptr, pteval) (*(pteptr) = pteval)
#define pte_clear(xp)      do { set_pte(xp, __pte(0)); } while (0)
```

There are a multitude of other such flags in /usr/src/linux/include/asm-i386/pgtable.h. As with many portions of the

Linux code base, these macros take different forms when the kernel is not running on a 32-bit Pentium.

There is also a significant amount of page metadata that is external to Intel's native paging data structures, which is to say that the metadata is relevant to Linux without being mandated by the processor. For example, Linux allows pages to be *locked*. A locked page of memory cannot be written out to disk. Kernel pages are locked. The kernel also keeps a record of how many processes are using a particular page of memory. These extra features are supported by the `page` structure:

```
typedef struct page
{
   struct list_head list;      /* -> Mapping has some page lists.*/
   struct address_space *mapping;  /* The inode (or ...)
                                      we belong to. */
   unsigned long index;        /* Our offset within mapping. */
   struct page *next_hash;     /* Next page sharing our hash bucket
                                  in the pagecache hash table. */
   atomic_t count;             /* Usage count, see below. */
   unsigned long flags;        /* atomic flags, some possibly
                                  updated asynchronously */
   struct list_head lru;       /* Pageout list, eg. active_list;
                                  protected by pagemap_lru_lock!!*/
   wait_queue_head_t wait;     /* Page locked?  Stand in line... */
   struct page **pprev_hash;   /* Complement to *next_hash. */
   struct buffer_head * buffers;  /* Buffer maps us to a disk
                                     block. */
   void *virtual;              /* Kernel virtual address (NULL
                                  if not kmapped, ie. highmem) */
   struct zone_struct *zone;   /* Memory zone we are in. */
} mem_map_t;
```

This structure is defined in /usr/src/linux/include/ linux/mm.h. The `count` member keeps track of how many processes are using a page. The `count` variable is zero if the page is free. The `flags` member stores 32 Boolean fields. Its first bit, the `PG_locked` field, is used to indicate if a page is locked.

```
#define PG_locked    0   /* Page is locked. Don't touch. */

#define UnlockPage(page)    unlock_page(page)
#define PageLocked(page)    test_bit(PG_locked, &(page)->flags)
#define LockPage(page)      set_bit(PG_locked, &(page)->flags)
```

The macros above are also defined in /usr/src/linux/ include/linux/mm.h.

Page Fault Handling

Page faults are the core mechanism that allow Linux to support memory protection and demand paging. The page fault handler in Linux is a function called do_page_fault() defined in /usr/src/linux/arch/i386/mm/fault.c:

```
void do_page_fault(struct pt_regs *regs, unsigned long
                   error_code);
```

The regs argument is a pointer to a structure containing the contents of the registers when the page fault was generated.

The error_code argument wraps a 3-bit value that was generated as a result of the page fault. It is this little 3-bit value that is absolutely crucial. It will determine what the kernel will do. If a memory access violation has occurred, the kernel will probably kill the process that made the illegal memory access. Sometimes this means putting the kibosh on the kernel! Linux uses the Supervisor/User flag in page table entries to implement the distinction between kernel code and user code.

If a process has attempted to access a page that is on disk (i.e., its present (P) flag is cleared), the kernel will need to take care of loading the page into memory. This is one feature that definitely separates Linux from MMURTL. MMURTL only uses paging as a way to divide up and manage memory. Linux takes things a step further and allows pages to be swapped to disk storage. Naturally, this requires a whole load of additional instructions and logic, making Linux a far more intricate operating system.

Table 2.3 explains the format of the 3-bit value passed to do_page_fault and the information that it stores.

Table 2.3

Bit	Value	Meaning
0	0	Page fault caused by accessing a page that has its present (P) flag cleared
0	1	Page fault caused by invalid access right
1	0	Page fault caused by access of type execute or type read
1	1	Page fault caused by access of type write
2	0	Page fault occurred while the processor was in kernel mode
2	1	Page fault occurred while the processor was in user mode

Memory Allocation

When Linux boots, the kernel reserves a region of physical memory to store its code and data structures. The pages of memory that constitute this region are locked and cannot be written to disk. The kernel is loaded into physical memory starting at physical address 0x00100000 (i.e., just above 1MB). This is done to avoid overwriting BIOS code at the bottom of memory and VRAM that lies within the first megabyte. The size of the kernel's image in memory is a function of the features that were built into it when it was compiled, so it is not really feasible to give a definite upper boundary to the kernel's region in physical memory. The remaining part of physical memory (not reserved by the kernel, BIOS, or VRAM) is known as *dynamic memory*. Figure 2.11 displays this basic organization of physical memory.

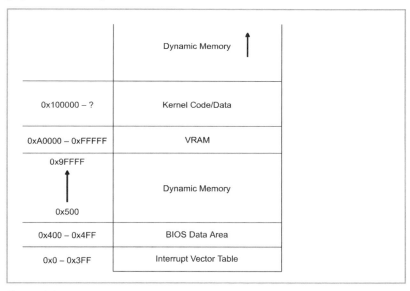

Figure 2.11

The linear address space is an alternate reality that is created by the kernel and the processor (the programs happen to think it is real). It has little or nothing in common with the actual arrangement of code and data in physical memory. The linear address space of Linux is broken into two basic regions. The linear address range from 0 to PAGE_OFFSET−1 is used for user programs. The linear address range from PAGE_OFFSET to 0xFFFFFFFF (4GB) is reserved for the kernel. The PAGE_OFFSET macro is defined in /usr/src/linux/include/asm-i386/page.h as 0xC0000000. This means that the kernel uses the last gigabyte of linear memory, and the user applications reside in the first three gigabytes. The layout of the Linux linear address space is displayed in Figure 2.12.

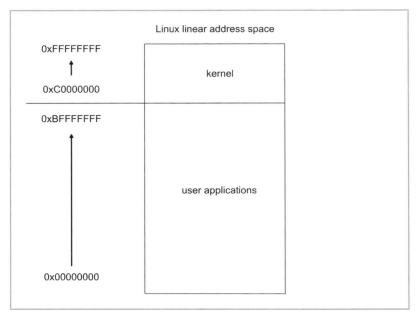

Figure 2.12

NOTE A gigabyte of linear address space does not necessarily translate into a gigabyte of physical memory. For example, if the kernel consumes 4MB of physical memory, only 4MB of linear address space will be active in the operating system's gigabyte of linear memory.

The kernel can allocate dynamic memory for itself by invoking one of three functions:

- `unsigned long __get_free_pages(unsigned int gfp_mask, unsigned int order);`
- `void * kmalloc (size_t size, int flags);`
- `static inline void * vmalloc (unsigned long size);`

The `__get_free_pages()` function is defined in /usr/src/linux/mm/page_alloc.c. It uses the buddy system algorithm to allocate 2^{order} pages of contiguous memory. The `gfp_mask` dictates how the free pages will be looked for. For example, if `gfp_mask` is set to `__GFP_HIGH`, the priority of the memory request is set to the highest level. There are a whole set of `gfp_mask` values in /usr/src/linux/include/linux/mm.h.

The `kmalloc()` function is defined in /usr/src/linux/mm/slab.c and allocates `size` number of bytes. Instead of a buddy system algorithm, it uses an approach similar to the *slab allocator* designed by Sun Microsystems in 1994. The `kmalloc()`

function manages 4KB pages internally so that smaller amounts of memory can be requested.

The `vmalloc()` function is defined in `/usr/src/linux/include/linux/vmalloc.h`. This function allows noncontiguous pages of memory to be allocated. The two previous functions deal only with contiguous regions of memory. The `size` argument indicates the number of pages to allocate.

The kernel allocates dynamic memory for user applications when the `sys_fork()` system call is made. The `sys_fork()` function causes a *process address space* to be requisitioned from memory for the user program. A process address space consists of a set of *memory regions* in the computer's linear address space. Each region is a contiguous set of linear addresses and is assigned a set of access rights. The size of each memory region is a multiple of 4KB.

Linux user applications traditionally have four memory regions. One is used to store the application's machine code, one is used to store the application's data, another serves as a stack, and the fourth region is used as a heap to provide space for run-time storage requests. The arrangement of these regions in the linear address space is a function of the development tools that were used to build the application and operating system's program loader. For example, Figure 2.13 displays two different ways to organize memory regions.

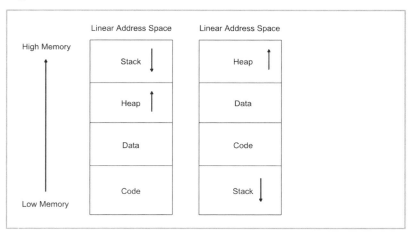

Figure 2.13

The `sys_fork()` function in `/usr/src/linux/arch/i386/kernel/process.c` is just a wrapper for `do_fork()`, which takes care of the real work. The `do_fork()` function calls a function named `copy_mm()` to take care of creating the new task's address space. The `copy_mm()` function, in turn, calls a function named `mm_init()`, which eventually ends up in a call to `__get_free_pages()`.

This string of function calls creates a memory descriptor for the new process and populates it. A memory descriptor, in terms of the C programming language, is just a `mm_struct` structure in the file `/usr/src/linux/include/linux/sched.h`.

```
struct mm_struct
{
    struct vm_area_struct * mmap;
    rb_root_t mm_rb;
    struct vm_area_struct * mmap_cache;
    pgd_t * pgd;
    atomic_t mm_users;
    atomic_t mm_count;
    int map_count;
    struct rw_semaphore mmap_sem;
    spinlock_t page_table_lock;

    struct list_head mmlist;

    unsigned long start_code, end_code, start_data, end_data;
    unsigned long start_brk, brk, start_stack;
    unsigned long arg_start, arg_end, env_start, env_end;
    unsigned long rss, total_vm, locked_vm;
    unsigned long def_flags;
    unsigned long cpu_vm_mask;
    unsigned long swap_address;

    unsigned dumpable:1;

    /* Architecture-specific MM context */
    mm_context_t context;
};
```

The `vm_area_struct` structure describes a given memory region. Because a process address space usually consists of several memory regions, the `mm_struct` process address space descriptor will need to keep a list of `vm_area_struct` variables. This is what the `mmap` member variable is for.

The `pgd` member variable points to the page global directory allocated to a process address space. Each process in Linux owns a single page global directory, and this points to one or more page tables. Each process also has its own CR3 value. This register's contents are saved in the task's TSS when its corresponding task is suspended.

Memory Management Policies

The `total_vm` member specifies how many pages have been allotted for a process, and the `locked_vm` field determines how many of these pages are locked. The `rss` member variable indicates the number of page frames in RAM that the process is actually using.

There are a number of fields, like `start_code` and `end_code`, that store the initial and final linear addresses of each memory region. The location of command line arguments on the task's run-time stack is specified by the `arg_start` and `arg_end` member variables.

Memory Usage

For a system-wide summary of memory usage, use the `free` command:

```
# free
                total       used       free     shared    buffers     cached
Mem:            62200      58916       3284        864       2692      17688
-/+ buffers/cache:         38536      23664
Swap:           96380       9480      86900
Total:         158580      68396      90184
```

`Mem` and `swap` are simply physical memory and disk swap space. Linux tends to keep things simple, and this is part of its appeal to me. The data displayed by `free` is actually an abbreviated version of what you would get by looking in the kernel's `/proc` directory:

```
# cat /proc/meminfo
            total:      used:       free:  shared: buffers:   cached:
Mem:    63692800   39899136   23793664  1110016  6172672  15433728
Swap:   98693120   39428096   59265024
MemTotal:       62200 kB
MemFree:        23236 kB
MemShared:       1084 kB
Buffers:         6028 kB
Cached:          8972 kB
SwapCached:      6100 kB
Active:         10664 kB
Inact_dirty:    11208 kB
Inact_clean:      312 kB
Inact_target:    1780 kB
HighTotal:          0 kB
HighFree:           0 kB
LowTotal:       62200 kB
LowFree:        23236 kB
SwapTotal:      96380 kB
SwapFree:       57876 kB
NrSwapPages:    14469 pages
```

If you are interested in looking at the memory usage of a particular process, the `ps` command can be applied:

```
# ps -o sz,vsz,pmem,pid -C init

 SZ   VSZ  %MEM    PID
353  1412   0.1      1
```

This command pumps out the size in bytes of physical memory used, the size in bytes of linear address space being used, percent of memory used, and the process ID of the `init` command. If you need to determine which tasks are running on a Linux machine in order to use the `ps` command that I just showed you, I would recommend using `pstree`. The `pstree` command displays an ASCII tree of all the tasks currently running.

Example: Siege Warfare

In the Middle Ages, siege warfare was a common form of battle. A siege would occur when a larger army surrounded a smaller army that was holed up inside a stronghold. The besiegers had two basic options: storm the fortifications or wait the enemy out. Both options could be expensive. War has always been, and still is, founded on financial concerns. Storming the stronghold could be costly in terms of lives. Starving an enemy into submission was also expensive because it cost a significant amount of money to sustain a standing army in terms of food and supplies. Although movies may favor the storming tactic, some of the more spectacular victories were obtained through patience.

"So, you think you could out-clever us French folk with your silly knees-bent running about advancing behavior?"
— French guard, *Monty Python and the Holy Grail*

Because Linux has a two-ring privilege scheme, the innards of the operating system are not exposed and vulnerable like they are in DOS. We cannot simply rip out entries in the interrupt vector table or write messages to the screen by modifying VRAM. We are back in elementary school: To do anything, we need permission. The kernel policies, in conjunction with Intel hardware, have built fortifications against malicious programs. The crown jewels, operating system data structures, have been hidden far behind thick, formidable walls.

In this example, I will lay siege to Linux in an attempt to demonstrate its memory protection facilities. As in the Middle Ages, I can either storm the walls or wait it out. I suspect that waiting it out and starving the kernel of resources is still the most effective way to bring a computer to its knees. An example of this kind of attack would be a memory leak.

I ran the following program on Linux:

```
/* --starve.c-- */

#include <stdio.h>
void main()
{
    unsigned long i;
    unsigned long j;
    char ch;
    unsigned char *ptr;

    for(i=0;i<0xFFFFFFFF;i++)
    {

        printf("malloc(%lu)\n",i);
        ptr = malloc(0x100000);
        for(j=0;j<0x100000;j++){ ptr[j]=0x7; }
        printf("press [enter] key\n");
        scanf("%c",&ch);
    }
    return;
}
```

The machine I tested this code on had 64MB of DRAM. At about 110MB of allocated virtual memory, my computer's paging subsystem began to thrash. A few moments later, I lost control of my machine; I couldn't even gain the attention of a terminal console to kill the process. I literally had to unplug my computer. A more insidious version of this program would sleep at odd intervals and only allocate small bits of memory. This kind of attack tends to creep up on systems that aren't being monitored carefully.

Next, I tried the more audacious approach of directly assaulting the kernel:

```
/* --brute.c-- */

void main()
{
    unsigned char *ptr;
    ptr = 0xC0000000;
    *ptr ='a';
    return;
}
```

Here is the console output that I received:

```
[root@localhost root]# cc -o brute brute.c
```

```
[root@localhost root]# ./brute
Segmentation fault
```

"You silly King..." As you can see, the Linux kernel has been heavily fortified against such brazen direct attacks. It noticed my attempt for access to the kernel's memory image and sent me to /dev/null. Trying this type of straightforward tactic is about as wise as starting a land war in Asia. Inconceivable.

> **NOTE** However, there is an option that I haven't mentioned. The goal of storming a stronghold is to get inside. There are other, less obtrusive ways of getting past a heavy stone barrier. At the end of the day, nothing beats a generous plateful of treachery. Why spend man-hours of effort to break down a wall when you can sneak by it?

Linux Loadable Kernel Modules (LKMs) present the besieging army with an opportunity to dress up like opposing troops and simply walk blithely through the main gate. LKMs are basically software components that can be dynamically added to the kernel image, which is loaded in memory, at run time. An LKM becomes a part of the executing kernel. Why spend all that effort trying to pass a fortification when you can start on the other side to begin with?

> **NOTE** Once an LKM has been merged with the kernel's image, the LKM's code is a DOS-like situation where the operating system is naked. In this state, we can write to any device files we want. This includes /dev/kmem, the kernel's coveted memory image. We can also modify the /proc file system or perhaps hook an internal kernel function. The potential number of uses is almost infinite. Ba ha ha ha ha (evil laugh).

An LKM is really just an ELF object file that is dynamically linked with the kernel. You can create an LKM simply by compiling with the -c option that prevents the linker from being invoked. For example, if you have an LKM source file named lkm.c, you can compile it into an object file with:

```
[root@localhost root]# gcc -c -Wall lkm.c
```

> **NOTE** The Executable and Linkable Format (ELF) was originally designed by the UNIX System Laboratories (USL) before it was bought by Novell. The ELF specification was a part of the Application Binary Interface (ABI) effort. ELF is a binary format like COFF or Microsoft's PE format. In 1995, the Tool Interface Standard (TIS) group came out with version 1.2 of the ELF specification.

LKMs can be loaded/inserted into the kernel at run time with the following command:

```
[root@localhost root]#   insmod   lkm.o
```

The `insmod` program invokes the `sys_init_module()` system call, which the kernel uses to register the LKM. If you look at this system call in `/usr/src/linux/kernel/module.c`, you will see that it invokes a similarly named function in the LKM — `init_module()`. Try not to get confused by all the various `init_module()` functions.

To verify that the module is loaded, you can issue the `lsmod` command:

```
[root@localhost root]# lsmod
Module                  Size    Used by
lkm                     880     0  (unused)
ide-cd                  27072   0  (autoclean)
cdrom                   28512   0  (autoclean) [ide-cd]
soundcore               4464    0  (autoclean)
binfmt_misc             6416    1
tulip                   39232   1
ds                      7056    2
yenta_socket            9488    2
pcmcia_core             41600   0  [ds yenta_socket]
autofs                  11520   0  (autoclean) (unused)
appletalk               20912   0  (autoclean)
ipx                     16448   0  (autoclean)
mousedev                4448    1
hid                     19024   0  (unused)
input                   3840    0  [mousedev hid]
usb-uhci                21536   0  (unused)
usbcore                 51712   1  [hid usb-uhci]
ext3                    64624   1
jbd                     40992   1  [ext3]
```

Equivalent results can be obtained via:

```
[root@localhost root]#  cat /proc/modules.
```

This will provide you with a list of currently loaded modules. Naturally, some modules can be written so that they modify the kernel and are not listed (just a thought). Ba ha ha ha (Neumann laugh).

To remove an LKM from the kernel's image, you can use the `rmmod` command:

```
[root@localhost root]#  rmmod lkm
```

Note how I did not include the `.o` suffix as I did with `insmod`. The `rmmod` command will cause the LKM's `cleanup_module()` function to be invoked. You should use this as an opportunity to restore the system to its previous state.

NOTE The `init_module()` and `cleanup_module()` are the only functions that are required in order for an object file to serve as an LKM.

In the following code, I use an LKM to intercept the `sys_chdir` system call. This is reminiscent of the DOS example where I stole the keyboard interrupt. I basically take my own version of `sys_chdir` and use it to wrap a call to the actual system call. This allows me to piggyback the system call code with my own instructions.

The key to system call swapping is the `sys_call_table` array, which is an array of pointers to system call functions in the kernel. It is analogous to the real mode interrupt vector table. We can change which address gets jumped to for a given system call by switching an entry in the `sys_call_table` pointer array. In my example code, I make sure to save the old function address so that I can restore the `sys_call_table` when I am done.

```
/* --lkmod.c-- */

#define __KERNEL__          /*instructions are in kernel*/
#define MODULE              /*type of kernel code is module code*/
#define LINUX               /*keep it portable*/

#include<linux/kernel.h> /*standard LKM include*/
#include<linux/module.h> /*standard LKM include*/
#include<stdio.h>        /*need for sprintf()*/

#include <sys/syscall.h> /*need for __NR_chdir*/
#include <linux/sched.h> /*need for "current" pointer in
                           printStr*/
#include <linux/tty.h>   /*need for tty_struct*/

extern void sys_call_table[];   /*array of function pointers*/

void printStr(char *str)
{
      struct tty_struct *my_tty;

      my_tty = current->tty;
      if (my_tty != NULL)
      {
         (*(my_tty->driver).write)(my_tty,0,str,strlen(str));
         (*(my_tty->driver).write)(my_tty,0,"\015\012",2);
      }
      return;
}

asmlinkage int (*getuid_call)();
```

```
asmlinkage int (*saved_call)(const char *);

asmlinkage int my_call(const char *dir)
{
    char *uid_str[8];
    int uid;

    uid = getuid_call();
    sprintf((const char*)uid_str,"%d",uid);
    printStr((const char*)uid_str);
    printStr(dir);

    return saved_call(dir);
}

int init_module()
{
    printStr("init_module()-start");

    saved_call = sys_call_table[__NR_chdir];
    sys_call_table[__NR_chdir] = my_call;

    getuid_call = sys_call_table[__NR_getuid];

    printStr("init_module()-end");
    return(0);
}

void cleanup_module()
{
    printStr("cleanup()-start");

    sys_call_table[__NR_chdir] = saved_call;

    printStr("cleanup()-end");
    return;
}
```

Example: Siege Warfare, More Treachery

We have waged a lengthy siege against Linux and have tried a number of tactics to defeat memory protection. Of the three approaches that I have presented, starving the enemy into submission is the path of least resistance. Then again, you never really get inside the castle walls (i.e., the kernel) with the wait-them-out tactic; you merely get to watch your quarry inside the castle spasm in their death throes. Memory leaks provide only a hollow victory in that they don't allow you to get past the protective walls of the operating system.

Brute force attacks are glaringly fruitless, seeing as how the Pentium and Linux were explicitly designed to protect against such overt methods. Trying to barge into the kernel's linear address space is akin to banging your head against an anvil — the anvil wins every time.

LKMs are a cunning solution, but you need to have root privileges to execute programs such as `insmod` (ah ha! there's a catch!). Most people who obtain root don't need LKMs once they achieve that vaunted status anyway.

An ingenious and more sophisticated approach is needed.

One of the most devious tactics that I can think of is the buffer overflow attack. In the medieval days, a buffer overflow attack would be implemented by poisoning the besieged army's supply of food and water. They would consume the bad provisions and start acting confused and irrational.

Buffer overflow techniques were made famous by Aleph One's article in issue 49 of *Phrack* magazine. They rely on a function that uses a call like `strcpy()` to copy an argument to a local buffer. If a large enough argument is fed to the function, you can overflow the local buffer so that the function's activation record is corrupted. This allows skillful attackers to place their own return addresses and executable code on the activation record and literally hijack the processor's path of execution.

Here is a fairly simple example:

```
/* --bufferFlow.c-- */

#include<stdio.h>
#include<stdlib.h>
#include<string.h>

void overflow(char *str)
{
    char buffer[4];
    strcpy(buffer,str);
    return;
}

void hijacked()
{
    printf("\tYou've been hijacked!\n");
    exit(0);
    return;
}

void main()
{
```

```
    char bigbuff[]={'a','b','c','d',                /*buffer*/
                    'e','f','g','h',                /* ebp */
                    '\x0','\x0','\x0','\x0'};       /*IP*/
    void *fptr;
    unsigned long *lptr;

    printf("bigbuff = %s\n",bigbuff);

    fptr = hijacked;
    lptr = (unsigned long*)(&bigbuff[8]);

    *lptr = (unsigned long)fptr;

    printf("In main()\n");
    overflow(bigbuff);
    printf("Back in main()\n");

    return;
}
```

When this program is run, the following output is streamed to the console:

```
bigbuff = abcdefgh
In main()
        You've been hijacked!
```

The key of this technique lies in the activation record of the function to which you are feeding arguments. Figure 2.14 displays the normal activation record of the `overflow()` function.

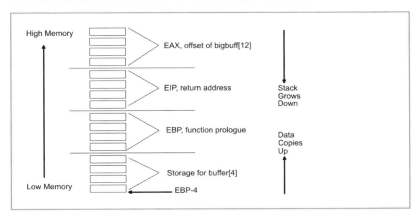

Figure 2.14

When the `overflow()` function is called from `main()`, the code in `main()` will pop the address of the string argument on to the stack and call `overflow()`. This will cause EIP to be indirectly placed on the stack also.

```
                        overflow(bigbuff);

0009d   8d 4d f4            lea    eax, DWORD PTR _bigbuff$[ebp]
000a0   51                  push   eax
000a1   e8 00 00 00 00      call   _overflow
000a6   83 c4 04            add    esp, 4
```

Once execution has jumped to `overflow()`, the EBP register will be popped on the stack so that it can be used as a frame of reference for the activation record. In addition, space will be allocated on the stack for the `buffer[4]` local array.

```
00000   55          push    ebp
00001   8b ec       mov     ebp, esp
00003   51          push    ecx
```

This leaves us with the 16-byte activation record in Figure 2.14. To alter the return address, we merely feed `overflow()` an argument that is 12 bytes in size. The `strcpy()` function does the rest by placing 12 bytes in memory starting at the storage allocated for buffer.

The best way to understand this is visually. The before and after `strcpy()` snapshots of the `overflow()` stack are displayed in Figure 2.15. Notice how the original return address bytes (ret1a, ... , ret1d) are replaced with four new bytes (ret2a, ..., ret2d).

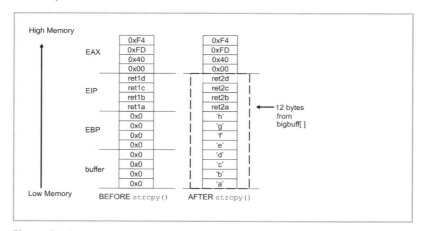

Figure 2.15

Imagine what would happen if the function to which we passed the oversized argument was in the kernel? You could jump to another function in the kernel. You can augment this technique by placing extra executable code on the stack and having execution jump to that code. This would allow you to execute any code of your choosing and have it execute in kernel mode. Performing a successful buffer overflow attack can give you ownership of a machine. Ba ha ha ha...

Do not lament. There is hope for those soldiers who are defending the walls of a besieged castle. Buffer overflow attacks can be foiled by replacing `strcpy()` with `strncpy()`. The general idea is to replace copying functions with functions that impose a specific boundary. This is more a matter of discipline and code audits than anything else. The people at OpenBSD know this more than anyone else (www.openbsd.com). Commercial vendors like Microsoft are so busy churning out new versions that they cannot invest the time needed to protect against these types of attacks.

In the Middle Ages, defenders of a fortress could rain arrows and boiling oil down on attackers. These defenses were very effective, seeing as how the aggressors typically had nowhere to hide. Having thick walls didn't hurt either. Likewise, Linux sysops can do a number of things to harden their production systems and make attacking them much more expensive:

Table 2.4

Measure	Benefit
Shut down unnecessary services	Decrease number of potential targets
Install an intrusion detection system	Detect Trojan horses and compromised binaries
Implement a VPN	Foil sniffers
Disable all dial-up servers	Remove the easy path around your firewall
Place public servers in a demilitarized zone	Limit damage done if public boxes are hacked
Disable zone transfers on DNS servers	Prevent information leakage
Implement password changes/checking	Prevent usage of weak and old passwords
Log data with a dedicated syslog machine	Save forensic evidence in the event of an attack
Enable port scan detection software	Preempt an attack before it happens
Disable NFS and sendmail	Use SSH and qmail
Establish phone call protocols	Reduce the risk of social engineering attacks
Install a dedicated firewall (i.e., CheckPoint)	Limit/monitor network traffic to the outside

Table 2.4 provides only a small sample of possible measures. If any of the items that I mentioned are foreign to you, then you will need to do a little homework. For an extended treatment of security on Linux, I recommend a couple of books in the reference section. Some exploits, like buffer overflows, are hard to prevent if you don't

have access to source code. This is why you will probably want to visit www.securityfocus.com and get on their *bugtraq* mailing list. This gives you a way to hear about problems as they are reported.

Case Study: Windows

Windows is a closed source operating system, and this will probably somewhat limit the depth of my examination. DOS is another closed source project from Microsoft, but DOS is literally so small that this fact doesn't have much of an impact. You could probably disassemble DOS in a few weeks. I am pretty sure that some of Microsoft's competitors actually took this route. With the Windows operating system, full-scale reverse engineering is just not feasible. In this case, all I have to go on is whatever Microsoft gives me. The rest will be pure detective work: picking up leads and seeing where they take me.

> "We work in the dark
> We do what we can
> We give what we have.
> Our doubt is our passion
> And our passion is our task.
> The rest is the madness of art."
>
> — Henry James

Of the four operating systems that are examined in this chapter, Windows is, by far, the largest and most complicated. The engineers who designed Windows should probably consider it an accomplishment just to have been able to successfully manage the construction of such a behemoth. Thus, I will spend more effort describing how this leviathan works.

Historical Forces

Microsoft's DOS operating system has never really died off. I have seen DOS 6.22 books at Barnes & Noble. In fact, you can still buy a copy of IBM's PC DOS. This is known as PC DOS 2000, found at http://www3.ibm.com/software/os/dos.

Unofficially, however, the death knell of DOS was sounded when Windows 1.0 was released on November 20, 1985. A little over two years later, Windows 2.0 was released. Windows 2.0 ran on an Intel 80286 in protected mode. The first truly popular version of Windows, 3.1, was presented to the public on April 6, 1992. It provided a modest GUI and ran on affordable hardware. Microsoft also made a foray into peer-to-peer networking with Windows 3.11. These versions of Windows all required one thing: an existing DOS installation. This is because Windows, during these early years, was more of a glorified DOS program than a stand-alone operating system. It is a well-known fact that Windows 3.11 and its predecessors used the file system manager (i.e., INT 21 system calls) provided by DOS.

In August of 1995, Windows 95 was made available to the public. It was a major facelift and was completely independent of DOS, although it did ship with MS-DOS 7.0. Windows 95 supported advanced features like pre-emptive multitasking and TCP/IP networking. Windows 95 also possessed a much more attractive user interface. It was a smashing success. Microsoft followed Windows 95 with Windows 98, whose success was not as celebrated.

The limitation of Windows 95 and 98 was that they targeted the average consumer. Windows 95 and 98 both ran a broad spectrum of desktop applications, but that was about it. The memory protection was still weak, and they had a tendency to crash, or freeze, when multiple applications were loaded (I am a voice of experience). In other words, neither of these operating systems was intended to run as a business server.

In the early 1990s, Microsoft did not have an industrial-strength, enterprise level operating system to sell, like UNIX, VMS, or OS/390. Computers that ran the Windows operating system were viewed by mainframe vendors as nothing more than embroidered clients. The high-end system vendors, like IBM and HP, could turn up their noses and smirk.

"Here's a nickel, kid. Buy yourself a better computer."
— UNIX Admin from "Dilbert"

Bill Gates decided that he wanted in; the potential for profit was too much to resist. So, like any political action committee, he went out and bought the best that money could buy. He hired Dave Cutler, the lead architect of Digital Equipment Corporation's (DEC) VMS operating system. Cutler also played a pivotal role in the development of DEC's RSX-11 system. Many people don't know about Cutler, and he doesn't get the publicity that someone like Ken Thompson commands. Nevertheless, hiring Cutler and his small group of engineers was the best money that Gates ever spent. In 1994, Windows NT 3.1 was released and marked the beginning of Microsoft's wildly profitable ascent into the server market.

ASIDE

In 1997, I was hired by an ERP company in the Midwest. I walked smack into the middle of a major effort to port their 16 million line, middleware code base to Windows NT 4.0. This, in and of itself, was enough to prove to me that NT was finally gaining attention. Porting a 16 million line code base is anything but cheap. In fact, it is more like getting married: You don't do it unless you are willing to make a significant long-term commitment.

There were complaints from the engineers undertaking the port. Their primary gripe was that NT was not a multiuser system. Microsoft, you see, was espousing a fundamentally different network model. Instead of having everyone log into a central machine, Microsoft wanted program components to be spread out so that applications could take advantage of the processing power on each machine in the network. This new paradigm was christened the *Distributed Network Architecture* (DNA). It sent some UNIX developers I know into conniptions.

Microsoft attempted to mainstream NT in an effort to appeal to a larger audience. The result of this attempt was Windows 2000, which was unleashed on the public in February of 2000. Windows 2000 was based heavily on the NT kernel, and it was originally referred to as Windows NT 5.0. However, Microsoft still was in the business of building and selling low-end operating systems belonging to the Windows 3.1/95/98 lineage. For example, in September of 2000, Microsoft released Windows Millennium Edition (ME), which was the next iteration of Windows 98.

On October 25, 2001, Microsoft unveiled its latest incarnation of Windows: Windows XP. XP is intended to target both consumers and businesses. It also offers Microsoft the opportunity to merge the Windows 2000 product line with the Windows ME product line. The Windows XP kernel is an extension of the Windows 2000 kernel. So in a way, it is more of a descendent of NT, with extra driver support to offer the plug-and-play features of Windows ME.

An abbreviated version of the family tree of Microsoft operating systems is displayed in Figure 2.16 on the following page.

Microsoft has historically made a point of jealously protecting their intellectual property. I am not making a judgment call, just stating a fact. The source code to Windows is carefully hidden away on a cluster of servers in Redmond. Only companies that Microsoft

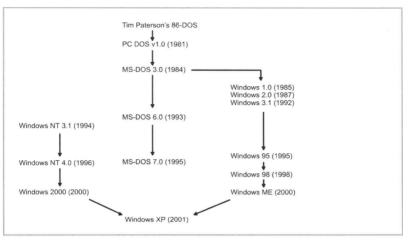

Figure 2.16

judges as being "organizations that have a long-term commitment to Windows" are allowed to view the source code. This includes OEMs, like Compaq, that need to tweak Windows to run on their hardware. The marketing people at Microsoft like to make a big deal when OEMs come to Redmond to pick up their source code CDs. The OEMs typically fly to Redmond in a helicopter and are handed special suitcases that resemble something you might use to carry radioactive material. Considering that Microsoft pours billions of dollars a year into Windows, this is not a bad analogy. Those CDs are worth their weight in weapons-grade plutonium.

ASIDE

Microsoft has recently announced that it will share the source code to its .NET tool suite with academic programs throughout the United States. My guess is that this is a response to the growing popularity of Linux, which is currently the system of choice for research. UNIX gained a strong following among universities in the 1970s, back when Bell Labs gave its UNIX source code to computer science departments. These same 1970s students went out into the marketplace and made UNIX the dominant high-end player that it is today. The same could happen with Linux, and I think this scares Microsoft.

On the other hand, what gains a stronghold at universities does not always gain a foothold in the real world. The RISC architecture is a darling in many academic programs, but unless you are looking at Apple PCs or high-end UNIX servers, you will be stuck with CISC. CISC is not going to die no mat-

> ter how much the professors want it to.
>
> Likewise, Microsoft is not going to die because Windows runs on CISC and the company knows how to support and document its products. Anyone who has an MSDN subscription knows that Microsoft's documentation is exhaustive and complete. This is more than I can say for the scattered collection of man pages, textinfo files, HOWTOs, and README files that you get with the typical Linux distribution. Bill Gates pours billions of dollars into Windows, and it shows.

For the following discussion, I am going to focus on the Windows NT/2000/XP family of operating systems. This branch of the Windows family tree does a better job of isolating and protecting applications from each other and the kernel. What else would you expect from a guy like Dave Cutler? So when I refer to "Windows," I am talking about Windows NT/2000/XP and not 95/98/ME.

Memory Map Overview

Windows uses both the segmentation and paging facilities of the Pentium processor. This means that, like Linux and MMURTL, applications see the world in terms of a "fake" linear address space instead of an actual physical address space. Again, like Linux and MMURTL, the Windows 32-bit, 4GB linear address space is broken up into two sections. For normal, consumer-based versions of Windows, the kernel occupies the upper 2GB of linear memory (0x80000000 to 0xFFFFFFFF). Each user process gets its own private linear address region in the lower 2GB (0x0 to 0x7FFFFFFF). This layout of memory is displayed in Figure 2.17.

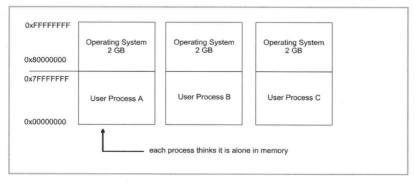

Figure 2.17

NOTE As I have mentioned before, 2GB of linear address space does not require 2GB of physical storage; it's more of a bookkeeping convention.

For applications that are memory intensive, like databases, there are versions of Windows (i.e., Windows 2000 Advanced Server and Windows 2000 Datacenter Server) that pack the kernel into the topmost gigabyte of linear address space so that the applications can have 3GB of linear address space. This feature is enabled via the following sort of entry in BOOT.INI:

```
multi(0)disk(0)rdisk(0)partition(2)\WINNT="Windows
        2000 Advanced Server" /3GB
```

```
0xFFFFFFFF
                Operating System
                      1 GB
0xC0000000
0xBFFFFFFF


                   User Process
                  (Big Database)


0x00000000
```

Figure 2.18

Windows is also able to take advantage of the PAE flag in CR4 that allows 36 address lines (i.e., 64GB) to be used instead of the normal 32. Naturally, Microsoft had to invent its own acronym so you would think they had invented it. The facility, in Windows, that allows a 32-bit application to use more than 2GB of physical memory is known as Address Windowing Extensions (AWE). In order to take advantage of AWE, one of the core kernel binaries has to be replaced. Specifically, the Ntoskrnl.exe executable must be replaced by Ntkrnlpa.exe. AWE is supported by all of the Windows 2000 implementations. It is enabled by the /PAE switch in BOOT.INI.

```
multi(0)disk(0)rdisk(0)partition(2)\WINNT="Windows
        2000 Advanced Server" /PAE
```

Windows supports two rings of memory protection. The operating system runs in *kernel mode*, which is another way to say that it executes at privilege level 0x0. User processes execute at privilege level 0x3 (also called *user mode*). I bet you see a pattern developing here. Both MMURTL and Linux used this same type of two-ring scheme so that the paging facilities of the Pentium could provide the bulk of memory management accounting work. MMURTL and Linux also make only minimal use of segmentation, seeing as how it is a somewhat redundant memory partitioning technology. I suspect that Windows will also eschew an involved segmentation approach in favor of using paging to divvy up memory. As we will see in the following section, my suspicions were correct.

The operating system is the only real universally visible construct. Applications might be isolated from each other, each one in its own private 2GB linear address space, but they all see the operating system as occupying the bottom portion of memory. Figure 2.19 displays the most common topography of the operating system's components.

High Memory	0xFFC00000 – 0xFFFFFFFF	HAL-specific data
	0xFFBE0000 – 0xFFBFFFFF	memory dump forensic data
	0xEB000000 – 0xFFBDFFFF	locked system heap operating system page tables
	0xE1000000 – 0xEAFFFFFF	pageable system heap
	0xC1000000 – 0xE0FFFFFF	system cache
	0xC0C00000 – 0xC0FFFFFF	system working set data
	0xC0800000 – 0xC0BFFFFF	not used
	0xC0400000 – 0xC07FFFFF	process working set data
	0xC0000000 – 0xC03FFFFF	process page directory, tables
	0xA4000000 – 0xBFFFFFFF	extra system page tables
	0xA0000000 – 0xA3FFFFFF	user session data
Low Memory	0x80000000 – 0x9FFFFFFF	kernel code

Figure 2.19

Some of the regions in Figure 2.19 are not exact in terms of their starting and stopping range because some components of the operating system address space are dynamic. The really important thing to take from Figure 2.19 is that the kernel's machine instructions are secluded in the basement of the operating system's linear address space. The remaining space is taken up by data structures of one form or another.

Windows and Segmentation

I don't have access to the full-blown source code distribution on Windows. However, I have lurked around in device driver header files shipped with the Windows 2000 DDK, and this is where I obtained my first lead with regard to how Windows manages its memory segments. This makes sense because device drivers, by their nature, access the kernel. In a header file named ntddk.h, the following macros are defined:

Table 2.5

Macro	Meaning
KGDT_NULL	Null selector (points to vacant entry at start of GDT)
KGDT_R0_CODE	Selector to kernel code segment descriptor
KGDT_R0_DATA	Selector to kernel stack segment descriptor
n0 KGDT_R3_CODE	Selector to user code segment descriptor
KGDT_R3_DATA	Selector to user stack/data segment descriptor
KGDT_TSS	Selector to segment descriptor storing the TSS (multitasking)
KGDT_R0_PCR	Selector to segment containing the Process Control Region
KGDT_R3_TEB	Selector to segment containing the Thread Environment Block
KGDT_VDM_TILE	Selector to segment containing the DOS virtual machine
KGDT_LDT	Selector to segment containing the LDT

As you can see, the number of selectors is pretty scarce. This implies that the number of descriptors is also small. However, I don't have enough evidence to support this assumption, so I am going to have to take drastic measures. I am going to have to use a kernel debugger (gasp, ... no, not that, ... not the kernel debugger!).

Special Weapons and Tactics

A *kernel debugger* is a special application that can debug the Windows operating system. You can get your hands dirty with a kernel debugger by downloading the Windows *Customer Support Diagnostics* tool set. It is free and available at Microsoft's web site. There are three debuggers that are included:

- NTSD (and CDB)
- KD
- WinDbg

NTSD is the *NT Symbolic Debugger*. CDB is a special version of NTSD that is intended to debug console applications (i.e., *Console Debugger*). NTSD and CDB are both geared toward looking at user mode applications, so we're not really interested in them. WinDbg is a Win32 GUI program that can be used to look at both kernel mode and user mode code. KD, *Kernel Debugger*, is the console equivalent of WinDbg. KD comes in three flavors: `I386KD.EXE`, `ALPHAKD.EXE`, and `IA64KD.EXE`. I am assuming that you are on a Pentium machine, so the one you would need to use is `I386KD.EXE`.

Debugging a live kernel typically requires a special setup. A *target machine*, which is running the kernel under scrutiny, is connected by a NULL modem to a *host machine*. The kernel debugger lives on the host machine so that it can watch the kernel without becoming part of the action if the target machine becomes unstable. A NULL modem is just a special kind of serial cable. This target-host machine installation is illustrated in Figure 2.20.

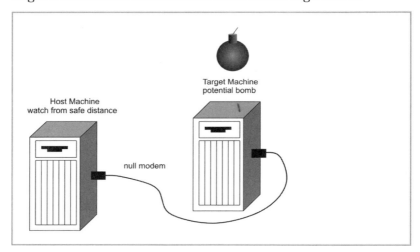

Figure 2.20

NOTE In discussions of kernel debugging, you may hear the term *checked build* mentioned. A checked build is just a specially compiled version of the Windows kernel that has been built with the DEBUG compile-time flag activated. Checked builds are only shipped with high-end MSDN subscriptions. This DEBUG setting results in a whole load of extra error-checking code being placed into the kernel binaries (i.e., `ASSERT()`). Normally when an error occurs in the retail version of the kernel, the system will become unstable and crash. The checked build is intended to catch errors that would normally cause a crash so that the operating system can be debugged. The cost of this extra supervision is memory and execution time, but this usually isn't a major issue for someone trying to see why their kernel mode driver is bringing Windows down.

Memory Management Policies

If you don't have access to a second machine, you can still use a kernel debugger to look under the hood. However, in this case, the kernel will be dead. Specifically, you will need to crash your Windows computer so that it dumps an image of memory to disk. This is exactly what happens when the infamous "Blue Screen of Death" (BSOD) appears. There are several types of memory dumps that can be performed:

- Complete memory dump
- Kernel memory dump
- Small memory dump

A *memory dump* is the snapshot of a system when it died. A complete memory dump makes sure that everything but the kitchen sink ends up in the dump file. A kernel memory dump limits its contents to the kernel code and data. The small memory dump is a 64KB file containing a minimal amount of system status information.

NOTE Regardless of the type of memory dump that occurs, the dump file will be placed in %SystemRoot%\memory.dmp.

To specify the type of memory dump that you want the kernel to write to disk during a crash, open the Windows Control Panel and double-click on the System icon. Select the Advanced tab and click on the Startup and Recovery button. The dialog box that should appear is displayed in Figure 2.21.

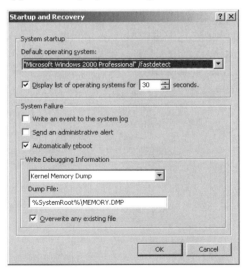

Figure 2.21

Crashing Windows with a Keystroke

Creating a memory dump is easier than you think. My favorite technique requires you to open up the registry to the following key:

HKEY_LOCAL_MACHINE\System\CurrentControlSet\Services\
i8042prt\Parameters

Once you are there, add the string value CrashOnCtrlScroll, and set it to the value 0x1. You have just added a *big red switch* to your keyboard. Back in the 1980s, the IBM PC shipped with a big red switch that turned the machine on and off. If DOS got corrupted, you could always hit the big red switch. To activate this switch (and I know you can't help yourself), press the *rightmost* Ctrl key and hold it down while pressing the Scroll/Lock key twice. This will crash your computer, and your screen will salute you with a BSOD. Let the screen countdown continue until your computer reboots.

When you log back into Windows, a Memory.dmp file should be waiting for you.

NOTE The author and publisher of this book take no responsibility for any damage produced by the information and source code in this text. If crashing your machine to produce a memory dump seems too precarious, please read the online help that accompanies the Customer Support Diagnostics tool kit.

Reverse Engineering the GDT

As I mentioned before, a memory dump is a snapshot of the machine's state when it crashed. The kernel debugger will allow you to sift through this information like Agent Scully performing an autopsy. I started in my quest for GDT information by loading the memory dump into memory with the kernel debugger.

```
E:\Program Files\Debuggers\bin>I386kd -z e:\winnt\memory.dmp

Microsoft(R) Windows 2000 Kernel Debugger
Version 5.00.2184.1
Copyright (C) Microsoft Corp. 1981-1999

Symbol search path is: E:\WINNT\Symbols

Loading Dump File [e:\winnt\memory.dmp]
Kernel Dump File Only kernel address space is available

Kernel Version 2195:   Service Pack 2  UP Free
Kernel base = 0x80400000 PsLoadedModuleList = 0x8046ccf0
Loaded kdextx86 extension DLL
Loaded userkdx extension DLL
```

```
Loaded dbghelp extension DLL
f70c20bd 5e                pop     esi
kd>
```

> **NOTE** You will need to make sure that you have the latest kernel symbols installed on your computer. These allow the debugger to map kernel symbols to addresses. It is important to make sure that you have the correct version of symbols too. If your kernel is `build 2195 SP 2` (Service Pack 2), you will need symbols for build `2195 SP 2`.
>
> You can determine your build and service pack number by opening the Windows Control Panel and clicking on the System icon. The panel marked General should specify the version status of your Windows installation. If your symbols are the wrong version or the debugger cannot find them, the kernel debugger will display an error message having to do with checksums or missing files. I spent several very frustrating hours figuring this out one particular Saturday.
>
> Finally, you will need to set the `_NT_SYMBOL_PATH` environmental variable to the directory containing your symbol files (i.e., `e:\winnt\symbols`). The kernel debugger will use this variable to find the symbol files at run time.

Once I had the kernel's state loaded up, I examined the GDTR register. This stores the base linear address and limit of the GDT. The debugger views GDTR in terms of two smaller registers (GDTR and GDTL). The `r` command is used to view the contents of registers:

```
kd> r gdtr
r gdtr
gdtr=80036000
kd> r gdtl
r gdtl
gdtl=000003ff
```

This told me that the GDT resides at a linear address of `0x80036000` and consists of 128 64-bit GDT entries (i.e., `3FF` bytes). I used the dump command to look at the actual GDT entries:

```
kd> d 80036000
d 80036000
80036000  00 00 00 00 00 00 00 00-ff ff 00 00 00 9b cf 00  ................
80036010  ff ff 00 00 00 93 cf 00-ff ff 00 00 00 fb cf 00  ................
80036020  ff ff 00 00 00 f3 cf 00-ab 20 00 20 24 8b 00 80  ......... . $...
80036030  01 00 00 f0 df 93 c0 ff-ff 0f 00 00 00 f3 40 00  ..............@.
80036040  ff ff 00 04 00 f2 00 00-00 00 00 00 00 00 00 00  ................
80036050  68 00 80 34 47 89 00 80-68 00 e8 34 47 89 00 80  h..4G...h..4G...
80036060  ff ff c0 2a 02 93 00 00-ff 3f 00 80 0b 92 00 00  ...*.....?......
80036070  ff 03 00 70 ff 92 00 ff-ff ff 00 00 40 9a 00 80  ...p........@...
kd>
```

After that, it was just a matter of sifting through 64-bit length strips of memory. What I came up with was a list of 25 live segment descriptors. The rest were vacant (i.e., the present flag was cleared). Given that a GDT is capable of storing 8,192 64-bit entries, Windows is only using a very small fraction of the possible total entries.

```
Kernel Segment Descriptors (Privilege = 0)
------------------------
0000  Bas=00000000 Lim=00000000 Bytes DPL=0 NP
0008  Bas=00000000 Lim=000fffff Pages DPL=0  P Code   RE A
0010  Bas=00000000 Lim=000fffff Pages DPL=0  P Data   RW A
0030  Bas=ffdff000 Lim=00000001 Pages DPL=0  P Data   RW A
0060  Bas=00022ac0 Lim=0000ffff Bytes DPL=0  P Data   RW A
0068  Bas=000b8000 Lim=00003fff Bytes DPL=0  P Data   RW
0070  Bas=ffff7000 Lim=000003ff Bytes DPL=0  P Data   RW
0078  Bas=80400000 Lim=0000ffff Bytes DPL=0  P Code   RE
0080  Bas=80400000 Lim=0000ffff Bytes DPL=0  P Data   RW
0088  Bas=00000000 Lim=00000000 Bytes DPL=0  P Data   RW
00e0  Bas=f7050000 Lim=0000ffff Bytes DPL=0  P Code   RE A
00e8  Bas=00000000 Lim=0000ffff Bytes DPL=0  P Data   RW
00f0  Bas=8042df4c Lim=000003b7 Bytes DPL=0  P Code   EO
00f8  Bas=00000000 Lim=0000ffff Bytes DPL=0  P Data   RW
0100  Bas=f7060000 Lim=0000ffff Bytes DPL=0  P Data   RW A
0108  Bas=f7060000 Lim=0000ffff Bytes DPL=0  P Data   RW A
0110  Bas=f7060000 Lim=0000ffff Bytes DPL=0  P Data   RW A

User Segment Descriptors (Privilege = 3)
----------------------
0018  Bas=00000000 Lim=000fffff Pages DPL=3  P Code   RE A
0020  Bas=00000000 Lim=000fffff Pages DPL=3  P Data   RW A
0038  Bas=00000000 Lim=00000fff Bytes DPL=3  P Data   RW A
0040  Bas=00000400 Lim=0000ffff Bytes DPL=3  P Data   RW

TSS Segment Descriptors (Used For Multitasking)
----------------------
0028  Bas=80242000 Lim=000020ab Bytes DPL=0  P TSS32      B
0050  Bas=80473480 Lim=00000068 Bytes DPL=0  P TSS32      A
0058  Bas=804734e8 Lim=00000068 Bytes DPL=0  P TSS32      A
00a0  Bas=8147d468 Lim=00000068 Bytes DPL=0  P TSS32      A
```

I discovered that my initial suspicions were warranted. Windows, for the most part, makes only minimal use of segmentation. The segmentation scheme that is implemented has only two privilege levels (0 and 3) so that it can rely on paging to do most of the actual memory management and protection.

Windows and Paging

The bulk of Windows memory management is built upon paging hardware. Windows uses the Pentium's paging facilities to implement both memory protection and demand paging. As with the last section, I do not have access to the source code that implements paging. This means that I'll have to try and validate the existence of features by looking for related API functions, special tools, and other indirect means.

Linear Address Space Taxonomy

The memory that constitutes the linear address space of a user application can be classified as one of three different species:

- Free
- Reserved
- Committed

Free memory is not being used by an application. To understand reserved and committed memory, it is helpful to use a restaurant analogy. When you call a restaurant and reserve a table, you are not actually sitting at the table, but you know it will be there when you need it. Not until you walk into the restaurant and sit down have you made a commitment to spend money.

Likewise, *reserved memory* is nothing more than a range of linear addresses that has been set aside for future use. Trying to access linear memory that is reserved produces a page fault because no physical memory has been allocated yet. *Committed memory* is a range of linear addresses for which physical storage in memory or on disk has been allocated. This two-phase commit, to borrow a phrase from transaction theory, allows memory to be reserved. This approach, which delays physical memory allocation until the last minute, belongs to a school of algorithms known as *lazy evaluation*.

The concepts of reserved and committed memory are reflected in the Win32 API. Specifically, there is a function called `VirtualAlloc()` that allows memory to be reserved or committed.

Given that allocation of linear address regions consists of two phases, it only makes sense that the freeing of linear memory is also comprised of two phases. Linear memory is de-committed so that the memory region has reverted to the reserved state, and then it is released. `VirtualFree()` is a Win32 API function that provides this mechanism to user applications.

Consider the following example:

```c
#include<windows.h>
#include<stdio.h>

void main()
{
    long *ptr;
    unsigned long nbytes = 1024;
    ptr = VirtualAlloc(NULL,nbytes,MEM_RESERVE,PAGE_READWRITE);
    /*
    memory is reserved: this will cause application to crash
    ptr[64]='a';
    */
    VirtualAlloc(ptr,nbytes,MEM_COMMIT,PAGE_READWRITE);
    ptr[64]='a';

    if(VirtualLock(ptr,nbytes)){ printf("page locked\n"); }
    else{ printf("lock failed\n"); }

    if(VirtualUnlock(ptr,nbytes)){ printf("page unlocked\n"); }
    else{ printf("unlock failed\n"); }

    VirtualFree(ptr,nbytes,MEM_DECOMMIT);
    /*
    memory is reserved: this will cause application to crash
    ptr[64]='a';
    */
    VirtualFree(ptr,nbytes,MEM_RELEASE);
    return;
}
```

If memory is accessed while it is in the reserved state, the application will crash. You can re-insert the code that has been commented out to prove this to yourself.

As with Linux, pages of memory can be locked. User programs can use the VirtualLock() and VirtualUnlock() functions to request that a region of linear memory is locked. However, the kernel is free to ignore this request. The only way to guarantee that a region of linear memory is locked is to invoke kernel mode functions like MmLockPageableCodeSection() and MmLockPageableDataSection(). Unfortunately, these calls are internal to the kernel and normally cannot be invoked from user space.

Musical Chairs for Pages

In the game of musical chairs, a large group of people compete to occupy a limited number of chairs. There are always a few people who end up without a chair. This is the kind of scenario that a page of memory faces. A page would like to be in physical memory, but there are a limited number of page frames available in DRAM.

A *working set* is the subset of pages in a linear address space that actually reside in physical memory. Each user application has a working set, known as a *process working set*. The operating system also has a working set, known as the *system working set*. If you look at Figure 2.19, you will see that regions of the operating system's linear address space are reserved for keeping track of process and system working sets. To make efficient use of physical memory, Windows tracks the number of pages allocated to each working set and can expand or trim the number of page frames allotted. The default minimum and maximum working set sizes are depicted in Table 2.6.

Table 2.6

Physical DRAM Available	Default Minimum	Default Maximum
Less than 20MB	20 pages	45 pages
20-32MB	30 pages	145 pages
More than 32MB	50 pages	345 pages

The default maximum values can be transgressed if enough free page frames are available. This can be initiated by a user application through a call to the `SetProcessWorkingSetSize()` function. The only catch is that the application making the call will pass its process handle to the function, and `SetProcessWorkingSetSize()` will verify that the invoking application has the necessary `PROCESS_SET_QUOTA` privileges. If you merely want to determine the size of a working set, you can use the `GetProcessWorkingSetSize()` Win32 function.

In addition to managing working sets, Windows also maintains data on all the pages that are located in physical memory as a whole. Windows uses what is known as the *Page Frame Number database* (PFN) to track information regarding pages in DRAM. The PFN database is an array of data structures. Each page in physical memory has an entry. You can use the kernel debugger to get a status report from the PFN database:

```
kd> !memusage
!memusage
loading PFN database
loading (99% complete)
           Zeroed:    1550  (  6200 kb)
             Free:       1  (     4 kb)
          Standby:   11424  ( 45696 kb)
         Modified:     683  (  2732 kb)
```

```
ModifiedNoWrite:        0 (      0 kb)
   Active/Valid:    19109 (  76436 kb)
     Transition:        0 (      0 kb)
        Unknown:        0 (      0 kb)
          TOTAL:    32767 (131068 kb)
```

As you can see, there are eight different types of page states. These types are enumerated and explained in Table 2.7.

Table 2.7

Page Frame Type	Meaning
Zeroed	Page is free and initialized with zero values
Free	Page is free but is uninitialized (stores garbage bytes)
Standby	Recently removed from a working set, and was not modified while in the set
Modified	Recently removed from a working set, and was modified while in the set
ModifiedNowrite	Like a "modified" page but will not be written to disk
Active/Valid	Page is part of a current working set
Transition	Page is in digital purgatory between the disk and physical memory
Unknown	Danger! danger!, bad page frame, has caused hardware errors

Memory Protection

Given Windows' rather minimal use of segmentation, I suspect that page faults provide the core memory protection mechanism. Remember that Windows has only two rings of privilege (kernel mode and user mode). This fits perfectly with the Supervisor/User privilege scheme that Intel paging supports. As with Linux and MMURTL, when a user program attempts to access memory belonging to the kernel, a page fault is generated and passed on to Windows to do what it sees fit. Typically, this means halting the program that caused the page fault.

The nature of the page directory and page table bookkeeping also serves to keep one process from accessing physical memory being used by another process. Each process in Windows is supplied with its own page directory. This ensures that the linear address space used by the process will map to a unique physical address space. This is particularly important because Windows places each process in an identical linear address space.

The additional protection supplied by the page table entry read/write flag, discussed in Chapter 1, is reflected in the Win32 API. Take a look at the call to `VirtualAlloc()` that was made in a previous example:

```
ptr = VirtualAlloc(NULL,nbytes,MEM_RESERVE,
    PAGE_READWRITE);
```

The last argument is a memory access specifier. This specifier can be one of the eight macros enumerated in Table 2.8.

Table 2.8

Macro	Meaning
PAGE_READONLY	Page region can only be read
PAGE_READWRITE	Page region can be read and written to
PAGE_EXECUTE	Page region can be executed
PAGE_EXECUTE_READ	Page region can be read and executed
PAGE_EXECUTE_READWRITE	Page region can be read, executed, and written to
PAGE_GUARD	Access raises a STATUS_GUARD_PAGE exception
PAGE_NOACCESS	Page region cannot be accessed
PAGE_NOCACHE	Page region cannot be placed in the cache

Violating any of the policies causes an access violation to be generated. This usually results in the offending program being killed.

The PAGE_GUARD macro requires a little extra explanation. This macro causes the memory region allocated to be shielded by a one-time exception. The first time that a program tries to read or write to a PAGE_GUARD memory region, a STATUS_GUARD_PAGE exception is generated. The catch is that the run time will turn off the PAGE_GUARD status of the memory region so that the exception can only be thrown once.

Demand Paging

Windows uses the Present (P) flag in page table entries to support demand paging. Windows also adds a twist to this mechanism by loading a cluster of pages in an effort to reduce the number of page faults that it handles. The size of the page cluster loaded depends on the amount of physical memory available. Given that most machines have at least 32MB of DRAM, page clusters will be either four or eight pages in size.

As I mentioned earlier, disk I/O is an extremely expensive operation and should be avoided by whatever means necessary. Each page fault translates into a read from the disk. Clustering is a clever way to save execution time. It is like shopping at a wholesale food distributor to save trips to the grocery store.

When there are plenty of unoccupied page frames in physical memory, the operating system will load disk-bound pages into these frames when they are requested. However, things get a little more complicated when there are no available page frames to spare. In this case, the operating system has to make a policy decision and decide which pages in physical memory will be removed to make way for the requested pages that are loaded from disk storage. How does the operating system decide which pages to write to disk in order to produce the necessary free space?

Once again, we are faced with a scenario that is like a game of musical chairs.

There are a few standard algorithms, including *first in, first out* (FIFO) and *least recently used* (LRU). The FIFO algorithm moves pages to disk that have been in memory the longest. The LRU algorithm is slightly more involved. The LRU algorithm takes into account the number of times that a page in physical memory has been modified. Those pages that have been modified the least are written to disk.

Which algorithm does Windows use? This depends on the number of processors that Windows can access on the motherboard. If Windows is running on top of a single processor, a variation of the LRU algorithm is utilized. If Windows has multiple processors at its disposal, it uses the FIFO algorithm. In both cases, the algorithms are applied in the context of working sets. If a page is requested that has been written to disk, Windows will look at the working set that the page belongs to in order to determine which members of the working set should be swapped to disk so that the requested page can be loaded into memory.

Memory Allocation

When the kernel allocates physical memory for a process, it sets up the allocated memory so that the first address (i.e., the lowest address) is a multiple of 64KB. In other words, processes are aligned in physical memory on a 64KB boundary. The size of the address space reserved for a process is a multiple of the native processor's page size. On a Pentium, an application would be given a plot of real estate in physical memory that is a multiple of 4KB. The Pentium does provide facilities for larger page sizes (i.e., 4MB), but everyone in their right mind sticks to 4KB page sizes (MMURTL, Linux, Windows, etc.).

One of the fringe benefits of being a user process is that each task is constructed with its own heap. Figure 2.22 displays one of the possible memory layouts for a user process. The stack grows down from the highest address, and the heap grows up toward the stack.

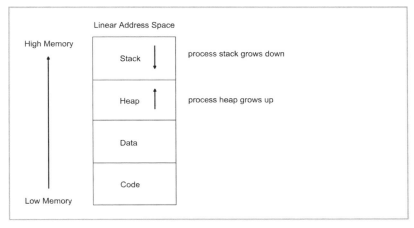

Figure 2.22

> **NOTE** The exact organization of a program's code, data, stack, and heap sections are a function of the development tools used to build the program. Linkers, in particular, can decide where to place an application's components. The linker will normally process object files in the order in which they appear on its command line. For each object file, the linker will embed program sections into the executable as it encounters them. The /DO linker option can be used to alter this behavior so the program's sections are arranged in the Microsoft Default Order.

Unlike MMURTL, which relies on user mode tool libraries, the Windows operating system provides kernel-level services to manage a task's heap. Windows exposes this functionality through a set of Win32 functions. These user-level calls end up invoking kernel mode code in Ntoskrnl.exe. A few of the more relevant functions include GetProcessHeap(), HeapAlloc(), and HeapFree(). The following short program demonstrates how these routines are used.

```
/* --heapFun.c-- */

#include<windows.h>
#include<stdio.h>

void main()
{
    HANDLE hHeap;
    unsigned char *buffer;

    hHeap = GetProcessHeap();
    if(hHeap==NULL){ printf("No heap!\n"); exit(1); }
```

```
    buffer = HeapAlloc(hHeap,HEAP_ZERO_MEMORY,1024);
    if(buffer==NULL){ printf("No heap space!\n"); exit(1);}

    printf("buffer[511]=%X, buffer has been
           zeroed\n",buffer[511]);
    buffer[512]=0xCA;
    printf("buffer[512]=%X\n",buffer[512]);

    if(HeapFree(hHeap,HEAP_NO_SERIALIZE,buffer))
    {
        printf("have returned memory to the collective\n");
    }
    return;
}
```

When this program is run, you will see:

```
buffer[511]=0, buffer has been zeroed
buffer[512]=CA
have returned memory to the collective
```

NOTE A process in Windows can also create additional heaps in its linear address space. The `HeapCreate()` function is used to this end.

NOTE There is a set of older heap management functions, like `Globalxxx()` and `Localxxx()`. The `Heapxxx()` functions are meant to replace these artifacts.

The Windows operating system also has a set of mechanisms so that kernel mode components can allocate memory for themselves. This includes:

- Look-aside lists
- Paged memory pool
- Non-paged (i.e., locked) memory pool

Look-aside lists are a special-purpose source of fixed-size memory blocks. Look-aside lists are fast because the kernel does not have to waste time searching for memory blocks of a particular size. Look-aside lists use memory borrowed from the kernel's paged and non-paged pools. To take a look at the look-aside lists that the kernel is using, you can use the `!lookaside` kernel debugger command.

```
kd> !lookaside
!lookaside

Lookaside "nt!CcTwilightLookasideList" @ 80475560 "CcWk"
    Type          =       0000 NonPagedPool
    Current Depth =          4   Max Depth   =          4
    Size          =         16   Max Alloc   =         64
```

```
        AllocateMisses  =           193    FreeMisses   =       185
        TotalAllocates  =           295    TotalFrees   =       291
        Hit Rate        =           34%    Hit Rate     =       36%

Lookaside "nt!IopSmallIrpLookasideList" @ 80478d00 "Irps"
        Type            =      0000 NonPagedPool
        Current Depth   =             0    Max Depth    =         4
        Size            =           148    Max Alloc    =       592
        AllocateMisses  =             9    FreeMisses   =         0
        TotalAllocates  =             9    TotalFrees   =         0
        Hit Rate        =            0%    Hit Rate     =        0%
.
.
.
Total NonPaged currently allocated for above lists =      2536
Total NonPaged potential for above lists           =      4048
Total Paged currently allocated for above lists    =         0
Total Paged potential for above lists              =       544
kd>
```

If you look back at Figure 2.19, you will see that the operating system reserves significant portions of memory for the paged and locked memory pools/heaps. These pools vary in size, but the maximum pool sizes are hard coded in the kernel's source code. The paged memory pool, whose storage can be written to disk, can be at most approximately 492MB in size. The non-paged memory pool, which is used by device drivers that require resident memory, can be at most 256MB in size.

The kernel's use of its memory pools can be examined with the `Poolmon.exe` program that ships with the Windows Support Tools package. But before you do, you will need to run `gflags.exe` (which also ships with the support tools) and enable *pool tagging*. Pool tagging allows the kernel to assign a tag to each type of data structure being allocated and freed within the kernel. Statistics can then be gathered for particular data structures. The `Poolmon.exe` program tracks the individual allocations that are made from the paged and non-paged memory pools. The output is character-based, as shown in Figure 2.23.

An explanation of the columns appearing in Figure 2.23 is provided in Table 2.9.

Table 2.9

Column	Meaning
Tag	Identifies a particular type of data structure
Type	Source of memory: paged or non-paged pool
Allocs	Number of data structure allocations made
Frees	Number of data structure releases made

Column	Meaning
Diff	Allocs — Frees
Bytes	Total number of bytes currently used by this type of data structure
Per Alloc	Number of bytes used by a single data structure of this type

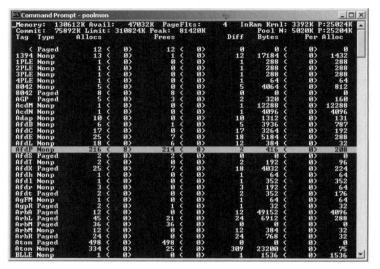

Figure 2.23

For an in-depth look at Poolmon.exe, I suggest you read the w2rksupp.chm help file that accompanies the support tools kit.

Memory Usage

Memory usage can be measured on a system-wide basis or on a process-by-process basis. System administrators tend to be concerned with the former and developers tend to be concerned with the latter.

The following three mechanisms can be used to track memory usage on a system-wide basis:

- Task Manager: Performance pane
- Win32 API
- Pmon.exe

There are also a couple of tools that can be used to measure the memory used by a process:

- Task Manager: Process pane
- Pviewer.exe

The Task Manager can be invoked by pressing the Ctrl+Alt+Del keys simultaneously. This combination of keys is known as the *three-finger salute*. The Performance dialog and Process dialog are really just panes within the Task Manager (see Figure 2.24).

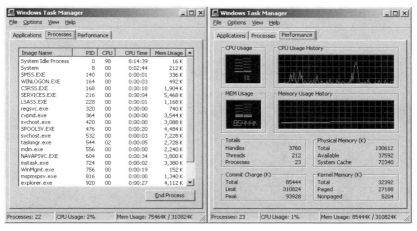

Figure 2.24

The Mem Usage column in the Process pane specifies the physical memory used by a process. The Kernel Memory section on the Performance pane specifies the size of the paged and non-paged kernel memory pools.

The Win32 API has a function called `GlobalMemoryStatus()` that will return the current memory usage by the system. An example of its usage is offered in the following short program.

```
#include<windows.h>
#include<stdio.h>

void main()
{
    MEMORYSTATUS mstatus;
    GlobalMemoryStatus(&mstatus);
    printf("percent of memory in use =%lu\n",
            mstatus.dwMemoryLoad);
    printf("bytes of physical memory =%lu\n",
            mstatus.dwTotalPhys);
    printf("free physical memory bytes =%lu\n",
            mstatus.dwAvailPhys);
    printf("max. bytes in paging file =%lu\n",
            mstatus.dwTotalPageFile);
    printf("free bytes in paging file=%lu\n",
            mstatus.dwAvailPageFile);
    printf("total bytes in user space =%lu\n",
            mstatus.dwTotalVirtual);
    printf("free user bytes =%lu\n",mstatus.dwAvailVirtual);
```

```
    return;
}
```

Pmon.exe and Pviewer.exe are both tools that are bundled with the Windows Support Tools package. Pmon.exe offers a snapshot of the operating system and all of its processes. The output is dynamically updated so that the statistics provided reflect the actual state of your computer (see Figure 2.25).

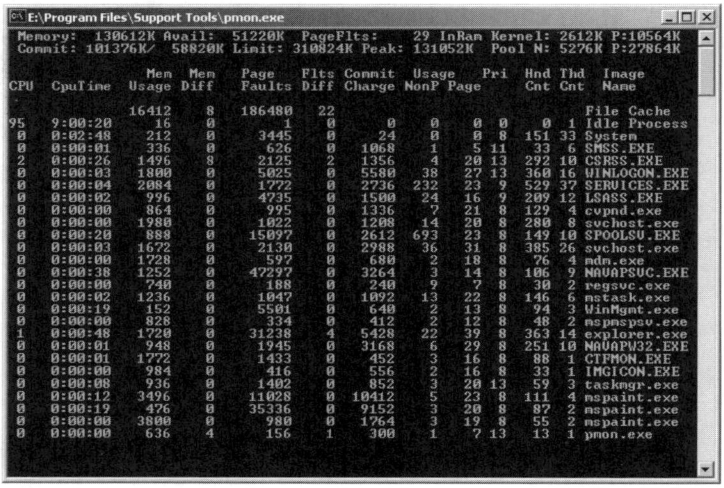

Figure 2.25

Pviewer.exe is a utility that offers an extremely detailed view of each process. To examine the memory consumption of a particular process, select a process in the Process scroll pane and click on the Memory Details button (see Figure 2.26).

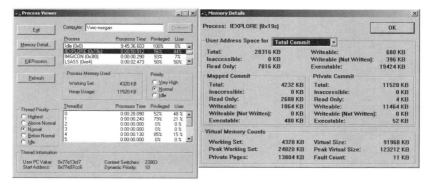

Figure 2.26

Turning Off Paging

Anyone who has ever read *Computer Architecture: A Quantitative Approach* by Patterson and Henessey knows that there is one true measure of performance: execution time. In light of this, disk storage I/O is probably the most expensive operation that a computer can execute (with the exception, maybe, of establishing a network connection). This makes demand paging a very costly feature in terms of performance. Barry Brey, an expert on the Intel chip set, told me that paging on Windows imposes an average execution time penalty of 10%.

NOTE The paging penalty can actually be even greater than 10% given that most programs are currently larger than 88KB (the amount of cached page relocations afforded by the look-aside cache in the paging unit). Take a program that calls many functions. Each time you access a function, there is a high probability that it will not be in the cache. This really drags out execution time. The only short-term solution that I can think of is to inline code with macros.

If you are interested in allowing your machine to handle multiple tasks without suffering the overhead incurred by demand paging, I recommend you buy as much physical memory as you can afford and turn off paging. I think that 512MB to 1GB of DRAM ought to do the trick for most people (at least for the time being). Paging memory to disk can be turned off by opening the Control Panel and clicking on the System icon. Select the Advanced tab and click on the Performance Options button. This will display the Performance Options dialog. Click on the Change button in the Virtual Memory section. The Virtual Memory dialog will appear (see Figure 2.27). This dialog will allow you to disable the use of disk storage for memory.

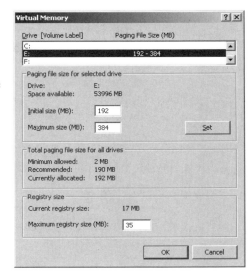

Figure 2.27

Example: Things That Go Thunk in the Night

Windows supports mixed memory models using a number of different subsystems. For example, Windows has a DOS subsystem, a Windows 3.1 subsystem, a POSIX subsystem, and an OS/2 subsystem. I am about to reveal to you a nasty trick that has brought dozens of different Intel debuggers to their knees. I am talking about *thunking*, which is a mechanism that allows 16-bit and 32-bit Windows code to interact.

There are three types of thunking techniques. They are distinguished based on the platforms on which they are used. Table 2.10 describes the three thunking methods.

Table 2.10

Thunk Type	Platform	Use
Universal	Windows 3.1	16-bit code calls a 32-bit DLL running under Win32s
Flat	Windows 95/98/ME	Allows 16-bit and 32-bit DLLs to call each other
Generic	Windows NT/2000/XP	API that allows a 16-bit program to use a 32-bit DLL

NOTE For those of you who were not on the scene in the early 1990s, Win32s was a special extension package that allowed 32-bit applications to run on Windows 3.1 and Windows 3.11. It was often bundled with development tools. I installed Win32s on my 80486 back in 1995 as an add-on to the Borland 4.5 C++ compiler.

Universal thunking is of little use, seeing as how Windows 3.1 is, for all intents and purposes, an extinct operating system.

Generic thunking is facilitated entirely by an API. Win32 functions like `LoadLibraryEx32W()`, `CallProc32W()`, and `FreeLibrary32W()` declared in `WOWNT16.H` allow 16-bit code to load and invoke a 32-bit Win32 DLL. Because this mechanism is API driven, most of the internal operation is hidden from view.

Flat thunking, however, uses a mechanism that is open to inspection, so dissecting this mechanism may offer some sort of insight.

Implementing flat thunking is a procedure that has five steps:

1. Write a thunk script.
2. Compile the thunk script with the `thunk.exe` compiler to produce an `.ASM` file.
3. Assemble the generated `.ASM` file twice (to create a 16-bit and a 32-bit `.OBJ` file).
4. Create a 16-bit DLL and link it with the 16-bit `.OBJ` file.
5. Create a 32-bit DLL and link it with the 32-bit `.OBJ` file.

The really interesting piece in this puzzle is the assembly code file that the thunk compiler generates. It is this assembly code that allows the 16-bit and 32-bit DLLs to interact.

> **NOTE** For those of you who have never written a DLL, I included the source code to a 32-bit DLL called `dll32.c` and a small program that uses it, called `usedll32.c`, in the downloadable files (www.wordware.com/memory). Reading this code should give you what you need to know.

The thunk script is just a text file that spells out the type of signature of the functions that the 16- and 32-bit DLLs wish to expose to each other. Consider the following thunk script called `script.thk`:

```
enablemapdirect3216 = true;

typedef char *LPSTR;
typedef unsigned long  ULONG;
typedef unsigned short USHORT;

ULONG function16(LPSTR cptr,USHORT n)
{
    cptr=input;
}
```

The first line (`enablemapdirect3216 = true`) indicates that we are thunking from 32-bit code to 16-bit code. In other words, the function prototype included in the thunk script represents a 16-bit DLL function that we wish to invoke from a 32-bit DLL.

The thunk script can be translated to assembly code using the thunk compiler. The thunk compiler ships as a part of the Windows ME SDK.

`C:\devstudio\thunk>thunk.exe script.thk`

This creates an assembly code file named `script.asm`.

> **NOTE** Copies of both `script.thk` and `script.asm` are in the downloadable files.

The assembly code in `script.asm`, which the 32-bit DLL will use to call the 16-bit DLL function (i.e., `function16()`), looks like this:

```
; dword ptr [ebp+8]:   cptr
; dword ptr [ebp+12]:  n
;
public IIfunction16@8
IIfunction16@8:
    push    ebp
```

```
mov     ebp,esp
push    ecx
sub     esp,60
call    SMapLS_IP_EBP_8
push    eax
push    word ptr [ebp+12]      ;n: dword->word
call    dword ptr [pfnQT_Thunk_script]
shl     eax,16
shrd    eax,edx,16
call    SUnMapLS_IP_EBP_8
leave
retn    8
```

You can tell that this assembly code must be called by the 32-bit DLL because the instructions use the extended registers. For example, EBP is used as a frame pointer instead of just BP, and ESP is used to point to the stack instead of just SP.

Keep in mind that the 16-bit DLL is native to 16-bit Windows. A 16-bit DLL does not run in real mode. It runs in a variation of protected mode. Before we begin, you need to read the following information carefully.

IMPORTANT! According to the MSDN documentation, a pointer in a 16-bit Windows environment consists of a 16-bit segment selector and a 16-bit offset (i.e., `selector:offset` form, or `16:16` for short).

Be careful! This is not the same as real mode, where an address is specified by a 16-bit segment address and a 16-bit offset address (i.e., `segment:offset` form). In real mode, a segment address is specified. In 16-bit Windows, a segment selector is specified. This is the crucial distinction.

Because an address in real mode is specified with a 16-bit segment address and 16-bit offset address, you might be tempted to also call this `16:16` addressing. In this discussion, however, I am using `16:16` to denote 16-bit Windows addressing. I will admit that the convention is completely arbitrary.

A pointer in a 32-bit Windows application only consists of a 32-bit offset because all the segment registers (CS, SS, DS, ES, etc.) contain selectors that point to segments with the same base address. Recall that Windows NT/2000/XP uses a variation of the flat segment model. In other words, all the function calls in 32-bit protected mode are NEAR.

Constructing a `16:16` Windows address from a 32-bit Windows offset address means that a new 16-bit selector must be allocated so that the memory location in question can then be specified by a 16-bit offset.

From this assembly code, we can glean a few things. The two function arguments, cptr and n, are both 4 bytes in size and have already been pushed onto the stack. The address of the character array is located at [ebp+8], and the length argument (i.e., n) is located at `[ebp+12]`. The return address of the invoking function is resident at `[ebp+4]`.

Next, the 32-bit offset address stored in `cptr` is mapped from protected mode `0:32` format to the older `16:16` Windows format via the `SMapLS_IP_EBP_8` function.

```
call    SMapLS_IP_EBP_8
```

This function, by the way, is located in the `THUNK32.LIB` library. You can verify this using the following command:

```
C:\DevStudio\VC\lib>dumpbin /linkermember thunk32.lib | more
```

The `SMapLS_IP_EBP_8` procedure in `THUNK32.LIB` is where the pointer acrobatics occur that map the 32-bit offset addresses to 16-bit Windows `selector:offset` addresses. I was hoping that the thunk script would reveal more details, but it seems like Microsoft has squirreled them all away inside of library code. The truth is out there... if you feel like disassembling.

The 4-byte integer argument n must be resized to a 16-bit word because the default integer size in real mode is 2 bytes. This transformation is realized in the following line of code:

```
push    word ptr [ebp+12]     ;n: dword->word
```

The actual real mode `function16()` routine is invoked when the machine executes the following:

```
call    dword ptr [pfnQT_Thunk_ script]
```

`pfnQT_Thunk_script` is a label in `script.asm` that stores the 32-bit address of the 16-bit function in memory. I assume that the 32 bytes designated by the `QT_Thunk_script` label are modified at run time to produce the necessary result.

```
pfnQT_Thunk_script    dd offset QT_Thunk_script
QT_Thunk_script label byte
    db     32 dup(0cch)    ;Patch space.
```

When the 16-bit function returns, we'll need to convert the `cptr` argument from its `16:16` format back to its original 32-bit offset format. This accounts for the following code:

```
call    SUnMapLS_IP_EBP_8
```

As you can see, Microsoft again has hidden the fine print away in the `THUNK32.DLL` library. I should have known better. If you are interested in taking the next step, you will need to crank up a disassembler and start reverse engineering `THUNK32.DLL`. Should you choose to accept this mission, I would recommend

DataRescue's IDA Pro interactive disassembler. It is a peach of a tool.

Closing Thoughts

Looking at the previous three protected mode operating systems (MMURTL, Linux, and Windows), you should notice a trend. Segmentation-based protection is not utilized to its full potential in any of the case studies. I suspect that this is because of the way that virtual memory works on Intel machines. The Pentium's paging facilities, in addition to supporting memory expansion via disk storage, also provide a degree of segmentation functionality. In fact, not only does Intel paging support memory segmentation, but it also does so at a much finer level of granularity. Access policies can be instituted on a 4KB page level.

> **NOTE** As I have mentioned several times before, operating system code serves as a policy maker that mandates how the hardware-based memory management tools will be used. Deciding not to use a given mechanism at all is still a policy decision in and of itself.

If you think about it, segmentation and paging both serve to break up a region of memory into smaller parts. Paging just partitions memory into smaller chunks. So, in a sense, investing in an elaborate segmentation scheme via GDTs and LDTs is somewhat of a wasted effort when the same type of services can be built on an existing service that is already being used for something else.

The trade-off to relying heavily on paging is that it only permits a two-ring privilege model. This is a far cry from the four-ring privilege scheme that segmentation hardware supports. Page directory and page table entries have only a single bit to specify privilege. This leaves us with a pretty limited user/supervisor implementation of access privileges. Paging also requires more memory within the kernel itself because the data structures that track pages of data are more numerous. Most operating systems give each process its own page directory, which necessarily implies a handful of page tables and their entries. A pure segmentation scheme could potentially only require a single entry in the GDT to delimit and manage an application in memory.

References

Books and Articles

Aleph One. "Smashing the Stack for Fun and Profit." *Phrack*, Issue 49.

    This is the groundbreaking article that put buffer overflow attacks on the map.

Barnaby, Jack. "Win32 Buffer Overflows: Location, Exploitation, and Prevention." *Phrack*, Issue 55.

Bovet, D. and M. Cesati. *Understanding the Linux Kernel: From I/O Ports to Process Management*. 2002, O'Reilly & Associates, ISBN: 0596000022.

    These authors do an exceptional job of presenting a conceptual view of how the Linux kernel operates. Generally this book should be read before you tackle Maxwell's.

Burgess, Richard. *MMURTL V1.0*. 2000, Sensory Publishing, Inc., ISBN: 1588530000.

    There were some people in the computer subculture that suspected that Richard's book had been suppressed by the powers that be. Thankfully, they were wrong. MMURTL is back and in print. Burgess does a particularly nice job of explaining the hardware interface.

Cesare, Silvio. "Runtime Kernel Kmem Patching." 1998, http://www.big.net.au/~silvio/runtime-kernel-kmem-patching.txt.

    This is the canonical article on kernel patching. Almost every article on Linux kernel patching can be traced to this article in one way or another.

Chebotko, Kalatchin, Kiselev, and Podvoisky. *Assembly Language Master Class*. 1994, Wrox Press Inc., ISBN: 1874416346.

    This book details a functional DPMI server for DOS.

halflife@infonexus.com. "Abuse of the Linux Kernel for Fun and Profit." *Phrack*, Issue 50.

    This article describes the steps needed to hijack a user-TTY via LKMs.

Hatch, B., J. Lee, and G. Kurtz. *Hacking Linux Exposed*. 2001, McGraw-Hill, ISBN: 0072127732.

Hoglund, Greg. "A *REAL* NT Rootkit: Patching the NT Kernel." *Phrack*, Issue 55.

This is an interesting article on NT kernel internals. The author also does a nice job of setting the tone of his article.

Maxwell, Scott. *Linux Core Kernel Commentary, 2nd Edition*. 1999, The Coriolis Group, ISBN: 1588801497.

This sizeable book is basically a guided tour of the source code. Be warned; you will need several book markers to read this text.

Palmers. "Sub proc_root Quando Sumus (Advances in Kernel Hacking)." *Phrack*, Issue 58.

This article focuses on manipulating the /proc file system using LKMs. The Latin title is fun too; there is nothing like a Pythonesque sense of humor. (Wink, wink, nudge, nudge.)

Patterson, D. and J. Hennessy. *Computer Architecture: A Quantitative Approach*. 1996, Morgan Kaufmann Publishers, ISBN: 1558603298.

Every hardware engineer I know has a copy of this book, and with good reason. This book provides a universally effective approach for analyzing processor performance.

Ray, J. and Anonymous. *Maximum Linux Security*. 2001, Sams, ISBN: 0672321343.

Schreiber, Sven. *Undocumented Windows 2000 Secrets: A Programmer's Cookbook*. 2001, Addison-Wesley, ISBN: 0201721872.

The title of this book is well deserved. This is an engrossing exploration of the Windows 2000 operating system by an author who knows what he's doing. Sven covers a lot more ground than I had space to. He also provides a number of handy tools. If you are hungry to find out more about Window's internals, get a copy of this book.

SD and Devik. "Linux on-the-fly kernel patching without LKM." *Phrack*, Issue 58.

This article is concerned with manipulating `/dev/kmem`. The bad news is that they assume that the reader has already attained root status.

Solomon, D. and M. Russinovich. *Inside Microsoft Windows 2000*. 2000, Microsoft Press, ISBN: 0735610215.

This book gives a detailed overview of Windows 2000. Unfortunately, there is no source code included. This is like trying to admire a painting blindfolded while listening to someone describe it to you. You can't extract any sort of concrete insight. This book does have a rare photo of Bruce Cutler.

Toxen, Bob. *Real World Linux Security: Intrusion Prevention, Detection and Recovery.* 2000, Prentice Hall, ISBN: 0130281875.

Villani, Pat. *FreeDOS Kernel; An MS-DOS Emulator for Platform Independence and Embedded Systems Development.* 1996, CMP Books, ISBN: 0879304367.

If you want to understand how DOS works without using a disassembler, this is a useful book. FreeDOS is a DOS clone. It's a good first step for readers who are not ready to jump into protected mode.

Web Sites

http://www.cs.vu.nl/~ast/minix.html
(the home page for MINIX)

http://www.delorie.com/djgpp
DJGPP is the Win32 version of GCC. This distribution offers a DPMI host called cwsdpmi.exe.

http://www.dunfield.com/downloads.htm
The MICRO-C compiler can be obtained from this site.

http://www.kernel.org
This site offers the most recent Linux kernel source code.

http://www.linux.org
This is one of the more popular Linux portals.

http://www.microsoft.com/
Microsoft provides a number of tool kits that can be downloaded for free.

http://www.phrack.com
Before there was hacking, there was phone phraking. This e-zine came into being when guys like John Draper were exploring the telecom systems. *Phrack* is one of the oldest and most respected underground zines in distribution. I found more than a few interesting articles at this site.

http://www.securityfocus.com
This is an excellent site for getting information on recent software exploits. Bugtraq is particularly useful.

http://standards.ieee.org
If you have a couple hundred dollars to spare, you can purchase the POSIX specification at this site.

http://www.tenberry.com/web/dpmi/toc.htm
　　The DPMI spec is available at this web site, as is the renowned DOS/4G DOS extender.

http://www.vci.com/products/pharlap.asp
　　The Phar Lap corporate name is still alive. Believe it or not, they are still selling a DOS extender.

Chapter 3

High-Level Services

"My problem is that I have been persecuted by an integer."
— George A. Miller

View from 10,000 Feet

A computer's memory management subsystem can be likened to a house. The foundation and plumbing are provided by the hardware. It is always there, doing its job behind the scenes; you just take it for granted until something breaks. The frame of the house is supplied by the operating system. The operating system is built upon the foundation and gives the house its form and defines its functionality. A well-built frame can make the difference between a shack and a mansion.

It would be possible to stop with the operating system's memory management facilities. However, this would be like a house that has no furniture or appliances. It would be a pretty austere place to live in. You would have to sleep on the floor and use the bathroom outside. User space libraries and tools are what furnish the operating system with amenities that make it easier for applications to use and execute within memory. High-level services like these are what add utility to the house and give it resale value (see Figure 3.1 on the following page).

There are two ways that user applications can allocate memory: compiler-based allocation and heap allocation.

We will spend this chapter analyzing both of these techniques.

The first approach is supported, to various degrees, by the development environment that is being used. Not all compilers, and the languages they translate, are equal. You will see a graphic demonstration of this later on in the chapter.

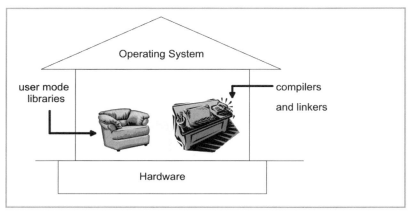

Figure 3.1

The second approach is normally implemented through library calls (i.e., like `malloc()` and `free()`) or by a resident virtual machine. Using this technique to implement memory management provides a way for storage allocation facilities to be decoupled from the development tools. For example, there are several different implementations of `malloc()` that can be used with the `gcc` compiler. Some engineers even specialize in optimizing `malloc()` and offer their own high-performance `malloc.tar.gz` packages as a drop-in replacement for the standard implementation.

In order to help illustrate these two approaches, I will look at several development environments. This will give you the opportunity to see how different tools and libraries provide high-level services to user applications. We will be given the luxury of forgetting about the hardware details and be able to look at memory from a more abstract vantage point. I will begin by looking at relatively simple languages, like COBOL, and then move on to more sophisticated languages, like C and Java.

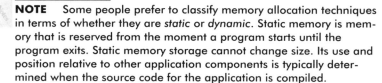

NOTE Some people prefer to classify memory allocation techniques in terms of whether they are *static* or *dynamic*. Static memory is memory that is reserved from the moment a program starts until the program exits. Static memory storage cannot change size. Its use and position relative to other application components is typically determined when the source code for the application is compiled.

Dynamic memory is memory that is requested and managed while the program is running. Dynamic memory parameters cannot be specified when a program is compiled because the size and life span factors are not known until run time.

While dynamic memory may allow greater flexibility, using static memory allows an application to execute faster because it doesn't have to perform any extraneous bookkeeping at runtime. In a production environment that supports a large number of applications, using static memory is also sometimes preferable because it allows the system administrators to implement a form of load balancing. If you know that a certain application has a footprint in memory of exactly 2MB, then you know how many servers you will need to provide 300 instances of the application.

I think that the static-versus-dynamic scheme makes it more complicated to categorize hybrid memory constructs like the stack. This is why I am sticking to a compiler-versus-heap taxonomy.

Compiler-Based Allocation

User applications typically have their address space divided into four types of regions:

- Code section
- Data section
- Stack
- Heap

An application may have more than one section of a particular type (see Figure 3.2). For example, an application may have multiple code sections and stacks.

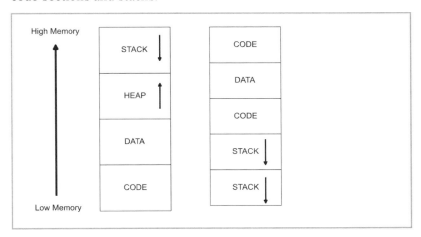

Figure 3.2

Sometimes an application may have only a single section that is a hybrid of different types (see Figure 3.3). For example, DOS .COM executables, loaded into memory, consist of a single section. Data, as long as it is not executed, can be interspersed with code. The stack pointer register (SP) is set to the end of the executable's image so that the last few bytes serve as an informal stack.

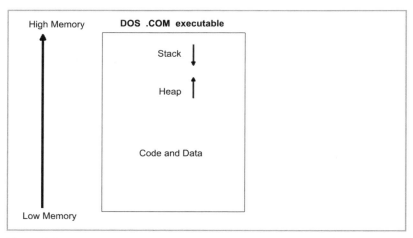

Figure 3.3

A .COM file has no official boundaries. If the stack overflows into the heap, or if the program is so large that the stack spills into the code, then you are out of luck. Here is a small .COM file program so that you can see what I am talking about:

```
; --smallCom.asm--
.386
mycode SEGMENT USE16
ASSUME CS:mycode,DS:mycode,SS:mycode,ES:mycode
ORG 100H

;code region---------------------------------
entry:
PUSH DS
MOV AH,0H
PUSH AX

MOV [oldstack],SP
MOV SP,OFFSET stktop

MOV AX,OFFSET string1
PUSH AX
CALL printStr

MOV AX,OFFSET string2
PUSH AX
CALL printStr

MOV SP,[oldstack]
RETF

;data region---------------------------------
oldstack    DW ?
```

```
string1     DB "the hot side stays hot--"
end1        DB '$'
string2     DB "the cool side stays cool"
end2        DB '$'

;stack region--------------------------------
stkbody     DB 31 dup ('01')
stktop      DB 01H

;code region--------------------------------
printStr:
PUSH BP
MOV  BP,SP
MOV  AH,09H
MOV  DX,[BP+4]
INT  21H
POP  BP
RET

mycode ENDS
END entry
```

Here is the build command with MASM: `C:\MASM\SRC> ML /AT smallCom.asm`

When you run this application, the following message is printed to the screen:

```
C:\MASM\SRC>smallCom
the hot side stays hot--the cool side stays cool
```

As you can see, I have placed data, not to mention a whole entire stack, dead in the middle of executable code. There are really very few rules in the case of a `.COM` binary. Most current executable formats, like the ELF file format or the PE file format, have more strict and established rules with regard to program section arrangement.

NOTE Regardless of how many or what type of sections a program has, the general rule is that the stack grows down from a high address and the heap grows up from a low address.

QUESTION

What does all of this memory partitioning have to do with development tools?

ANSWER

A compiler is a development tool that acts as a translator. It consumes human-readable source code, moves the source through its compound digestive track, and then emits native machine instructions (or some other type of bytecode). A compiler also determines how the emitted binary values will be organized to provide the four types of memory sections described previously. *In general, compilers control how memory is arranged, allocated, accessed, and updated in every section, except the heap.* Managing the heap is the domain of user libraries and virtual machines.

Data Section

The data section of an application traditionally supplies what is known as static memory. As I mentioned earlier, static memory regions are fixed in size and exist for the duration of an application's life span.

Given these two characteristics, most compilers will construct data sections to serve as storage for global data. For example, consider the following C program:

```
#include<string.h>

struct employee
{
    char firstname[32];
    char lastname[32];
    unsigned char age;
    unsigned int salary;
};

struct employee architect = {"Gil","Bates",45,100000};
struct employee ceo = {"Reed","Almer",42,95000};
struct employee drone;

void main()
{
    strcpy(drone.firstname,"bill");
    strcpy(drone.lastname,"blunden");
    drone.age=35;
    drone.salary=(int)(3.5);
    return;
}
```

If we look at a listing file, it is clear that the global variables above have been isolated in their own reserved program section called _DATA. This section will have a fixed size and exist from the time the program starts until the time that it exits.

```
.386P
.model FLAT
PUBLIC _architect
PUBLIC _ceo
```

```
_DATA   SEGMENT
COMM    _drone:BYTE:048H
_architect DB 'Gil', 00H
        ORG $+28
        DB  'Bates', 00H
        ORG $+26
        DB  02dH
        ORG $+3
        DD  0186a0H
_ceo    DB  'Reed', 00H
        ORG $+27
        DB  'Almer', 00H
        ORG $+26
        DB  02aH
        ORG $+3
        DD  017318H
_DATA   ENDS
PUBLIC  _main
EXTRN   _strcpy:NEAR
_DATA   SEGMENT
$SG117  DB  'bill', 00H
        ORG $+3
$SG118  DB  'blunden', 00H
_DATA   ENDS
_TEXT   SEGMENT
_main   PROC NEAR

; 16   : {

        push    ebp
        mov     ebp, esp

; 17   :     strcpy(drone.firstname,"bill");

        push    OFFSET FLAT:$SG117
        push    OFFSET FLAT:_drone
        call    _strcpy
        add     esp, 8

; 18   :     strcpy(drone.lastname,"blunden");

        push    OFFSET FLAT:$SG118
        push    OFFSET FLAT:_drone+32
        call    _strcpy
        add     esp, 8

; 19   :     drone.age=35;

        mov     BYTE PTR _drone+64, 35    ; 00000023H
; 20   :     drone.salary=(int)(3.5);
```

```
                mov     DWORD PTR _drone+68, 3
; 21   :        return;
; 22   :    }

                pop     ebp
                ret     0
_main   ENDP
_TEXT   ENDS
END
```

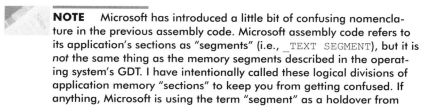

NOTE   Microsoft has introduced a little bit of confusing nomenclature in the previous assembly code. Microsoft assembly code refers to its application's sections as "segments" (i.e., _TEXT SEGMENT), but it is *not* the same thing as the memory segments described in the operating system's GDT. I have intentionally called these logical divisions of application memory "sections" to keep you from getting confused. If anything, Microsoft is using the term "segment" as a holdover from DOS, where addresses were specified with a segment and offset address.

The data section has a long and venerable history as the second oldest type of application memory section. In the old days, programs were just code and a fixed clump of static storage. The sysop was the only person with a console, punch cards were considered high-tech, and a top-of-the-line Dietzgen-Tyler Multilog slide rule with enamel finish cost $35.

Code Section

At the end of the day, an application's various sections are just bytes in memory. So in some special cases, you can get away with using a code section for data storage. In other words, it is possible to turn a code section into a data section. The magic rule to keep in mind is: It is data as long as you don't execute it. Here is an example:

```
/* --codedata.c-- */

#include<stdio.h>

void code()
{
    /*
    on Intel, each instruction is 4 bytes:
    encoded as 0x66 0xb8 0x07 0x00
    */
    _asm MOV AX,0x07
    _asm MOV AX,0x07
    _asm MOV AX,0x07
    _asm MOV AX,0x07
```

```
        /* 16 bytes total */
        return;
}

void main()
{
    char *cptr;
    short reg;

    code();
    _asm MOV reg,AX
    printf("reg=%d\n",reg);

    cptr = (char*)code;
    cptr[0]='d'; cptr[1]='a';cptr[2]='t';cptr[3]='a';
    cptr[4]=(char)0;
    printf("cptr[]=%s\n",cptr);
    return;
}
```

This can be built as a 16-bit DOS app with Turbo C++.

```
C:\TCC\codeData>TCC -ms codedata.c
```

The output you will get will look like this:

```
C:\TCC\codeData>codedata
reg=7
cptr[]=data
```

Before you rush out and try to write your own self-modifying app, I think you should know something: In the first chapter, I demonstrated how segments and pages can be marked as read-only, read-write, execute-only, etc. Some operating systems designate the pages belonging to code sections as execute-only, so you cannot always use the previously described trick because the memory in question cannot be read or modified. The above application worked fine running under DOS 6.22 because DOS has absolutely no memory protection.

If you try to run the previous application on Windows via Visual Studio as a Win32 console application, the operating system will stop you in your tracks and present you with a dialog box like the one shown in Figure 3.4.

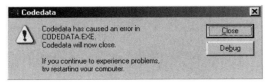

Figure 3.4

Stack

A stack is a sequence of bytes in memory that act like a first-in-last-out (FILO) data structure. Computer stacks typically "grow down." Each stack has a stack pointer (i.e., SP in Figure 3.5) that stores the lowest address of the last item allocated on the stack. When a new item is added to the stack, the stack pointer is decremented to point to that item's first byte.

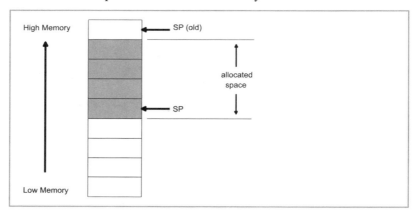

Figure 3.5

There are two basic ways to manipulate a stack so memory can be allocated and freed: PUSH/POP instructions and integer arithmetic.

Every machine instruction set has a set of PUSH and POP instructions. The PUSH instruction causes the stack pointer to be decremented. The space created by this operation will be populated by the PUSH instruction's operand. The stack pointer will always point to the first byte of the data item on the top of the stack.

The POP instruction causes the stack pointer to be incremented. The storage reclaimed has its data stored in the POP instruction's operand. The PUSH and POP operations are displayed in Figure 3.6 to give you a better idea of how they function.

NOTE In Figure 3.6, I am assuming that I'm dealing with a native host that is *little endian*. Little endian architectures store the low-order bytes of a value in lower memory. For example, a value like 0x1A2B3C4D in memory would store 0x4D at byte (n), 0x3C at byte (n+1), 0x2B at byte (n+2), and 0x1A at byte (n+3).

address	n	n+1	n+2	n+3
byte	0x4D	0x3C	0x2B	0x1A

A *big endian* architecture stores the high-order bytes of a value in low memory:

address	n	n+1	n+2	n+3
byte	0x1A	0x2B	0x3C	0x4D

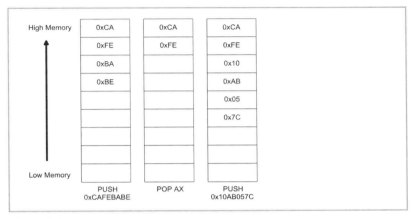

Figure 3.6

With manual stack pointer manipulation via direct arithmetic, storing and retrieving data is not as automated. Adding or subtracting values from the stack pointer does effectively change where `SP` points, and this is a very fast way to allocate and free large amounts of storage on the stack. However, transferring data to and from the stack must be done manually. This is illustrated in Figure 3.7.

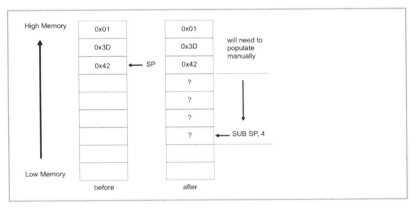

Figure 3.7

The stack is a kind of temporary scratch pad that applications can use to keep track of short-lived values. The stack is particularly useful for operations that must be done and then undone. Thus, it is a good way to store and then reclaim temporary data. What distinguishes the stack from a free-for-all storage region, like the heap, is that there are rules that enforce a certain degree of regularity. In other words, the stack is predictable and the heap is chaotic. With the stack, you pretty much always know where the next chunk of memory will start, regardless of how big or small the data item to be allocated is.

The stack, though it might seem simple, is an extremely powerful concept when applied correctly. Stacks are used to implement high-level features like recursion and variable scope. Some garbage collectors use them as an alternative to a heap for more efficient allocation.

Activation Records

If you wanted to, you could use registers to pass parameter information to a function. However, using registers to pass parameters does not support recursion. Using the stack is a more flexible and powerful technique. Managing the stack to facilitate a function call is the responsibility of both the procedure that is invoking the function and the function being invoked. Both entities must work together in order to pass information back and forth on the stack. I will start with the responsibilities that belong to the invoking function.

The following steps can be used to invoke a procedure and pass it arguments:

1. Push the current function's state onto the stack.
2. Push the return value onto the stack.
3. Push function arguments onto the stack.
4. Push the return address onto the stack.
5. Jump to the location of the procedure.

Using Intel's CALL instruction will typically take care of the last two steps automatically. The function being invoked must also take a few steps to ensure that it can access the parameters passed to it and create local storage:

1. Push EBP on to the stack (to save its value).
2. Copy the current ESP value into EBP.
3. Decrement ESP to allocate local storage.
4. Execute the function's instructions.

The code that performs these four steps is known as the invoked function's *prologue*.

The result of all this stack manipulation is that we end up with a stack arrangement similar to that displayed in Figure 3.8.

The region of the stack used to store a function's parameters and local storage is referred to as the *activation record* because every time a procedure is activated (i.e., invoked), this information must be specified. An activation record is also known as a *stack frame*.

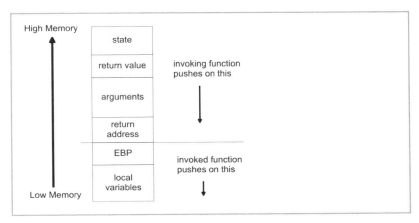

Figure 3.8

The stack region displayed in Figure 3.8 is an example of an activation record.

NOTE On Intel machines, the EBP register is pushed on the stack so that it can serve as a reference point. EBP is known as the *stack frame pointer*, and it is used so that elements in the activation record can be referenced via indirect addressing (i.e., MOV AX, [EBP+5]).

NOTE The arrangement of elements in the activation record does not necessarily have to follow the conventions that I adhere to in this section. Different languages and compilers will use different ordering for items in the activation record.

When the function has done its thing and is ready to return, it must perform the following stack maintenance steps:

1. Reclaim local storage.
2. Pop EBP off the stack.
3. Pop the return address off the stack.
4. Jump to the return address.

The Intel RET instruction will usually take care of the last two steps.

The code that performs the previous four steps is known as the invoked function's *epilogue*.

Once the invoked function has returned, the invoking function will need to take the following steps to get its hands on the return value and clean up the stack:

1. Pop the function arguments off the stack.
2. Pop the return value off the stack.
3. Pop the saved program state off the stack.

Another way to handle the arguments is to simply increment the stack pointer. We really have no use for the function arguments once the invoked function has returned, so this is a cleaner and more efficient way to reclaim the corresponding stack space.

This whole process can be seen in terms of four compound steps:

1. Invoking function sets up stack
2. Function invoked sets up EBP and local storage (prologue)

-----called function executes-----

3. Function invoked frees local storage and restores EBP (epilogue)
4. Invoking function extracts return value and cleans up stack

Here is a simple example to illustrate all of the previous points. Consider the following C code:

```
/* ---stkfram.c--- */

unsigned char array[] = {1,2,3,4,5};

unsigned short sigma(unsigned char *cptr,int n)
{
    int i;
    int sum;
    sum= 0;
    for(i=0;i<n;i++){ sum = sum+ cptr[i]; }
    return(sum);
}

void main()
{
    int retval;
    retval = sigma(array,5);
    return;
}
```

If we look at a listing file, we can see how activation records are utilized in practice:

```
.386P
.model  FLAT
PUBLIC  _array
_DATA   SEGMENT
_array  DB      01H
        DB      02H
        DB      03H
        DB      04H
        DB      05H
_DATA   ENDS
PUBLIC  _sigma
```

```
_TEXT   SEGMENT
_cptr$ = 8
_n$ = 12
_i$ = -8
_sum$ = -4
_sigma   PROC NEAR
; 7    : {

        push    ebp
        mov     ebp, esp
        sub     esp, 8

; 8    :     int i;
; 9    :     int sum;
; 10   :
; 11   :     sum= 0;

        mov     DWORD PTR _sum$[ebp], 0

; 12   :     for(i=0;i<n;i++){ sum = sum+ cptr[i]; }

        mov     DWORD PTR _i$[ebp], 0
        jmp     SHORT $L31
$L32:
        mov     eax, DWORD PTR _i$[ebp]
        add     eax, 1
        mov     DWORD PTR _i$[ebp], eax
$L31:
        mov     ecx, DWORD PTR _i$[ebp]
        cmp     ecx, DWORD PTR _n$[ebp]
        jge     SHORT $L33
        mov     edx, DWORD PTR _cptr$[ebp]
        add     edx, DWORD PTR _i$[ebp]
        xor     eax, eax
        mov     al, BYTE PTR [edx]
        mov     ecx, DWORD PTR _sum$[ebp]
        add     ecx, eax
        mov     DWORD PTR _sum$[ebp], ecx
        jmp     SHORT $L32
$L33:

; 13   :     return(sum);

        mov     ax, WORD PTR _sum$[ebp]

; 14   : }

        mov     esp, ebp
        pop     ebp
        ret     0
_sigma ENDP
```

```
_TEXT   ENDS
PUBLIC  _main
_TEXT   SEGMENT
_retval$ = -4
_main   PROC NEAR

; 17   : {

        push    ebp
        mov     ebp, esp
        push    ecx

; 18   :       int retval;
; 19   :
; 20   :       retval = sigma(array,5);

        push    5
        push    OFFSET FLAT:_array
        call    _sigma
        add     esp, 8
        and     eax, 65535              ; 0000ffffH
        mov     DWORD PTR _retval$[ebp], eax

; 21   :
; 22   :       //printf("retval=%d\n",retval);
; 23   :       return;
; 24   : }

        mov     esp, ebp
        pop     ebp
        ret     0
_main   ENDP
_TEXT   ENDS
END
```

OK, let us look at each step as it occurs to understand what the compiler is doing. The first important thing that happens is the call to `sigma()`. The invoking function, `main()`, has to set up its portion of the activation record:

```
; 20   :       retval = sigma(array,5);

        push    5
        push    OFFSET FLAT:_array
        call    _sigma
```

The invoking function pushes on the arguments. The CALL instruction automatically pushes a return address onto the stack. What about the return value? As it turns out, the compiler is smart enough to realize that recursion does not exist and uses the EAX register to pass a return value back to `main()`.

Once execution has reached `sigma()`, the sigma function sets up the bottom part of the stack frame:

```
push    ebp
mov     ebp, esp
sub     esp, 8
```

The index variable `i` requires 4 bytes and the integer variable `sum` requires 4 bytes. This accounts for the 8 bytes of local storage allocated by the prologue of `sigma()`.

The activation record produced in this example resembles the one detailed in Figure 3.9.

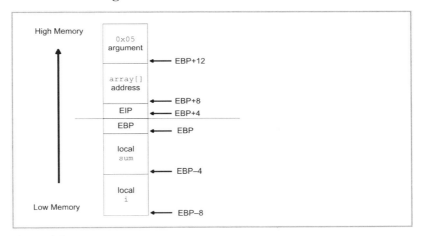

Figure 3.9

Once `sigma()` has calculated its sum, it places the return value in `EAX` and cleans out the local storage. The `RET` instruction automatically pops the return address off the stack.

```
; 13   :       return(sum);

        mov     ax, WORD PTR _sum$[ebp]

; 14   : }

        mov     esp, ebp
        pop     ebp
        ret     0
```

When `main()` has things back under its control, it cleans up the arguments placed on the stack and extracts the return value from `EAX`:

```
        call    _sigma
        add     esp, 8
```

```
            and     eax, 65535                  ; 0000ffffH
```

You should be able to appreciate the amount of bookkeeping done by the compiler to compute the size of each activation record and the location of each element in them. These calculations are all performed at compile time while the source code is being processed. You should also keep in mind that some compilers have very intelligent optimizers that will take advantage of certain circumstances (for example, by doing sneaky things like using registers to return values).

Scope

The *scope* of a program element (a variable declaration, a function, etc.) determines both the visibility and, potentially, the life span of the element. When a program element is visible, it can be accessed and manipulated. The life span of a program element determines when the element is created and destroyed.

The one caveat to this rule is for program elements that have their storage space allocated off the heap, dynamically, during execution. In this case, scope only defines the visibility of the program element. The element will exist until it is reclaimed, which may or may not be related to the scope of the element.

To explore the meaning of scope, let us examine how scope rules apply to variables in the C programming language. Scope rules in C are implemented through the use of code blocks. A *block* of code is a region of source code that lies between a pair of brackets (i.e., between a "{" and a "}"). A function definition is an example of a block of code.

```
void myfunction()
{
    # block of code
    return;
}
```

In fact, functions are actually at the top of the block hierarchy in C. Functions may contain other blocks of code, as long as the blocks of code are not function definitions (which is to say that function definitions *cannot* be nested in C). For example, the following function definition contains a few sub-blocks:

```
void myfunction()
{
    int i;
    for(i=0;i<10;i++)
    {
```

```
            if((i%2)==0)
            {
                printf("%d is even\n",i);
            }
    }
    {
        int j=10;
        printf("j=%d\n",j);
    }
    return;
}
```

From the previous function definition, we can see that blocks of code may be nested. In addition, although blocks of code are usually associated with program control statements, it is possible for blocks of code to exist independently of a program control statement. For example, the code that prints out the value of "j" is a stand-alone block.

Even though functions may contain other blocks of code, blocks of code (that are not function definitions) cannot independently exist outside of a function definition. For example, you would *never* see:

```
void myfunction1()
{
    # block of code
    return;
}

int i;
for(i=0;i<10;i++){ printf("%d\n",i); }

void myfunction2()
{
    # block of code
    return;
}
```

An ANSI C compiler processing the previous code would protest that the `for` loop does not belong to a function and would refuse to compile the code.

The scope of variables in C is block based. A variable declared inside of a block of code is known as a *local variable*. A local variable is visible in the block in which it is declared and all the sub-blocks within that block. A variable cannot be accessed outside of the block in which it was declared. For example, the following snippet of C code is completely legal:

```
void main()
{
```

```
    int i;
    for(i=0;i<10;i++)
    {
        int j=i*i;
        printf("i=%d, i^2=%d\n",i,j);
    }
    return;
}
```

The following snippet of C code, however, is *illegal*:

```
void main()
{
    int i;
    for(i=0;i<10;i++)
    {
        int j=i*i;
        printf("i=%d, i^2=%d\n",i,j);
    }
    printf("i=%d, i^2=%d\n",i,j);
    return;
}
```

In the first case, we are perfectly within the syntactical rules of C when the variable "i" is accessed in a sub-block. In the second case, however, if we try to access the variable "j" outside of its declaring block, the compiler will emit an error. Naturally, there are two special cases to this rule: global variables and the formal parameters of a function.

A *global variable* is a variable defined outside of any block of code. As such, a global variable is visible throughout a program by every section of code. Global variables also exist for the duration of a program's execution path.

Formal parameters are the variables specified in the prototype of a function. They are the variables that receive the arguments passed to a function when it is invoked. Formal parameters have visibility and a life span that is limited to the body of the function they belong to.

Two basic techniques exist with regard to managing scope within the body of a procedure: the all-at-once approach and additional stack frames.

One way to manage scope is to allocate storage for all of a function's local variables in the prologue code. In other words, we use the function's activation record to provide storage for every local variable defined inside of the function, regardless of where it is used. To support this approach, a compiler will use its symbol table to make sure that a local variable is not accessed outside of its declaring block.

High-Level Services

Here is an example to help illustrate this:

```c
/* ---localvars.c--- */

void main(int argc, char *argv[])
{
    unsigned char arr1[20];
    unsigned long int i;

    arr1[0]='a';
    i=argc;

    if(i<4)
    {
        unsigned char arr2[7];
        unsigned long int j;
        unsigned long int k;
        arr2[0]='b';
        j=5;
        k=6;
    }
    else
    {
        unsigned char arr3[17];
        arr3[0]='c';
    }
}
```

By looking at its assembly code equivalent, we can see how storage for all these variables was allocated:

```
.386P
.model FLAT
PUBLIC _main
_TEXT   SEGMENT
_argc$ = 8
_arr1$ = -24
_i$ = -4
_arr2$31 = -40
_j$32 = -28
_k$33 = -32
_arr3$35 = -60
_main   PROC NEAR
; Line 4
        push    ebp
        mov     ebp, esp
        sub     esp, 60                         ; 0000003cH
; Line 8
        mov     BYTE PTR _arr1$[ebp], 97 ; 00000061H
; Line 9
        mov     eax, DWORD PTR _argc$[ebp]
```

```
                mov     DWORD PTR _i$[ebp], eax
; Line 11
                cmp     DWORD PTR _i$[ebp], 4
                jae     SHORT $L30
; Line 16
                mov     BYTE PTR _arr2$31[ebp], 98     ; 00000062H
; Line 17
                mov     DWORD PTR _j$32[ebp], 5
; Line 18
                mov     DWORD PTR _k$33[ebp], 6
; Line 20
                jmp     SHORT $L34
$L30:
; Line 23
                mov     BYTE PTR _arr3$35[ebp], 99     ; 00000063H
$L34:
; Line 25
                mov     esp, ebp
                pop     ebp
                ret     0
_main   ENDP
_TEXT   ENDS
END
```

The compiler places all of the local variables, even the ones that may not be used, on the procedure's activation record. We end up with an activation record like the one in Figure 3.10. Notice how the compiler pads entries so that they always begin on an address that is a multiple of 4 bytes. This is particularly true for the arr2[] and arr3[] arrays.

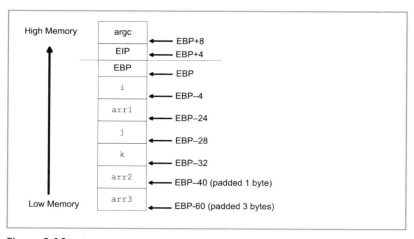

Figure 3.10

The alternative to the all-at-once approach is to give each sub-block its own private activation record. In the "Activation Records" section, we saw how procedure-based scope was implemented. By using the stack, we were able to create storage that had a scope and life span limited to the function. By using this same type of technique on a smaller scale, we can implement visibility and life span on a block-by-block basis.

NOTE In a way, stacks are really about storage life span. Visibility restrictions follow naturally as a result of life span constraints. Recall that stacks are good for situations in which you need to do, and then undo, an operation. This makes them perfect for creating temporary storage. The limited visibility is more of a side effect of the limited life span. Once a variable has been popped off the stack, it is gone and any reference to it can yield garbage.

The easiest way to think of a block of code is like a stripped-down type of function that has no return value and no return address. It only has local variables. Table 3.1 presents a basic comparison of functions and code blocks.

Table 3.1

	Saved State	Return Value	Arguments	Return Address	Variables
Function	yes	yes	yes	yes	yes
Sub-block	yes	no	yes	no	yes

As you can see from the table, a code block has saved program state information and local variables in its stack frame. Local variables declared outside the block but accessed inside the block can be treated as arguments. Figure 3.11 displays a comparison of the stack frames used by a function and a code block.

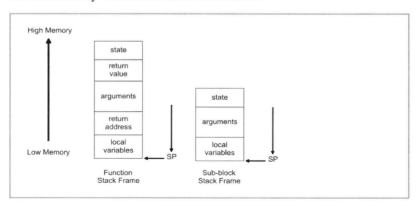

Figure 3.11

QUESTION

What are the trade-offs between the all-at-once approach and the additional stack frame approach?

ANSWER

The extra stack frame technique requires that stack manipulation be performed every time a block is entered or exited. If a section of code has a heavily nested set of blocks, this translates into a lot of extra push and pop operations. This means the extra stack frame tactic will create an executable that is larger and slower because more instructions will need to be executed.

Another downside of using the all-at-once tactic is that it requires a lot of storage overhead. Space in the activation record will be reserved even if a variable is not used. If a function has several different possible execution paths, a lot of storage is wasted.

Table 3.2 summarizes a comparison of these two techniques.

Table 3.2

	All-at-once Allocation	Extra Stack Frames
Speed	faster	slower
Stack memory usage	more	less
Executable size	smaller	larger

In the final analysis, real estate on the stack is relatively cheap compared to execution speed, which is why most compilers opt for the all-at-once approach.

Static or Dynamic?

The stack is a hybrid between a purely static and a purely dynamic form of storage. It is not purely static because the amount of occupied storage on a stack varies with each function call. Each time a function is invoked, a new activation record is pushed on to the stack. When a function returns, its activation record vanishes and all of its associated data goes out of scope.

However, the way in which stack storage is allocated and freed obeys a strict first-in-last-out (FILO) policy. In addition, the regions of storage consumed on a stack are almost completely dictated by the compiler. In a structured language like C, the stack is populated with nothing but activation records, and the size of each activation record is fixed at compile time. Thus, there is a lot more regularity with a stack than there is with a dynamic storage mechanism like a heap. The stack, as I have said before, is a predictable creature. In addition, because of the presence of a stack pointer, you always know where your next byte will be allocated or released from.

Because of its close connection to the machine instructions emitted by the compiler in terms of prologue and epilogue code, I like to think of the stack as being a memory component whose utilization is tied to the development tools being used. This is why I included a discussion of the stack in this section of the chapter.

Heap Allocation

Heap memory allocation, also known as *dynamic memory allocation* (DMA), consists of requesting memory while an application is running from a repository known as the *heap*. A heap is just a collection of available bytes (i.e., a bunch of bytes piled into a heap). Unlike the data segment or the stack, the size and life span of memory allocated from the heap is completely unpredictable. This requires the agent that manages the heap to be flexible, and this, in turn, translates into a lot of extra memory management code.

The data segment requires no special management code, and stack management is limited primarily to the prologue and epilogue code of functions. The heap, however, normally has its own dedicated set of elaborate routines to service memory requests.

Table 3.3

Storage	Size	Life Span	Bookkeeping
data section	fixed	program life span	none
stack	fixed size stack frames	function-based	all at compile time
heap	varies	varies	significant at run time

The heap relies heavily on user mode libraries. These libraries (like `malloc()` and `free()` declared in `stdlib.h`) may be invoked directly by programs or called indirectly by a virtual machine. Either way, these libraries normally end up utilizing facilities provided by the underlying operating system. Thus, before we dive straight into managing memory through user libraries, it would help to understand how they communicate with the operating system.

System Call Interface

Most user applications are blissfully unaware of what really goes on to support their execution. They never see the GDT or the page table entries. User applications are strictly memory *consumers*. Like a pizza-hungry college freshman, applications ask for memory takeout, and the operating system gives it to them; they don't care about the details. User programs have a perspective that is roughly 10,000 feet above the operating system level. At this altitude, the system call interface is all that user-space code sees.

In his book on MINIX, *Operating Systems: Design and Implementation*, Tanenbaum asserts that the system call interface is what defines an operating system. I would tend to agree with him. The system call interface of an operating system is a set of function prototypes that completely specify every service that the operating system can provide to the outside world. An operating system is nothing more than the implementation of its system calls. If you were a human resources professional, you would view the system call interface as the kernel's formal job description. It dictates the actions that the operating system must be able to perform.

Let us look at a simple example. Take, for instance, the NACHOS operating system. NACHOS was developed by Tom Anderson at Berkeley for instructional use in computer science courses. Its system call interface consists of just 11 routines.

Process Management

```
void Halt()
void Exit(int status)
SpaceId Exec(char *name)
int Join(SpaceId id)
```

File Input/Output

```
void Create(cha *name)
OpenFileId Open(char *name)
void Write(char *buffer, int size, OpenFileId id)
int Read(char *buffer, int size, OpenFileId id)
void Close(OpenFileId id)
```

Threads

```
void Fork(void (*func)())
void Yield()
```

That is it. Everything that NACHOS is capable of doing is described by the previous 11 functions. Naturally, production grade operating systems have a system call interface that is much larger. Linux, for example, has more than 200 routines defined in its system call interface. You can read descriptions of these 200+ system calls in the Linux man pages (i.e., `man2`).

NOTE In case you are wondering, NACHOS stands for Not Another Completely Heuristic Operating System. I think Richard Burgess is correct; we are running out of good acronyms.

System calls are not always spelled out with tidy C prototypes. Some operating systems, like DOS, have a system call interface that is specified strictly in terms of interrupts. Consider the following DOS system call:

```
Interrupt: 0x21 (i.e., INT 0x21)
Function: 0x09
Description: prints a string terminated by a $
Inputs: AH = 9
DS = segment address of string
DX = offset address of string
```

A wise system engineer will attempt to ward off complexity by banishing the system-related assembly code to the basement of the OS. There, in the darkness, only a trained plumber with a flashlight can muck around with the pipes. Even then, an experienced developer will attempt to wrap the assembly code in C/C++ to make it more palatable. Tanenbaum, for instance, did an excellent job of wrapping assembly routines when he implemented MINIX.

> **NOTE** I had the opportunity to speak with an engineer who helped manage the construction of the original OS/2 platform. He told me that around 20% of the kernel code was assembler. This is a lot of assembler, especially when you consider that UNIX operating systems, like FreeBSD, have less than 2% of the kernel coded in assembly language. I am sure that the proliferation of assembly code in OS/2 had an impact on the development team's ability to port the code and institute design changes.

> **NOTE** Cloning is not limited to the bio-tech sector. An operating system *clone* is typically constructed by taking the system call interface of the original OS and performing a clean-room implementation of those calls. The clone differs from the original because those system calls are implemented using different algorithms and data structures. For example, FreeDOS is a clone of Microsoft's DOS. Tanenbaum's MINIX is actually a UNIX clone. It is a well-documented fact that Microsoft's 1982 release of its DOS operating system was a clone of IBM's PC-DOS.

System calls are the atomic building blocks that all other APIs rely on. The user libraries that help to manage memory are built upon the relevant system calls. The layering effect that is generated by building one set of functions on top of another is illustrated in Figure 3.12.

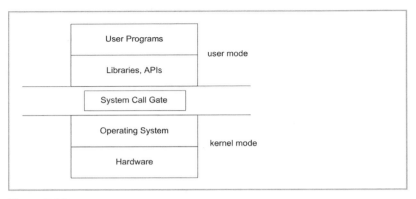

Figure 3.12

User libraries cannot directly access system calls. They must all travel through a choke point called the *system call gate*. If an operating system were a fortress, the system call gate would be its drawbridge. Everything outside the gate runs in user mode, and everything inside the fortress runs in kernel mode.

The system call gate is the only way in and out of the kernel. This is because memory management at the operating system level, in conjunction with the processor, prevents user code from making a FAR JMP directly to kernel functions. For the most part, this keeps the Viking pillagers at a safe distance from the inhabitants of the kernel. Occasionally, however, there are curious explorers like Sven Schreiber who find a hole in the castle wall. Sven found a way around the Windows 2000 system call gate. He describes this discovery in his book, *Undocumented Windows 2000 Secrets*.

NOTE In an operating system like DOS, which has no memory protection, it is possible to execute an interrupt service routine by using a FAR JMP instruction with some assorted assembly language acrobatics. There's nothing in place to prevent a program from jumping to the location of the system call's instructions and executing them.

Typically, a system call gate is implemented as an interrupt handler. The ISR that mans the system call drawbridge checks to see if the user request is valid. If the service request is valid, the call gate ISR then reroutes the request and its arguments to the appropriate system call in kernel space. When the requested system call is done, it hands off execution back to the system call gate, which then returns execution control to the user program.

user library ↔ system call gate ↔ system call
restaurant customer ↔ waiter ↔ cook

The C programming language's standard library is a classic example of this tactic. Let's look at a somewhat forced implementation of the putchar() function to see how library functions build upon system functions. To begin with, most standard library implementations define putchar() in terms of its more general sibling, putc(), which writes a character to a given output stream. In the case of putchar(), the output stream is fixed as standard output (stdout).

```
#define putchar(c) putc(c,stdout)
```

Thus, to understand putchar(), we must dissect putc():

```
int putc(int ch, FILE *stream)
{
    int ret;
    ret = write(stream,&ch,1);
    if(ret!=1){ return(EOF); }else{ return(c); }
}
```

The putc() function, in turn, wraps a system call called write(). A recurring theme that you will notice is the tendency of functions with specific duties to invoke more general and primitive routines.

```
/*
stream  = output stream to write to
buffer  = buffer of bytes to write to stream
nbytes  = number of bytes to write
returns: number of bytes written to stream
*/

int write(FILE *stream, void *buffer, int nbytes)
{
    struct call_struct;
    call_struct.type = FILE_SYSTEM;
    call_struct.subtype = BUFF_OUTPUT;
    call_struct.param1 = (long)stream;
    call_struct.param2 = (long)buffer;
    call_struct.param3 = nbytes;

    asm
    {
        MOV ECX,USER_LIBRARY
        LEA EAX,call_struct
        INT SYSTEM_GATE
    }
}
```

Notice how the write() function is actually a front man for a more general system call gate called SYSTEM_GATE.

The Heap

The heap is just a region of bytes. It is a portion of an application's address space that has been set aside for run-time memory requests. As mentioned previously, the general nature of possible memory requests forces the code that manages the heap to have to deal with a number of possible contingencies. The heap manager cannot handle every type of request equally well, and concessions have to be made. As a result of this, heap management is beset by three potential pitfalls:

- Internal fragmentation
- External fragmentation
- Location-based latency

Internal fragmentation occurs when memory is wasted because a request for memory resulted in the allocation of a block of memory that was much too big, relative to the request size. For example, let's say you request 128 bytes of storage and the run-time system gives you a block of 512 bytes. Most of the memory you've been allocated will never be used. Management schemes that allocate fixed-sized memory blocks can run into this problem.

External fragmentation occurs when a series of memory requests leaves several free blocks of available memory, none of which are large enough to service a typical request.

Latency problems can occur if two data values are stored far apart from one another in memory. The farther apart two values are in memory, the longer it takes for the processor to perform operations that involve those values. In an extreme case, one value may be so far away that it gets paged-out to disk and requires a disk I/O operation to bring it back into the ball game.

Latency problems can also occur because of complexity. If an algorithm takes extensive measures to ensure that internal and external fragmentation are both minimized, the improvement in memory utilization will be offset by the additional execution time necessary to perform the requisite accounting.

Depending on the allocation technique used by the heap management code, it will suffer from one or more of these problems. Rarely can you have your cake and eat it too.

Figure 3.13 displays these three pitfalls.

In the end, what makes the heap an interesting problem is not the heap itself, but the algorithms used to manage it. There are two different approaches to managing heap memory: manual memory management and automatic memory management.

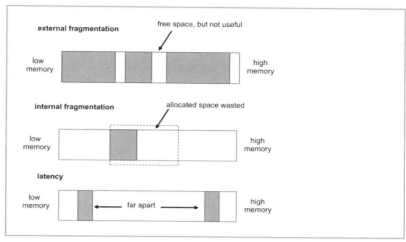

Figure 3.13

In the next two sections, I will examine both of these techniques and offer examples of how they are used in practice.

Manual Memory Management

Manual memory management, also known as *explicit memory management*, requires the programmer to explicitly allocate and recycle heap storage. This is performed through function calls like `malloc()` and `free()`. Explicit memory management shifts responsibility onto the shoulders of the developer with regard to keeping track of allocated memory.

The result of this is that the algorithms implemented by the run-time systems are simpler and involve less bookkeeping. This is both a blessing and a curse. Explicit memory management allows programs to be smaller because the compiler does not have to emit any extra instructions or data to handle garbage collection. In addition, explicit memory management also gives the programmer a better idea of what is actually going on behind the curtain.

The curse of this extra complexity is that it can lead to mistakes (this is an understatement).

If a dynamically allocated variable leaves its scope before being recycled, the memory cannot be recycled and the program will gradually drain away memory until the computer halts. This is known as a *memory leak*, and is an insidious problem to try to correct (the author is a voice of experience in this matter). In Chapter 2 we encountered a program that created a memory leak during the discussion of siege warfare.

If a dynamically allocated variable is recycled before it goes out of scope, the variable will become an invalid reference and can potentially crash the program (or produce incorrect results, which is even worse). The invalid reference in this kind of situation is known as a *dangling pointer*.

Memory leaks and dangling pointers are the bugaboos of every C programmer's working hours. Trying to find these problems by inspection alone can entail many frustrating debugging sessions. Fortunately, there are specialized tools that can be used to track down memory leaks. These tools tend to be platform specific, so it is hard to recommend a universal solution. The Boehm-Demers-Weiser (BDW) conservative garbage collector, described later, can be used as a memory leak detector on several platforms.

Example: C Standard Library Calls

The ANSI C standard library, whose prototypes are spelled out in `stdlib.h`, supports manual memory management through a series of four functions:

```
void *calloc(size_t num, size_t size);
void free(void *);
void malloc(size_t);
void *realloc(void *block, size_t size);
```

The `calloc()` function allocates an array of `num` elements, each element being `size` bytes long, and initializes everything to zero. The `free()` function releases an allocated block of memory. The `malloc()` function allocates `size` number of bytes from the heap. The `realloc()` function changes the `size` of an allocated block of memory. As you can see, there are very few amenities. Calls to `calloc()` and `realloc()` typically end up indirectly calling `malloc()`. So most of the behind-the-scenes work is actually done by `malloc()` and `free()`.

```
void *calloc(size_t num, size_t size)
{
    void ptr;
    size_t nbytes;
    nbytes = num*size;
    ptr = malloc(nbytes);
    if(ptr!=NULL){ memset(ptr, 0x0,nbytes); }
    return ptr;
}

void *realloc(void *ptr, size_t size)
{
    unsigned char *cptr;
```

```
        int oldsize;
        if (ptr == NULL){ return malloc(size); }
        oldsize = sizeMem(ptr);
        if (size <= oldsize){ return ptr; }
        cptr = (char *)malloc(size);
        memcpy(cptr, ptr, oldsize);
        free(ptr);
        return cptr;
}
```

The implementation of `malloc()` and `free()` varies greatly from one distribution to the next, so it is a little harder for me to offer reference implementations. The `malloc()` and `free()` functions on UNIX platforms are front men for the `brk()` system call. Its prototype usually resembles something like this:

```
        int brk(void *end_heap);
```

The `brk()` system call is responsible for modifying the size of a program's heap by either increasing or decreasing its end point. The `end_heap` value can be changed as long as it does not infringe on other sections of the application.

NOTE The POSIX standard does not include `brk()` on the grounds that it dictates a certain underlying memory model implementation. On most flavors of UNIX, however, you will find the `brk()` system call. If you are interested in looking at an implementation of `brk()`, I would recommend taking a look at the one that accompanies Linux. It is located in the `/usr/src/linux/mm/mmap.c` file.

Now that you are familiar with C's manual memory allocation functions, I can demonstrate how dangling pointers occur and what happens when they do. Consider the following example:

```
/* --dangleptr.c-- */

#include<stdio.h>
#include<stdlib.h>

void main()
{
    char *cptr1;
    char *cptr2;

    cptr1 = malloc(10);
    printf("address=%p\n",cptr1);

    cptr1[0]='a'; cptr1[1]='b'; cptr1[2]=0;
    printf("cptr1=%s\n",cptr1);

    free(cptr1); /* whoops! */
```

```
            cptr2 = malloc(10);
            printf("address=%p\n",cptr2);

            cptr2[0]='c'; cptr2[1]='d'; cptr2[2]=0;
            printf("cptr1=%s\n",cptr1);
            return;
}
```

This program will produce the following output when it is run:

```
address=00770670
cptr1=ab
address=007706A0
cptr1=
```

As expected, the contents of memory pointed to by `cptr1` were corrupted after it was prematurely set free. Imagine what would happen with a dangling pointer to a database handle in a large ERP application...

Automatic Memory Management

Automatic memory management, also called *garbage collection*, takes care of all the memory recycling details. This allows the programmer to focus on domain-specific problem solving. An analyst who is writing a purchase-order system already has enough complexity to deal with just trying to get the logic of the purchase-order application to function. Having to manage low-level details like memory only makes the job more difficult.

NOTE Scientists like George Miller have claimed that the average human can only keep track of about seven things at any point in time. By forcing the developer to keep track of memory recycling, the number of things the developer has to juggle increases. Garbage collection is an effective solution to this problem.
  Don't take my word for it. Here is what Bertrand Meyer, the inventor of Eiffel, has to say:
  "Manual memory management — that is to say, the absence of automatic garbage collection — suffers from two fatal flaws: it is dangerous (as it is all too easy to make a mistake, causing errors that are often missed during testing and arise only when the system goes operational, usually in erratic and hard-to-reproduce conditions); and it is extremely tedious, forcing the developer to concentrate on mundane yet complex tasks of bookkeeping and garbage collection instead of working on their application. These deficiencies are bad enough to cancel out any benefit that is claimed for the application of object-oriented techniques."

A significant benefit of using a garbage collector is that the recycling problems that plague manual memory management are eliminated. Memory leaks and dangling pointers do not exist in a program that uses automatic memory management. Automatic memory takes care of freeing allocated memory so the programmer isn't given the opportunity to make a recycling error.

Garbage collection was entirely theoretical until 1959, when Dan Edwards implemented the first garbage collection facilities. It just so happened that Dan was involved with John McCarthy in the development of the LISP programming language. LISP, which was intended for algebraic LISt Processing, started off as a notational concept that evolved into a computer language. When compared to other programming languages that existed during its development, LISP was way ahead of its time.

There were, however, problems with LISP's performance, and this was probably the price that LISP paid for its advanced features. The garbage collection schemes in early implementations of LISP were notoriously slow. One response to this problem was to push basic operations down to the hardware level. There were companies that attempted to follow this route, like Symbolics, which sold LISP machines. LISP machines were manufactured in the 1970s and 1980s. The idea, unfortunately, never really caught on. In the mid-1990s, Symbolics went bankrupt.

There are a number of programming environments that support automatic memory management. This includes popular virtual machines like Java's and more obscure run times, like the one that Smalltalk utilizes. There are even garbage collectors than can be plugged into native code via user mode libraries. This brings us to the Boehm-Demers-Weiser conservative garbage collector.

Example: The BDW Conservative Garbage Collector

The Boehm-Demers-Weiser (BDW) conservative garbage collector is a drop-in replacement for `malloc()` that eliminates the need to call `free()`. This allows old, moldy C programs to have their memory management scheme upgraded with minimal effort. The only catch is that the BDW collector has to be ported, which is to say that the collector has platform dependencies. If you are working on an obscure platform, like Trusted Xenix, you will not be able to use it.

NOTE The BDW garbage collector can also be modified to detect memory leaks.

You can download a copy of the distribution and view additional information by visiting http://reality.sgi.com/boehm/gc.html.

The BDW distribution has been ported to a number of different platforms. Each one has its own makefile. On Windows, the BDW garbage collector can be built into a single-threaded, static library (gc.lib) using the following command:

```
C:\DOCS\bdw\gc6.0>nmake /F NT_MAKEFILE
```

NOTE You will need to make sure that the necessary environmental variables have been set up. You can do so by executing the VCVARS32.BAT batch file before you invoke NMAKE.

Here is a short example to demonstrate the BDW collector in action:

```
/* --testbdw.c-- */

#include<stdio.h>
#define GC_NOT_DLL
#include<gc.h>

unsigned long oldmem=0;

void printMemSize()
{
    unsigned long nfree;
    nfree = GC_get_free_bytes();

    printf("total heap=%7lu\t",GC_get_heap_size());
    printf("free bytes=%7lu\t",nfree);
    if(oldmem!=0)
    {
        printf("change=%ld",(oldmem-nfree));
    }
    printf("\n");
    oldmem = nfree;
    return;
}/*end printHeapSize*/

#define KB     16*1024          /* 16KB = 16384 bytes */

void main()
{
    short j;
    unsigned long i;

    for(j=0;j<15;j++)
    {
```

```
            unsigned char *bdwptr;
            bdwptr = GC_malloc(KB);
            for(i=0;i<KB;i++){ bdwptr[i]='a'; }
            printMemSize();
    }
    printf("\nforcing collection\n");
    GC_gcollect();
    printMemSize();
    return;

}/*end main*/
```

In the previous code example, I reuse the `bdwptr` pointer repeatedly in an effort to create a memory leak. If you compile and run this program on Windows, you will get output like the following:

```
total heap=  65536      free bytes=  45056
total heap=  65536      free bytes=  24576      change=20480
total heap=  65536      free bytes=   4096      change=20480
total heap=  65536      free bytes=  24576      change=-20480
total heap=  65536      free bytes=   4096      change=20480
total heap= 131072      free bytes=  49152      change=-45056
total heap= 131072      free bytes=  28672      change=20480
total heap= 131072      free bytes=   8192      change=20480
total heap= 131072      free bytes=  90112      change=-81920
total heap= 131072      free bytes=  69632      change=20480
total heap= 131072      free bytes=  49152      change=20480
total heap= 131072      free bytes=  28672      change=20480
total heap= 131072      free bytes=   8192      change=20480
total heap= 131072      free bytes=  90112      change=-81920
total heap= 131072      free bytes=  69632      change=20480

forcing collection
total heap= 131072       free bytes= 110592
change=-40960
Press any key to continue
```

As you can see, the amount of free memory does not just descend downward, as it normally would if you were using `malloc()`. Instead, it increases a couple of times, which indicates that garbage collection has occurred. At the end of the sample code, I explicitly force collection to illustrate this.

NOTE   You will need to make sure that the linker includes `gc.lib` in its list of libraries. Also, I could only get this to work with the *release* version of Visual Studio's libraries. Trying to link `gc.lib` to Microsoft's debug libraries gave my linker a fit.

Manual Versus Automatic?

I cannot think of a better way to start a heated argument at an engineering meeting than to bring up this topic. Within minutes, people will go from calm and deliberate to emotional and violent. Although I have my own opinion, I am going to back up my conclusions with source code that you can test yourself. Nothing beats empirical evidence.

Both explicit memory management and automatic memory management involve explicit allocation of memory; the difference between the two methods is how they deal with memory that isn't needed anymore and must be discarded back into the heap.

Garbage collection advocates claim that the energy committed to dealing with memory leaks and dangling pointers would be better spent on building a garbage collection mechanism. This is a very powerful argument — if the performance hit from garbage collection bookkeeping is not noticeable.

This is a big "if."

Early garbage collection implementations like the one for LISP were notoriously slow, sometimes accounting for almost 50% of execution time. Not to mention that explicit memory management proponents will argue that the emergence of tools that detect memory leaks have eliminated traditional problems. Thus, performance is a key issue.

Garbage collection supporters will jump up and down in an effort to demonstrate that the performance problems that plagued LISP are no longer an issue. It is as though they are personally insulted that you are questioning their position.

Let's try to avoid arm waving and examine some published results.

I found two articles that take a good look at the Boehm-Demers-Weiser conservative garbage collector. The first, a 1992 paper by Benjamin Zorn, demonstrates that the BDW collector is, on average, about 20% slower than the fastest explicit memory manager in each experimental trial. The second, published by Detlefs et. al. in 1993, indicates that the BDW collector is, on average, about 27% slower than the fastest explicit memory manager in each experimental trial. In these articles, this was what the authors claimed was the "comparable" performance of the BDW garbage collector.

Table 3.4 presents a comparison of manual and automatic memory management.

Table 3.4

	Manual Memory Management	Automatic Memory Management
Benefits	size (smaller) speed (faster) control (you decide when to free)	constrains complexity
Costs	complexity memory leaks dangling pointers	larger total memory footprint "comparable" performance

Garbage collection is not a simple task. It requires the garbage collector to ferret out memory regions that were allocated but are no longer needed. The bookkeeping procedures are complicated, and this extra complexity translates into executable code. Hence, the total memory image of a program using garbage collection will be larger than one that uses automatic memory management.

Let us look at an example. This way, I cannot be accused of supporting my conclusions with arm waving. Consider the following program that uses traditional memory management facilities:

```
#include<stdio.h>
#include<stdlib.h>

#define KB     16*1024          /* 16KB = 16384 bytes */

void main()
{
    short j;
    unsigned long i;

    for(j=0;j<15;j++)
    {
        unsigned char *bdwptr;
        bdwptr = malloc(KB);
        for(i=0;i<KB;i++){ bdwptr[i]='a'; }
    }
    return;

}/*end main*/
```

Now look at one that uses the BDW collector:

```
#include<stdio.h>
#define GC_NOT_DLL
#include<gc.h>

#define KB     16*1024          /* 16KB = 16384 bytes */
```

```
void main()
{
    short j;
    unsigned long i;

    for(j=0;j<15;j++)
    {
        unsigned char *bdwptr;
        bdwptr = GC_malloc(KB);
        for(i=0;i<KB;i++){ bdwptr[i]='a'; }
    }
    return;

}/*end main*/
```

When I built both of these programs on Windows, the executable that used manual memory management calls was 27,648 bytes in size. The executable that used the BDW collector was 76,800 bytes in size. This is over twice the size of the other program. *QED*.

With manual memory management, the programmer is responsible for keeping track of allocated memory. None of the bookkeeping manifests itself in the source code as extra instructions. When the programmer wants to release memory, they call `free()`. There is no need to execute a lengthy series of functions to sweep through memory looking for "live" pointers.

In the process of hunting down memory to free, the garbage collector will also find many allocated regions of memory that are still needed, and it will not free these blocks of memory. However, this means that the collector will repeatedly perform unnecessary procedures every time it attempts collection. This suggests to me that these superfluous actions will cause automatic memory collection to be necessarily slower than manual memory management.

Again, I would like to rely on empirical data instead of just appealing to your sense of intuition. Consider the following source code:

```
#include<stdio.h>
#include<windows.h>
#include<stdlib.h>

#define KB    1024

void main()
{
    short j;
    unsigned long i;
    long msecs1,msecs2;
    unsigned char *bdwptr[16*KB];
```

```
        msecs1 = msecs2 = 0;
        msecs1 = GetTickCount();

        for(j=0;j<(16*KB);j++)
        {
            bdwptr[j] = malloc(KB);
            for(i=0;i<KB;i++){ (bdwptr[j])[i]='a'; }
        }
        msecs2 = GetTickCount();
        printf("msec elapsed=%ld\n",(msecs2-msecs1));
        return;

}/*end main*/
```

Now consider another program that uses the BDW collector:

```
#include<stdio.h>
#include<windows.h>
#define GC_NOT_DLL
#include<gc.h>

#define KB      1024

void main()
{
    short j;
    unsigned long i;
    long msecs1,msecs2;

    msecs1 = msecs2 = 0;
    msecs1 = GetTickCount();

    for(j=0;j<(16*1024);j++)
    {
        unsigned char *bdwptr;
        bdwptr = GC_malloc(KB);
        for(i=0;i<KB;i++){ bdwptr[i]='a'; }
    }
    msecs2 = GetTickCount();
    printf("msec elapsed=%ld\n",(msecs2-msecs1));
    return;

}/*end main*/
```

The program that used `malloc()` completed execution in 427 milliseconds. The program that used the BDW garbage collector took 627 milliseconds to execute. I ran each of these programs several times to prove to myself that this wasn't some kind of fluke.

- Manual memory program times: 432, 427, 426, 443, 435, 430, 437, 430
- BDW collector program times: 633, 622, 624, 650, 615, 613, 630, 627

Time units are in milliseconds. I could have performed more trials and included an extended statistical analysis of mean values, but I think the results are already pretty clear.

NOTE I ran the previous two programs on a 700MHz Pentium. If you used more recent (GHz) processors, you would still see the same degree of lag.

Finally, garbage collection takes control away from the developer. The heap manager decides when to free memory back to the heap continuum, not the developer. For example, Java has a `System.gc()` call, which can be used to *suggest* to the Java virtual machine that it free its surplus memory. However, the JVM itself still has the final say as to when memory is actually set free. This can be a good thing for an engineer who doesn't want to be bothered with details, but it is a bad thing if you actually do want to dictate when an allocated block of memory is released.

NOTE In the end, using explicit or automatic memory management is a *religious question,* which is to say that deciding to use explicit or automatic methods reflects the fundamental beliefs, values, and priorities of the developer. As I've stated before, there are no perfect solutions. Every approach involves making some sort of concession. Explicit memory management offers speed and control at the expense of complexity. Manual memory management forsakes performance in order to restrain complexity.

The Evolution of Languages

The fundamental, core issue encountered in software engineering is *complexity*. The evolution of programming languages has been driven by the need to manage and constrain complexity. Initially, programs were hard-coded in raw binary. This was back in the days of Howard Aiken's MARK I, which was unveiled in 1944. As the years wore on, programs got to a size where coding in raw binary was simply too tedious.

In 1949, the first *assembly language* was developed for the UNIVAC I. Assembly language made programming less complicated by replacing raw binary instructions with terse symbolic mnemonics. Originally, a programmer would have had to manually write something like:

```
10010110    10101110    01101011
```

Using assembly language, the previous binary instruction could be replaced with:

```
INC AR 0x6B
```

This primitive symbolic notation helped to make programming easier. Again, programs became larger and more complicated to the extent that something new was needed. This something new reared its head in the next decade. In the 1950s, with the emergence of transistor-based circuits, higher-level languages emerged. Two such languages were COBOL and FORTRAN. All of these early high-level languages were *block-based* and used the GOTO statement, or something resembling it, to move from block to block.

The emergence of block-based languages led to the development of *structured programming* in the late 1960s. The essay that led to the birth of structured programming was written by Dijkstra in 1968. It was a letter in the *Communications of the ACM* titled "GOTO Statement Considered Harmful." This revolutionary paper caused quite a stir. The state-of-the-art languages at the time, like COBOL II and FORTRAN IV, used GOTOs liberally.

NOTE Structured programming is an approach to writing procedure-based code where the use of the GOTO statement is either minimized or excluded entirely. History sides with Dijkstra. Structured programming was the paradigm that characterized software development in the 1970s and 1980s.

When a software team in the 1970s wanted to design a business application, they would first model the data that the application would manage. This usually meant designing database tables and memory resident data structures. This initial collection of schemas and data types would be the starting point around which everything else would revolve. Next, the team would decide on the algorithms and corresponding functions that would operate on the data.

Structured programming is notably either data-oriented or procedure-oriented, but never both.

Even though structured programming was supposed to be a cure-all, it fell short of its expectations. Specifically, the structured approach proved to be inadequate with regard to maintaining large projects. This is a crucial flaw because most of the money invested in a software project is spent on maintenance. During the 1980s, structured programming was gradually replaced by the object-oriented approach that was promoted by languages like C++ and Smalltalk.

Can you see the trend I'm trying to illuminate?

I am of the opinion that every programming language has a complexity threshold. After a program reaches a certain number of lines of code, it becomes difficult to understand and modify. Naturally, lower-level languages will have a lower complexity threshold than the higher ones. To get an idea of what the complexity threshold is for different types of programming languages, we can take a look at a collection of well-known operating systems (see Table 3.5).

Table 3.5

OS	Lines of Code	Primary Language	Source
DOS	20,000	assembler	Modern Operating Systems (Andrew Tanenbaum)
MINIX	74,000	C	Operating Systems, Design and Implementation (Andrew Tanenbaum)
FreeBSD	200,000 (kernel only)	C	The Design and Implementation of 4.4BSD Operating System (McKusick et. al.)
Windows 98	18 million lines (everything)	C/C++	February 2, 1999 (A.M. Session) United States vs. Microsoft et. al.

From Table 3.5, it seems that the number of lines of code that can be efficiently managed by a language increase by a factor of 10 as you switch to more sophisticated paradigms (see Table 3.6).

Table 3.6

Language	Paradigm	Complexity Threshold
Raw binary	no-holds-barred	10,000 instructions
Assembler	block-based using GOTO	100,000 lines
C	structured (no GOTO)	1,000,000 lines
C++	object-oriented	10,000,000 lines

Inevitably, the languages that survive, and perhaps pass on their features to new languages, will be the ones that are the most effective at managing complexity. In the early days of UNIX, almost every bit of system code was written in C. As operating systems have grown, the use of C, as a matter of necessity, has given way to implementation in C++. According to an article in the July 29, 1996, *Wall Street Journal*, the Windows NT operating system consists of 16.5 million lines of code. It is no surprise, then, that Microsoft has begun building some of its primary OS components entirely in C++. For example, a fundamental component of the Windows NT kernel, the

Graphics Device Interface (GDI32.DLL), was written completely in C++.

QUESTION

What does any of this have to do with memory management?

ANSWER

The evolution of programming languages has basically mirrored the development of memory management since the 1950s. As I mentioned earlier, higher-level languages like COBOL and FORTRAN were born around the same time as the transistor. In the beginning, computer memory was entirely visible to a program. There was no segmentation and no protection. In fact, the program typically took up all the available memory. Likewise, the first computer programming languages were also fairly primitive. As time passed, both memory management and programming languages matured into the powerful tools that they are today. There are memory managers today that allow dozens of tightly coupled processors to share the same address space, and there are elegant object-oriented languages that allow complexity to be constrained.

In the following sections, I am going to provide a brief survey of several programming languages in order to demonstrate how different languages make use of the different high-level memory services. I will begin with early languages and work my way slowly to the present day. Along the way, I will try to offer examples and insight whenever I have the opportunity.

Case Study: COBOL

COBOL — this one word stirs up all sorts of different reactions in people. COmmon Business Oriented Language was formally defined in 1959 by the Conference On DAta SYstems Language (CODASYL). COBOL has its roots in the FLOW-MATIC language that was developed by Rear Admiral Grace Murray Hopper. Admiral Hopper is considered the mother of modern business computing.

"It's always easier to ask forgiveness than it is to get permission."
— Grace Murray Hopper

In 1997, the Gartner Group estimated that there were over 180 billion lines of COBOL code in use and five million new lines of COBOL code being written each year. Authors like Carol Baroudi even estimated the number of lines of legacy COBOL code at 500 billion lines. Needless to say, this mountain of code has taken on a life of its own and probably developed enough inertia to last at least another hundred years.

The preponderance of COBOL is partially due to historical forces. COBOL was adopted by the United States Department of Defense (DoD) in 1960 and became a de facto standard. The reason for this is that the DoD, the largest purchaser of computer hardware both then and now, would not buy hardware for data processing unless the vendor provided a COBOL compiler. Another reason COBOL is so widespread is due to the fact that COBOL is very good at what it is designed for — executing business calculations. When it comes to performing financial computations to fractions of a cent without introducing rounding errors, COBOL is still the king of the hill. The language features that support financial mathematics in COBOL are a very natural part of the language and extremely easy to use.

QUESTION
Will COBOL ever die? Will it be replaced?

ANSWER
I would like to assume that someday COBOL will be retured. However, I suspect that COBOL houses will probably, fundamentally, stay COBOL houses. 180 billion lines is a lot of source code. They may occasionally renovate with Object COBOL or slap on a new layer of paint with Java, but replacing the plumbing of an aging mansion is a very expensive proposition. In fact, it's often cheaper to just tear the house down and build a new one. Try explaining this to the CFO of a Fortune 100 company.

Legacy code may be old, but it supports core business functionality and has been painstakingly debugged. In this kind of situation, legacy code is seen as a corporate asset that represents the investment of hundreds of thousands of man-hours. An architect who actually does want to overhaul a system will, no doubt, face resistance from a CFO whose orientation tends toward dollars and cents. If a system does what it's supposed to and helps to generate income, then why fix it? Throwing everything away for the sake of technology alone is a ridiculously poor excuse.

Another factor that inhibits the replacement of legacy code is the sheer size of an existing code base. In order to replace old code with new code, you have to completely understand the functionality that the old code provides. In a million-line labyrinth of 80-column code, business logic is hard to extract and duplicate. Often, the people who wrote the code have left the company or have been promoted to different divisions. Instituting even relatively simple changes can prove to be expensive and involve months of reverse engineering and testing. I've known Y2K programmers who were too scared to modify legacy code. The old code was so convoluted that they didn't know what kind of repercussions their changes would have.

COBOL has been through several revisions. In 1968, the American National Standards Institute (ANSI) released a standard for COBOL. This COBOL standard was revisited in 1974. The current ANSI standard for COBOL, however, is a combination of the ANSI standard that was developed in 1985 coupled with some extensions that were added on in 1989. There have been moves toward a form of object-oriented COBOL and vendors have come out with their own forms of it. Nevertheless, when someone talks about ANSI COBOL, they are referring to COBOL 85 with the additions that were made in 1989. In the following discussion, I will use COBOL 85. I will also compile my code using Fujitsu's COBOL85 V30L10 compiler. If you are running Windows, you can download a copy from Fujitsu's web site.

COBOL is a structured language that does not use a stack or a heap. All that a COBOL program has at its disposal is a single global data section and blocks of instructions. In COBOL parlance, a program consists of four divisions:

1. Identification division
2. Environment division
3. Data division
4. Procedure division

The *identification division* is used to let the COBOL compiler know the name of the program it is translating. The identification division doesn't get translated in machine code; it is more of a directive. The environment division is used to describe the platform that a program will be built on and run on, as well as to specify the files that it will use. Again, this is mostly metadata that is intended for use by the compiler.

The data division contains, among other things, a working storage section that is basically a large static memory region that serves all of a program's storage needs. As I said before, there is no heap and no stack that a COBOL program can utilize. All that exists is one big chunk of fixed-size, global memory.

The procedure division consists of blocks of instructions. These blocks of code do not have formal parameters or local variables like functions in C. This would require a stack, which COBOL programs do not have. If you want to create storage for a particular block of code, you will need to use some sort of naming convention in the working storage section to help distinguish all the global variables. So the next time someone asks you "what's in a name?", you can tell them.

In general, divisions are composed of sections and sections are composed of paragraphs. Paragraphs are likewise composed of sentences in an effort to make COBOL resemble written English. To this end, COBOL sentences are always terminated with periods.

Division → Section → Paragraph → Sentence.

Here is a simple example so that you can get a feel for how these divisions, sections, and paragraphs are implemented in practice.

```
000010 @OPTIONS MAIN
000013 IDENTIFICATION DIVISION.
000020 PROGRAM-ID. FIRSTAPP.
000021*-------------------------------------------------
000022 ENVIRONMENT DIVISION.
000023 CONFIGURATION SECTION.
000024 SOURCE-COMPUTER. INTEL.
000025 OBJECT-COMPUTER. INTEL.
000026 INPUT-OUTPUT SECTION.
000027*-------------------------------------------------
000028 DATA DIVISION.
000029 WORKING-STORAGE SECTION.
000030 01 ASSETS   PIC 9(3)v99    VALUE 000.00.
000031 01 DEBT     PIC 9(3)v99    VALUE 000.00.
000032 01 NET      PIC S9(3)v99   VALUE 000.00.
000033 01 PRINT    PIC ZZZ.ZZ.
000034*-------------------------------------------------
000035 PROCEDURE DIVISION.
000036 MAIN-CODE SECTION.
000037 MAIN.
000038 MOVE 120.34 TO ASSETS.
000039 MOVE 50.20  TO DEBT.
000040 PERFORM COMPUTE-NET-WORTH.
000050 STOP RUN.
000060 SUBROUTINE SECTION.
000070 COMPUTE-NET-WORTH.
000080 MOVE ASSETS TO NET.
000090 SUBTRACT DEBT FROM NET.
000091 MOVE NET TO PRINT.
000100 DISPLAY  " NET: " PRINT.
```

The above program prints out:

```
NET:   70.14
```

I have tried to help delineate the different program divisions using comment lines. As you can see, the program consists primarily of data and code. The memory model that this program uses is probably closely akin to the one displayed in Figure 3.14.

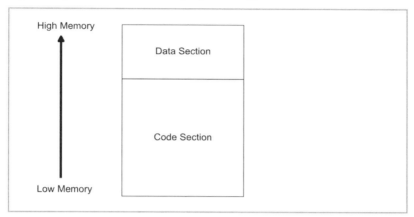

Figure 3.14

NOTE You might notice line numbers in the previous program's listing. This is a holdover from the days when punch cards were fed to mainframes. The motivation was that if you dropped your box of cards and they became mixed up, you could use the line numbering to sort your cards back to the proper order.

NOTE The arrangement of a COBOL application is closer to that of an assembly language program than it is to any structured language. Data is clumped together in one section, and the code consists of very crude blocks of instructions. Take a look at the following Intel assembly language program, and you will see what I mean. COBOL is, without a doubt, a prehistoric language.

```
;likeCob.asm--------------------------

.MODEL small, c
.STACK

;working storage----------------------
.DATA
assets  DW  0H
debt    DW  0H
net     DW  0H

;procedure division-------------------
.CODE
.STARTUP

MOV AX,07H
```

```
            MOV [assets],AX

            MOV AX,03H
            MOV [debt],AX

            MOV DX,[assets]
            MOV CX,[debt]
            SUB DX,CX

            ADD DX,'0'

            MOV AH,0EH
            MOV AL,DL
            INT 10H

            .EXIT
            END
```

This programming approach might not seem so bad. In fact, at first glance, it may appear like an effective way to organize an application. Do not be fooled by such naïve first impressions. With only a single section of working storage to provide read/write memory, a program can become very difficult to read if you want to do anything even remotely complicated.

Consider the following COBOL program that takes a list of values and prints out the average of those values and the maximum value in the list. You should be able to see how COBOL's limitations make simple array manipulation nowhere near as straightforward as it would be in C.

```
000012 IDENTIFICATION DIVISION.
000020 PROGRAM-ID. STATISTICS.
000021*-----------------------------------------------------
000022 DATA DIVISION.
000023 WORKING-STORAGE SECTION.
000024 01 AVERAGE   PIC 9(2) VALUE 0.
000025 01 ARRAY-SIZE PIC 9(1) VALUE 5.
000027 01 ARRAY.
000028 03 ARRAY-ELM  PIC 9(2) OCCURS 5 TIMES.
000029 01 COUNT-INDEX PIC 9(1) VALUE 1.
000030 01 ARRAY-MAX  PIC  9(1) VALUE 0.
000031*-----------------------------------------------------
000032 PROCEDURE DIVISION.
000033 SOURCECODE SECTION.
000034 MAIN.
000035     PERFORM INIT-ARRAY.
000040     PERFORM COMPUTE-AVERAGE.
000041     PERFORM GET-MAX.
000050     STOP RUN.
```

```
000051*-----------------------------------------------------
000052 SUBROUTINES SECTION.
000053 INIT-ARRAY.
000054     MOVE 5 TO ARRAY-ELM (1).
000055     MOVE 6 TO ARRAY-ELM (2).
000056     MOVE 3 TO ARRAY-ELM (3).
000057     MOVE 7 TO ARRAY-ELM (4).
000058     MOVE 4 TO ARRAY-ELM (5).
000060 COMPUTE-AVERAGE.
000062     PERFORM COMPUTE-AVERAGE-SUM ARRAY-SIZE TIMES.
000064     DIVIDE ARRAY-SIZE INTO AVERAGE.
000065     DISPLAY "average is: " AVERAGE.
000070 COMPUTE-AVERAGE-SUM.
000071     ADD ARRAY-ELM(COUNT-INDEX) TO AVERAGE.
000081     ADD 1 TO COUNT-INDEX.
000091 GET-MAX.
000101     MOVE 1 TO COUNT-INDEX.
000102     MOVE ARRAY-ELM(1) TO ARRAY-MAX.
000111     PERFORM GET-MAX-EXAMINE-CURRENT ARRAY-SIZE
           TIMES.
000112     DISPLAY "max is: " ARRAY-MAX.
000121 GET-MAX-EXAMINE-CURRENT.
000131     IF ARRAY-ELM(COUNT-INDEX) > ARRAY-MAX
000132        MOVE ARRAY-ELM(COUNT-INDEX) TO ARRAY-MAX
000141     END-IF
000151     ADD 1 TO COUNT-INDEX.
```

When this source code (`statistics.cob`) is compiled and linked into an executable, it will produce the following output when run:

```
average is: 05
max is: 7
```

The absence of the stack and heap may be a good thing from the view of a sysadmin, who does not have to worry about memory leaks or buffer overflow exploits, but from the perspective of a programmer, COBOL's spartan memory arrangement is a curse. Very large COBOL applications can quickly become impossible to maintain or even understand. As a veteran Y2K COBOL programmer, I can attest to this fact. Some of the programs I looked at were so large, complicated, and crucial to business operations, that I was often scared to touch anything.

Case Study: FORTRAN

FORTRAN has the distinction of being considered one of the first compiled computer languages. The development of FORTRAN began in 1954 and was initiated by a team of engineers at IBM led by John Backus. FORTRAN originally stood for "IBM Mathematical

FORmula TRANslation system." Within 10 years, every hardware manufacturer in creation was shipping their computers with a FORTRAN compiler. Naturally, each vendor had to tweak FORTRAN so that they could call their compiler "value added." To help reign in chaos, a standards committee stepped in. In 1966, the first draft of the FORTRAN standard was released by the ASA (a predecessor to ANSI). This version of FORTRAN is known as FORTRAN 66. FORTRAN was the first high-level language to be specified by a standards committee.

> **NOTE** Any computer science student who has ever studied compiler theory will recognize the name Backus. This is because John Backus helped invent a notation called *Backus-Naur Form* (BNF), which is used to specify the context-free grammar of a programming language.

In 1977, the ANSI committee in charge of FORTRAN released a revised standard. It added several new features to the language including the `CHARACTER` data type and flow-control constructs like IF-ELSE blocks (i.e., `IF...THEN...ELSE...ENDIF`). FORTRAN 77 is also known as F77.

In 1990 and 1995, ANSI released new standards for FORTRAN. FORTRAN 90 (F90) was a major revision. FORTRAN 95 (F95) merely added a few extensions. F90, as specified in ANSI X3.198-1992, supplemented F77 with new features like dynamic memory allocation (via `ALLOCATE` and `DEALLOCATE`) and a stack to support recursion. However, because of the time lag between the F77 and the F90 standard, other languages were able to win popularity, which pushed FORTAN into the backwaters of history.

For the sake of illustration, I will be looking at FORTRAN 77. F77 occupies the next level of sophistication above COBOL 85 in terms of language features, and this will make it a good stepping-stone.

> **NOTE** A Control Data veteran once confided in me that, in his day, FORTRAN programmers looked down on COBOL programmers. This was because FORTRAN is geared toward analytic programs that perform sophisticated numerical computation, instead of the mundane dollars-and-cents math that is a core component of COBOL programs. FORTRAN programmers were scientists in white coats, and COBOL programmers were corporate schlubs who sat in cubes.

F77, from an organizational standpoint, actually provides much better procedure modularity when compared to COBOL 85. Specifically, an F77 program consists of:

- A single `PROGRAM` procedure
- Zero or more external procedures

An external procedure can be a function or a subroutine. A *function* is a procedure that can possess multiple arguments but returns only a single output value via its name identifier. A subroutine is invoked by a CALL statement and can accept an arbitrary number of input and output parameters.

Here is a simple program to help illustrate these concepts:

```
*-- metrics.F ----------------------------------------
      PROGRAM METRICS
      INTEGER ARRAY(5)
      INTEGER MAX
      ARRAY(1)=4
      ARRAY(2)=10
      ARRAY(3)=26
      ARRAY(4)=8
      ARRAY(5)=3
      MAX=0
      WRITE(*,*) "val= ", GETAVG(ARRAY,5)
      CALL GETMAX(ARRAY,5,MAX)
      WRITE(*,*) "max= ", MAX
      END
*------------------------------------------------------
      REAL FUNCTION GETAVG(ARR,NELM)
      INTEGER ARR(NELM)
      INTEGER INDEX
      REAL SUM
      SUM=0
      DO 10,INDEX = 1,NELM
      SUM=SUM+ARR(INDEX)
10    CONTINUE
      GETAVG = SUM/NELM
      END
*------------------------------------------------------
      SUBROUTINE GETMAX(ARR,NELM,MX)
      INTEGER ARR(NELM)
      INTEGER MX
      MX=ARR(1)
      DO 20,INDEX =2,NELM
      IF(ARR(INDEX)>MX) THEN
      MX = ARR(INDEX)
      END IF
20    CONTINUE
      END
```

If you run this program, you will see:

```
val=   10.1999998
max=   26
```

As you can see, F77 provides much better encapsulation than COBOL 85. Each procedure is capable of declaring its own arguments, local variables, and return values. By placing these variables where they are relevant, instead of in a global data section, the code is much easier to read and reuse.

QUESTION

How does FORTRAN support procedure arguments and local variables without a stack?

ANSWER

In F77, each routine has its own private stash of static memory that serves as a storage space for local variables and arguments. This precludes F77 from implementing recursion, but it does allow an F77 program to utilize a more sophisticated memory model than COBOL 85. An example F77 memory model is displayed in Figure 3.15.

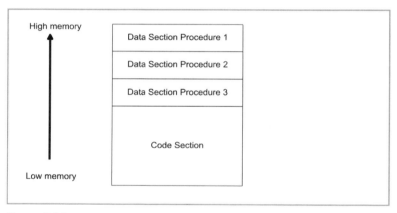

Figure 3.15

One feature that this per-procedure static memory space supports is the SAVE statement. The SAVE statement allows the local variables of a procedure to sustain their values between function calls. If FORTRAN used an activation record for local variables, it wouldn't be possible to implement SAVE.

Here is a short example demonstrating the SAVE statement:

```
      PROGRAM RUNSUM
      WRITE(*,*) SIGMA(3)
      WRITE(*,*) SIGMA(5)
      WRITE(*,*) SIGMA(2)
      WRITE(*,*) SIGMA(7)
      END
*-----------------------------------------------------
      FUNCTION SIGMA(VAL)
```

```
            INTEGER VAL
            INTEGER SUM
            SAVE SUM
            SUM=SUM+VAL
            SIGMA = SUM
            END
```

When the previous program is run, the following output is displayed:

```
            3.
            8.
            10.
            17.
```

Case Study: Pascal

In 1971 Niklaus Wirth presented the world with his specification of a structured language named after a French mathematician who lived during the 17th century. Pascal was inspired heavily by a programming language called ALGOL. This seems only natural when you consider that Wirth was part of the group that originally created ALGOL. During the 1960s, FORTRAN had supplanted ALGOL as the mathematical programming language of choice. As a result, the designers of ALGOL were looking for ways to extend the language.

Pascal supports heavy use of the stack and, unlike F77, allows function calls to be recursive. Pascal also provides manual access to the heap via the NEW and DISPOSE statements. Pascal allows global variables to be defined, which are stored in a static data segment. Pascal is the first language that we have examined that uses the stack, the heap, and a data section.

Wirth admits, however, that Pascal is really a toy language that is intended for educational purposes. The language has a limited set of features, and this handicap is compounded by the fact that the Pascal compiler enforces a rigid set of syntax rules. Pascal is not a suitable language for developing large projects and has been called a bondage-discipline language by some engineers. Wirth ended up moving on to invent other languages like Modula and Oberon. Borland, which marketed a very successful Pascal compiler in the 1980s, currently sells an object-oriented variation of Pascal called Delphi.

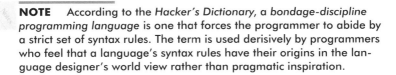

NOTE According to the *Hacker's Dictionary*, a *bondage-discipline programming language* is one that forces the programmer to abide by a strict set of syntax rules. The term is used derisively by programmers who feel that a language's syntax rules have their origins in the language designer's world view rather than pragmatic inspiration.

A Pascal program lies entirely within the boundaries of its
PROGRAM procedure. Inside of the PROGRAM routine are a number
of functions that may be arbitrarily nested. This nesting is particularly annoying to a C programmer like me. A FUNCTION is a routine
that returns a single value via its identifier, and a PROCEDURE is a
function that does not. As with COBOL, procedural code is always
prefixed by variable declarations and definitions.

Consider the following program:

```pascal
program main;
    var
        value:integer;

    procedure callNested;
        function nested1:integer;
            function nested2:integer;
            begin
                writeln('inside nested2()');
                nested2 := value+1;
            end;
        begin
            writeln('inside nested1()');
            nested1 := nested2+1;
        end;
    begin
        writeln('inside callNested()');
        writeln('value= ',nested1);
    end;

begin
    value:=5;
    callNested;
end.
```

When run, this program will generate the following output:

```
inside callNested()
value= inside nested1()
inside nested2()
7
```

Here is another brief example that demonstrates how Pascal can
use different memory components:

```pascal
program ptour;
    const
        size=6;
    type
        intPointer=^integer;
    var
        iptr:intPointer;
```

```
            index:integer;

    function factorial(arg:integer):integer;
    begin
        if arg>1 then
            factorial := arg * factorial(arg-1)
        else
            factorial :=1;
    end;

begin
    index:=10;
    iptr:=new(intPointer);
    iptr^:=0;
    for index:= 1 to size do
    begin
        iptr^:= iptr^ + factorial(index);
        writeln('factorial(',index,')= ',factorial
            (index))
    end;
    writeln('iptr^=',iptr^);
    dispose(iptr);
end.
```

If you run this program, the following output will be sent to the console:

```
factorial(1)= 1
factorial(2)= 2
factorial(3)= 6
factorial(4)= 24
factorial(5)= 120
factorial(6)= 720
iptr^=873
```

The `factorial()` function is recursive, which proves that Pascal implements activation records on the stack. I also manually allocate an integer off the heap and store its address in the variable `iptr^` to show how Pascal's manual memory management scheme works.

Pascal's variety of memory management facilities and its easy-to-read structured format place it above COBOL 85 and F77 on the scale of sophistication. However, Pascal is not a language that you would use to construct production software. The organization of heavily nested routines in Pascal source code does not lend itself to constructing large-scale applications. This is why I decided to present Pascal before my discussion of C and Java. Pascal may possess memory management bells and whistles, but it is not a prime-time language.

Case Study: C

The C programming language is the Swiss army knife of programming languages. It is compact, versatile, and you can do darn near everything with it. Perhaps this is why every operating system being sold today has been written mostly in C. Part of C's utility is based on the language's provision for low-level operations like bit-wise manipulation and inline assembly code. C also possesses a syntax that allows memory addresses to be symbolically manipulated in a number of intricate ways. Furthermore, the fairly simple function-based granularity of scope is a straightforward alternative to Pascal's tendency toward heavy procedure nesting.

NOTE In a sense, C can be viewed as a nifty macro language for assembly code. C elevates you far enough from assembly code that you don't have to worry about maintaining stack frames or keeping track of offset addresses. You are given enough programming amenities that you don't feel like you are being forced to sleep on the floor. However, C doesn't really take you any higher than a few floors above the basement. You can still hop down and tinker with the rusty old furnace, if you so desire.

NOTE If you are interested in the history of C, I offer a brief synopsis in the "Prerequisites" section of this book's introduction. For those of you who want the short version, a guy at Bell Labs named Ken Thompson wrote an operating system named Unics in assembly code back in the late 1960s. He discovered that porting assembly code is no fun, so he hacked a language called BCPL into a new language that he called B. Soon afterward, two of Ken's friends at Bell Labs (Dennis Ritchie and Brian Kernighan) got mixed up in Ken's project, and C was born. They rewrote Unics in C, Bell Labs trademarked the resulting product as UNIX, and the rest is history.

The C language can use all of the high-level memory constructs mentioned in this chapter. C supports global data, local variables, recursion, and dynamic memory allocation. In other words, C can make ample use of data sections, the stack, and the heap. As you saw earlier, there are even tools like the BDW garbage collector, that can be plugged into C as a set of library functions.

Throughout the chapter, we have used C to illustrate different high-level services. Now we have the opportunity to bring everything together and look at all the services in a single example. Consider the following code:

```
#include<stdio.h>
#include<stdlib.h>
#include<string.h>
```

```c
#define ERR_STK_SZ    64
#define ERR_STR_SZ    128

#define ERR_LVL_WARN     0
#define ERR_LVL_ERROR    1
#define ERR_LVL_FATAL    2

struct ErrData
{
    char *info;
    unsigned char  level;
};

struct ErrData *stack[ERR_STK_SZ];
int SP;
char *ErrLvl[]={"WARN","ERROR","FATAL"};

void bldErr();
void checkStack();

int main()
{
    SP=0;
    bldErr();
    checkStack();
    return(0);
}/*end main*/

void bldErr()
{
    stack[SP]=(struct ErrData*)malloc(sizeof(struct
            ErrData));
    (*stack[SP]).info = malloc(ERR_STR_SZ);
    (*stack[SP]).level = ERR_LVL_ERROR;
    strncpy((*stack[SP]).info,"testing",ERR_STR_SZ-1);
    SP++;
    return;
}/*end bldError*/

void checkStack()
{
    int i;
    for(i=0;i<SP;i++)
    {
        printf("%s\n",(*stack[i]).info);
        printf("%s\n",ErrLvl[(*stack[i]).level]);
    }
    return;
}/*end checkstack*/
```

When this program is executed, the following output will be produced:

```
testing
ERROR
```

The previous code implements a basic error stack. As errors occur, they are popped onto the stack and the stack pointer is incremented. In this example, I run through the full gamut of memory usage. There is global data (i.e., stack[]), heap allocation via malloc(), and the stack is used to provide storage for function activation records.

To get a better idea of how this code is realized at the machine level, let's look at an assembly code listing. Don't be concerned if you can't immediately "see" everything that is going on. I will dissect this code shortly and point out the important things. When I am done, you can come back and take a better look. For now, just skim the following assembly code:

```
.386P
.model   FLAT
PUBLIC   _ErrLvl
_DATA    SEGMENT
COMM     _stack:DWORD:040H
COMM     _SP:DWORD
_ErrLvl  DD      FLAT:$SG336
         DD      FLAT:$SG337
         DD      FLAT:$SG338
$SG336   DB      'WARN', 00H
         ORG $+3
$SG337   DB      'ERROR', 00H
         ORG $+2
$SG338   DB      'FATAL', 00H
_DATA    ENDS
PUBLIC   _bldErr
PUBLIC   _checkStack
PUBLIC   _main
_TEXT    SEGMENT
_main    PROC NEAR
         push ebp
         mov  ebp, esp
         mov  DWORD PTR _SP, 0
         call _bldErr
         call _checkStack
         xor  eax, eax
         pop  ebp
         ret  0
_main    ENDP
_TEXT    ENDS
```

```
        EXTRN   _malloc:NEAR
        EXTRN   _strncpy:NEAR
_DATA   SEGMENT
    ORG $+2
$SG344  DB      'testing', 00H
_DATA   ENDS
_TEXT   SEGMENT
_bldErr PROC NEAR
        push    ebp
        mov     ebp, esp
        push    8
        call    _malloc
        add     esp, 4
        mov     ecx, DWORD PTR _SP
        mov     DWORD PTR _stack[ecx*4], eax
        push    128                     ; 00000080H
        call    _malloc
        add     esp, 4
        mov     edx, DWORD PTR _SP
        mov     ecx, DWORD PTR _stack[edx*4]
        mov     DWORD PTR [ecx], eax
        mov     edx, DWORD PTR _SP
        mov     eax, DWORD PTR _stack[edx*4]
        mov     BYTE PTR [eax+4], 1
        push    127                     ; 0000007fH
        push    OFFSET FLAT:$SG344
        mov     ecx, DWORD PTR _SP
        mov     edx, DWORD PTR _stack[ecx*4]
        mov     eax, DWORD PTR [edx]
        push    eax
        call    _strncpy
        add     esp, 12                 ; 0000000cH
        mov     ecx, DWORD PTR _SP
        add     ecx, 1
        mov     DWORD PTR _SP, ecx
        pop     ebp
        ret     0
_bldErr ENDP
_TEXT   ENDS
        EXTRN   _printf:NEAR
_DATA   SEGMENT
$SG350  DB      '%s', 0aH, 00H
$SG351  DB      '%s', 0aH, 00H
_DATA   ENDS
_TEXT   SEGMENT
_i$ = -4
_checkStack PROC NEAR
        push    ebp
        mov     ebp, esp
        push    ecx
        mov     DWORD PTR _i$[ebp], 0
```

```
                jmp     SHORT $L347
$L348:
                mov     eax, DWORD PTR _i$[ebp]
                add     eax, 1
                mov     DWORD PTR _i$[ebp], eax
$L347:
                mov     ecx, DWORD PTR _i$[ebp]
                cmp     ecx, DWORD PTR _SP
                jge     SHORT $L349
                mov     edx, DWORD PTR _i$[ebp]
                mov     eax, DWORD PTR _stack[edx*4]
                mov     ecx, DWORD PTR [eax]
                push    ecx
                push    OFFSET FLAT:$SG350
                call    _printf
                add     esp, 8
                mov     edx, DWORD PTR _i$[ebp]
                mov     eax, DWORD PTR _stack[edx*4]
                xor     ecx, ecx
                mov     cl, BYTE PTR [eax+4]
                mov     edx, DWORD PTR _ErrLvl[ecx*4]
                push    edx
                push    OFFSET FLAT:$SG351
                call    _printf
                add     esp, 8
                jmp     SHORT $L348
$L349:
                mov     esp, ebp
                pop     ebp
                ret     0
_checkStack ENDP
_TEXT   ENDS
END
```

If you look for the global variables (i.e., stack[], SP, ErrLvl), you will notice that the compiler places them in data sections. However, one thing you might not be aware of is that the compiler also places other various in-code constants (like the string constant "testing") in data sections. This prevents any sort of data from being embedded in a code section. There are good reasons for this. For instance, on Windows, code sections are execute-only, so there is no way that data could be accessed if it were mixed in with the code. The assembler will merge these three different data sections into a single, global _DATA section when the application is built.

```
_DATA    SEGMENT
COMM     _stack:DWORD:040H
COMM     _SP:DWORD
_ErrLvl  DD      FLAT:$SG336
```

```
            DD      FLAT:$SG337
            DD      FLAT:$SG338
$SG336      DB      'WARN', 00H
       ORG  $+3
$SG337      DB      'ERROR', 00H
       ORG  $+2
$SG338      DB      'FATAL', 00H
_DATA       ENDS
;---------------------------------------
_DATA       SEGMENT
       ORG  $+2
$SG344      DB      'testing', 00H
_DATA       ENDS
;---------------------------------------
_DATA       SEGMENT
$SG350      DB      '%s', 0aH, 00H
$SG351      DB      '%s', 0aH, 00H
_DATA       ENDS
```

If you look at the assembly code for any of the functions, you will notice that they all have prologue and epilogue code to manage activation records. This is irrefutable evidence that the stack is being used. For example, take a look at the assembly code for checkStack():

```
_checkStack PROC NEAR

    ; prologue - set up frame pointer and allocate
                 local storage
    push    ebp
    mov     ebp, esp
    push    ecx   ; makes room for 4-byte local variable "i"

    ;-----------------------------------
    ; function body implementation here
    ;-----------------------------------

    ; epilogue - reclaim local storage and reset
                 frame pointer
    mov     esp, ebp
    pop     ebp
    ret     0

_checkStack ENDP
```

Finally, the heap allocation that occurs is facilitated by the malloc() library call, which is prototyped in stdlib.h. This may resolve to a system call behind the scenes, such that:

```
stack[SP]=(struct ErrData*)malloc(sizeof(struct
          ErrData));
```

becomes:

```
push    8                       ; # bytes to allocate
call    _malloc                 ; call malloc()
add     esp, 4                  ; clean up stack from call
mov     ecx, DWORD PTR _SP      ; set up index to access stack[]
mov     DWORD PTR _stack[ecx*4], eax ; address was returned
                                            in EAX
```

Before the actual library call is made, the number of bytes to be allocated is pushed onto the stack. Once the call is over, the address of the first byte of the allocated memory region is placed in EAX.

C has supported all of its memory features since its inception. Stack frames and heap allocation were not extensions amended to the language by a standards committee 10 years after the first specification was released. Instead, C was the product of a few inspired individuals who truly understood the utility of terse and simple language syntax. Compare the grammar of C to that of a committee-based language like COBOL. In contrast to C, COBOL is a behemoth.

But, as Stan Lee would say, "With great power, comes great responsibility." C's flexibility does not come without a price. The very features that allow C to manage memory so effectively can also produce disastrous consequences if they are not used correctly. Memory leaks and dangling pointers are just two of the perils that we have seen. The syntax of C also allows addresses to be cast and moved around so that you might not be sure what a program is referencing.

Here is an example of what I am talking about:

```
/* ---mess.c--- */

#include<stdio.h>
#include<stdlib.h>
#include<string.h>

void function4()
{
    printf("called function4()\n");
    return;
}/*end function4*/

void* function3()
{
    char *cptr;
    cptr = malloc(16);
    strcpy(cptr,"now a string");
    return(cptr);
```

```
}/*end function3*/

void* function2()
{
    void *fptr;
    fptr = function4;
    return(fptr);
}/*end function2*/

void* function1()
{
    int* iptr;
    iptr = malloc(sizeof(int));
    *iptr = 1012;
    return(iptr);
}/*end function1*/

typedef void (*fptr)();

void main()
{
    void *vptr;
    fptr addr;

    vptr = function1();
    printf("%lu\n",(*((int*)vptr)));

    vptr = function2();
    addr = vptr;
    (addr)();

    vptr = function3();
    printf("%s\n",(char *)vptr);
    return;
}/*end main*/
```

When this program is executed, the following output is generated:

```
1012
called function4()
now a string
```

When it comes to pointers of type void, you often cannot tell what is being referenced. The first call (i.e., function1()) returns the address of an integer. The second call (i.e., function2()) returns the address of a function. The third call (i.e., function3()) returns the address of a string. Without looking at the function implementations themselves, you would have no idea what kind of value you are dealing with.

C's simple, function-based organization can also lead to problems. For instance, if the code base you are working with grows beyond a million lines, it can become difficult to control. The tendency to abuse the global nature of C functions can very quickly transform a large project into a morass of tightly interwoven execution paths. You might be confronted with a scenario where one function calls another function that is a distant portion of the source code tree, and this function calls a function that belongs to another distant branch of the source tree. Without C being able to enforce encapsulation, which it can't, everyone can call everyone else. The resulting spaghetti code is difficult to maintain and almost impossible to modify.

Case Study: Java

The Java programming language originally started off as a skunk works project at Sun Microsystems in the early 1990s. Scott McNealy, the CEO of Sun, told James Gosling to go off somewhere and create something brilliant. In May of 1995, Sun released the Java SDK to the public. I can remember downloading my first copy of the SDK in December of 1995. It had an install program that executed from a DOS console, and the virtual machine ran on Windows 95. Heck, the first SDK didn't even touch the Windows registry when it installed (this is a feature I kind of miss).

NOTE Releasing a new development environment to the public wasn't exactly what Gosling had originally intended. According to Patrick Naughton, one of the original Java engineers, Gosling initially developed the Java virtual machine (JVM) to support a programming language called Oak that was geared toward building embedded programs for consumer appliances. Thus, Java was somewhat of a serendipitous creation.

Language Features

Java is an object-oriented (OO) language. Specifically, it is a fairly puritanical OO language. With the exception of atomic data types, like `char` or `int`, everything is instantiated as an object. In addition, there are no stand-alone functions in Java; every function must belong to a class. Like other OO languages, Java supports certain kinds of object encapsulation, polymorphism, and inheritance. However, the Java compiler (`javac`) also enforces a number of conventions that make it much easier to manage large projects.

Having worked at an ERP company that maintained a code base consisting of 16 million lines of K&R C, I dread the prospect of hunting down header files and obscure libraries, which were invariably spread across a massive, cryptic, and completely undocumented source tree. In the past, sometimes I would spend several hours just trying to find one source file or function definition. There were times where I would start `grep` at the root of a machine's file system and go have lunch. In fact, I distinctly remember spending an entire afternoon trying to locate the following macro:

    #define PrcBInNdNbr 14

In case you're wondering, this ridiculous macro stands for Process Binary Instruction Node Number. Java eliminated this problem in one fell swoop by enforcing a one-to-one mapping between package names and directory names. When I discovered that Java enforced this convention, I felt like jumping and shouting "Amen!"

Some engineers may decry the package directory naming scheme, claiming that it is a characteristic of a bondage-discipline language. These engineers have obviously never worked on a large project. On a large project, you need to maintain organization, even if it is instituted at the cost of flexibility. Sometimes, the only thing between a million lines of code and absolute chaos is a set of well-enforced conventions.

In the past, it has been up to the software engineers involved on a project to be good citizens and obey the informal organizational schemes. However, there was usually nothing stopping a programmer from breaking the rules and introducing complexity into the system. Sure enough, there's always at least one guy who has to do things "his way." As part of the language's masterful design, the founding fathers at JavaSoft decided that the Java run time would take an active role in maintaining an organized source tree by enforcing the package directory naming scheme.

Another design decision that the founding fathers made was to eliminate explicit pointer manipulation. This was another wise decision. As you saw from the example in the last section, pointers are easy to abuse. A sufficient dose of pointer arithmetic can make source code both ambiguous and platform dependent. By allowing only implicit references to objects, Java is able to safeguard programs from all sorts of pointer tomfoolery.

Finally, I think that Gosling had C++ in mind when he decided that Java would not support multiple inheritance and operator overloading. As far as complexity is concerned, these two features tend to make matters worse instead of making them better. There is nothing scarier than looking at the twisting cyclic relationships that multiple inheritance can generate. It is almost as ugly as spaghetti code. The developer is forced to compensate by using awkward mechanisms like virtual base classes and resolution operators. Likewise, operator overloading tends to make source code more difficult to interpret and understand. If you see a "+", you cannot always be sure if the engineer who wrote the code is talking about integer addition or some "special" operation that might not have anything to do with arithmetic.

NOTE   Java can almost be characterized in terms of what features it does not have, as opposed to the features it does have. By constraining the language's features and instituting a set of additional conventions, the architects of Java were attempting to force a certain level of organization. Having worked with both C++ and Java, I think that Gosling and his coworkers succeeded in doing this.

I have often listened to debates concerning the relative merits of C++ and Java. As far as I am concerned, these two languages are different tools used for different jobs. It is like asking, "Which is better, a hammer or a screwdriver?" Both Java and C++ are OO languages, but the primary distinction between them lies in their orientation. Java, first and foremost, is an *application language*. C++ works better as a *system language*. Java programs are compiled to run on a virtual machine. "Write once, run anywhere" is a fundamental benefit of implementing a project with Java. The downside to this is that you cannot directly interact with native hardware. By striving for portability, Java has isolated itself from hardware. Building system software requires that you have the ability to insert inline assembly code, explicitly manipulate memory, and generate a native executable. It just so happens that C++ provides these features. Table 3.7 summarizes the differences between C++ and Java.

Table 3.7

Language	Domain	Hardware	Motivation	Binary Format
Java	application	insulate from via virtual machine	portability abstraction	bytecode
C++	system software	intimate access to native CPU	control flexibility	native format

Virtual Machine Architecture

Java applications are compiled to run on a virtual machine. The Java virtual machine (JVM) provides high-level memory services to Java applications. Thus, to understand how Java applications use memory, we must first understand the operation of the virtual machine.

In terms of the virtual machine's artificial environment, the memory components that the virtual machine provides for Java applications can be divided into two categories: system-wide resources and thread-specific resources (see Figure 3.16).

A Java application consists of one or more executing threads. System-wide resources can be accessed by all of an application's thread. The primary system-wide memory components are the JVM's *heap* and the *method area*.

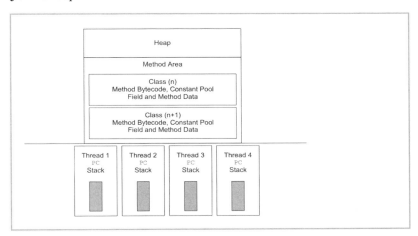

Figure 3.16

The heap is a large chunk of memory that is used to supply storage for object instantiation. Every time that a new object is created, space on the heap is allocated. The heap is supposed to be supervised by an automatic memory manager. Unfortunately, the JVM specification does not go any further than this. The engineer constructing a JVM has to decide which garbage collection algorithm to use and how to implement that algorithm.

The method area is a mixture between a code section and a static data section. Each class stores the bytecode instructions to its methods in this area. In addition, each class stows its run-time constant pool and field/method metadata in the method area. A constant pool stores, among other things, compile-time literals and indices used to reference other methods/fields.

Each thread has a program counter (PC), its own virtual machine stack. A thread may also possess zero or more native machine stacks to handle native method execution. The program counter is very much like Intel's EIP register. It points to the index of the bytecode instruction being executed by the thread. If native code is being executed instead of bytecode, the program counter's value is undefined.

Each thread has its own stack to provide support for activation records. The JVM spec refers to activation records as *frames*, as in stack frames. As usual, frames are utilized to provide storage for function arguments, local variables, and return values.

Java Memory Management

A Java application uses the heap and its own private stack for dynamic memory needs. Specifically, an object's field values are stored in its memory region located in the heap. An object's method implementations are stored in the method area. An object's local storage is provided by its private stack frame. Any other static data is placed in a constant pool of the object's corresponding class in the method area. Table 3.8 provides a summary of how Java applications use the different high-level services provided by the virtual machine.

Table 3.8

Object Element	Storage Space
fields	system-wide heap
methods	system-wide method area
local variables	thread stack
arguments	thread stack
return value	thread stack
return address	thread stack
static data (i.e., literals)	system-wide method area, constant pool

Objects are really just the sum of their field values. Two different objects of the same type can share the same method area because it is their field values that distinguish them. To give you a feel for this, the following code shows how you could implement this type of setup in C:

```
/* --objects.c-- */

#include<stdio.h>
#include<stdlib.h>
#include<string.h>

struct MyObject
{
    int value;
    char name[16];
```

```c
};

struct MyObject *constructor()
{
    return((struct MyObject*)malloc(sizeof(struct
            MyObject)));
}/*end constructor*/

void setValues(struct MyObject *ptr, int val, char *str)
{
    (*ptr).value = val;
    strcpy((*ptr).name,str);
    return;
}/*end setValues*/

void toString(struct MyObject *ptr)
{
    printf("value=%d, name=%s\n",(*ptr).value,
            (*ptr).name);
    return;
}/*end constructor*/

void main()
{
    struct MyObject *obj1;
    struct MyObject *obj2;

    obj1 = constructor();
    setValues(obj1,5,"object1");
    toString(obj1);

    obj2 = constructor();
    setValues(obj2,6,"object2");
    toString(obj2);

    return;
}/*end main*/
```

If this program is executed, the following output will be produced:

```
value=5, name=object1
value=6, name=object2
```

The objects in this case are collections of fields (i.e., structures). They both use the same member functions (i.e., `constructor()`, `setValues()`, `toString()`), but they are different because their fields are different.

The best way to see how a Java application uses memory services in practice is to take a small Java program, disassemble it, and examine its bytecode entrails. Consider the following Java program that consists of a single thread of execution. Both the heap and stack are utilized.

```java
public class MemDemo
{
    public int[] array;
    public int sum;

    public MemDemo(int size)
    {
        array = new int[size];
        return;
    }/*end constructor*/

    public int demoFrameUsage(int first)
    {
        int i;
        int j;
        sum = 0;
        for(i=0;i<array.length;i++)
        {
            array[i]=first;
            first++;
            sum = sum+array[i];
        }
        return(sum);
    }/*end demoFrameUsage*/

    public static void main(String[] args)
    {
        MemDemo md = new MemDemo(11);
        System.out.println("sum="+md.demoFrameUsage(1));
        return;
    }/*end main*/
}
```

When this application is executed, the following output is produced:

```
C:\j2sdk1.4.0\src>SET
CLASSPATH=C:\j2sdk1.4.0\src;%CLASSPATH%
C:\j2sdk1.4.0\src>javac MemDemo.java
C:\j2sdk1.4.0\src>java MemDemo
sum=66
```

> **NOTE** Do not forget to include the current working directory in your CLASSPATH environmental variable when you run the previous code.

Now I will look at each method of MemDemo.java in chronological order and analyze the corresponding bytecode instructions. To generate the necessary bytecode, I used the javap tool that ships with the Java 2 SDK. You will need to pass javap the name of the class file without an extension. The following command line disassembles `MemDemo.class`:

```
C:\j2sdk1.4.0\src>javap -c MemDemo
```

Instruction opcodes that are prefixed by a hash sign (i.e., "#") represent indices into the run-time constant pool. The item that the index references is placed in brackets to the right of the instruction (i.e., <Method Memdemo(int)>). I will also sprinkle the assembler with single- and double-line comments to help explain what is going on.

Execution begins in the `main()` method:

```
public static void main(String[] args)
{
   MemDemo md = new MemDemo(11);
   System.out.println("sum="+md.demoFrameUsage(1));
   return;
}/*end main*/

Method void main(java.lang.String[])
0 new #4 <Class MemDemo>       //create an object, don't initialize
3 dup                          //duplicate top operand, push on stack
4 bipush 11                    //push argument (11) on stack
6 invokespecial #5 <Method MemDemo(int)>  //initialize object we
                                              just created
9 astore_1                     //save reference to md object

10 getstatic #6 <Field java.io.PrintStream out>//get static
                                              field from class
13 new #7 <Class java.lang.StringBuffer>   //create StringBuffer
                                              object
16 dup                         //duplicate top operand, push on stack
17 invokespecial #8 <Method java.lang.StringBuffer()>
                       //initialize

StringBuffer
20 ldc #9 <String "sum="> //push reference to literal on stack
22 invokevirtual #10 <Method java.lang.StringBuffer append(java.
                  lang.String)>

25 aload_1                  //push reference to md on stack
26 iconst_1                 //push argument (1) on stack

/* rest of these instructions handle System.out.println()
statement*/

27 invokevirtual #11 <Method int demoFrameUsage(int)>
30 invokevirtual #12 <Method java.lang.StringBuffer append(int)>
33 invokevirtual #13 <Method java.lang.String toString()>
```

```
36 invokevirtual #14 <Method void println(java.lang.String)>
39 return
```

The first function that is invoked from `main()` is the constructor for `MemDemo()`. Let's take a look at its Java code and the associated bytecode assembler. All of the push instructions are nothing but setup work for the non-push instructions.

```
public MemDemo(int size)
{
    array = new int[size];
    return;
}/*end constructor*/

Method MemDemo(int)
0 aload_0                    //push reference to 'this' on stack
1 invokespecial #1 <Method java.lang.Object()> //call superclass
                                                constructor
4 aload_0                    //push reference to 'this' on stack
5 iload_1                    //push 'size' on stack
6 newarray int               //create an integer array object
8 putfield #2 <Field int array[]>  //set array field for 'this'
                                    object
11 return
```

After `MemDemo()` has returned, the `demoFrameUsage()` method is invoked next. Let's take a look at its Java code and the associated bytecode assembler. As before, most of the push instructions are setups for other instructions.

```
public int demoFrameUsage(int first)
{
    int i;
    int j;
    sum = 0;
    for(i=0;i<array.length;i++)
    {
        array[i]=first;
        first++;
        sum = sum+array[i];
    }
    return(sum);
}/*end demoFrameUsage*/

Method int demoFrameUsage(int)
0 aload_0                    //push 'this' reference on stack
1 iconst_0                   //push 0 on to stack
2 putfield #3 <Field int sum>  //set 'sum' field to 0
5 iconst_0                   //push 0 onto stack
6 istore_2                   //pop 0 into variable 'i'
7 goto 38                    //jump to bytecode index 38
```

```
10 aload_0                              //push 'this' reference on stack
11 getfield #2 <Field int array[]>      //push reference to 'array'
                                          on stack
14 iload_2                              //push value of 'i' on stack
15 iload_1                              //push value of 'first' on stack
16 iastore                              //store 'first' in array[i]
17 iinc 1 1                             //increment 'first' by 1
20 aload_0                              //push 'this' reference on stack
21 aload_0                              //push 'this' reference on stack
22 getfield #3 <Field int sum>          //push value of 'sum' on stack
25 aload_0                              //push 'this' reference on stack
26 getfield #2 <Field int array[]>      //push reference to 'array'
                                          on stack
29 iload_2                              //push value of 'i' on stack
30 iaload                               //push array[i] onto stack
31 iadd                                 //add 'sum' to 'array[i]', push
                                          on stack
32 putfield #3 <Field int sum>          //set 'sum' field to new value
35 iinc 2 1                             //increment 'i' by 1

38 iload_2                              //push value of 'i' on stack
39 aload_0                              //push 'this' reference on stack
40 getfield #2 <Field int array[]>      //push reference to 'array'
                                          on stack
43 arraylength                          //get length of array[]
44 if_icmplt 10                         //if 'i' < array.length, goto
                                          index 10
47 aload_0                              //push 'this' reference on stack
48 getfield #3 <Field int sum>          //push value of 'sum' on stack
51 ireturn                              //push value on invoker's frame,
                                          return
```

To summarize what has happened, we started in `main()`, where an object of type `MemDemo` is allocated off the heap. The thread's stack is used to pass the integer argument (11) to the constructor of `MemDemo`. Within the constructor, the heap is used again to allocate an integer array. The call to `demoFrameUsage()` makes ample use of the stack to support an argument, local variables, and a return value. The value returned by `demoFrameUsage()` and a string literal reference are used to supply a string argument to `System.out.println()` using the stack. (See Figure 3.17.)

 NOTE If you are interested in the specifics of a certain bytecode instruction, you should take a look at the JVM specification. It is distributed by Sun Microsystems as an aid to help third parties construct a clean-room implementation of the JVM. The JVM specification is the final word as to the functionality that a JVM has to provide.

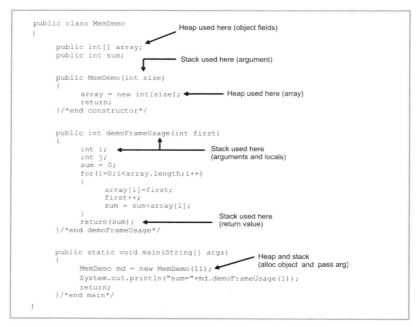

Figure 3.17

Memory Management: The Three-layer Cake

You have just spanned the spectrum of memory services that a computer provides. The previous chapters have been relatively dense, and it would be easy to let the details overwhelm you. To help illuminate the big picture, I am going to dedicate this section to pulling everything together.

Memory management occurs at three levels. In the basement lies the processor. The processor provides a set of system registers (i.e., GDTR) and dedicated instructions (i.e., LGDTR) that support the construction of memory management data structures. These data structures include descriptor tables, page directories, and page tables. The processor cannot actually create these data structures; instead, it merely supports their creation and use.

Upstairs, on the street level, is the operating system. The operating system is responsible for taking the raw materials provided by the hardware and constructing an actual memory management implementation. The operating system has to decide which processor features to use and to what extent. For example, both segmentation and paging can be used to institute memory protection. The Intel Pentium supports four levels of privilege for memory segments via the DPL field in descriptor table entries and two levels of privilege for paging via the Supervisor/User flag in page table entries. All three of the protected mode operating systems that we looked at in Chapter 2 used paging as the primary mechanism to implement privilege and access protocols.

Several floors up, sunning themselves on the balcony of a penthouse suite, are the user applications. User applications have it easy. They are insulated from the ugly details of memory management that occur down in the boiler room. When a user application needs memory, it sends a request to the operating system through a third party known as the system call interface. Why leave the penthouse for dinner when you can have the butler pick it up?

User applications view their own address space in terms of a set of memory regions. Most applications can see a stack, heap, data section, and code section. The extent to which they use these regions is determined both by the development tools being used and the run-time libraries that the applications invoke. As we saw in this chapter, older languages tend to possess very primitive memory models. Languages like COBOL 85 and F77 really only use a code section and a static data section. Contemporary languages, like Java, have very sophisticated memory models that make heavy use of the heap and stacks.

The "three-layer cake" of memory management is displayed in Figure 3.18.

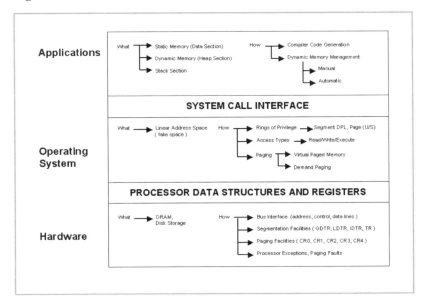

Figure 3.18

References

ANSI, X3.23-1985 (R1991), Programming Languages — COBOL.
This is the COBOL 85 ANSI standard; when someone talks about ANSI COBOL, they are referring to this standard and the 1989 amendments.

ANSI, X3.23b-1993 (R1998), amendment to ANSI X3.23-1985, updated with ANSI X3.23a-1989.

ANSI/ISO/IEC 1539-1:1997, Programming languages — Fortran — Part 1: Base language.
This is the most recent FORTRAN specification.

ANSI, ISO/IEC 9899:1999, Programming languages — C.
This is the most recent C specification.

Baroudi, Carol. *Mastering Cobol*. 1999, Sybex, ISBN: 078212321X.
According to Carol, there are 500 billion lines of COBOL code in existence. Unfortunately, she does not reference her sources (bad move). I believe that the Gartner Group's figure of 180 billion has more credibility.

Cooper, Doug. *Oh! Pascal*. 1993, W.W. Norton & Company, ISBN: 0393963985.

Diwan, A., D. Tarditi, and E. Moss. *Memory Subsystem Performance of Programs with Intensive Heap Allocation*. 1993, Carnegie Mellon University, Technical Report CMU-CS-93-227.

Graham, Paul. *ANSI Common LISP.* 1995, Prentice Hall, ISBN: 0133708756.

Joy, B. (Ed.), G. Steele, and J. Gosling. *The Java Language Specification*. 2000 Addison-Wesley, ISBN: 0201310082.

Lindholm, T. and F. Yellin. *The Java Virtual Machine Specification*. 1999, Addison-Wesley; ISBN: 0201432943.
For a specification, and I have waded through many, this one is not too difficult to digest. Still, you might want to have Meyer and Downing's book sitting next to you.

Metcalf, M. and J. Reid. *Fortran 90/95 Explained*. 1999, Oxford University Press, ISBN: 0198505582.

Meyer, J. and T. Downing. *Java Virtual Machine*. 1997, O'Reilly & Associates, ISBN: 1565921941.
This is an excellent companion to the actual JVM specification.

Microsoft. *Programmer's Guide, Microsoft MASM.* 1992, Microsoft Corp., Document No. DB35747-1292.

This is not a book for beginners, primarily due to the way that it is organized and presented. However, it is still a good reference if you know what you are looking for. The one complaint that I have about this book is that it invests little or no effort in explaining protected mode assembler. Most of the book is devoted to real mode topics. Considering that almost every application currently being written on Windows is a 32-bit protected mode application, I find this horribly negligent.

Naughton, Patrick. *The Java Handbook.* 1996, McGraw-Hill Professional Publishing, ISBN: 0078821991.

The last section of this book includes an engrossing personal recount of Java's creation by one of the principal engineers.

Ritchie, Dennis M. *The Evolution of the Unix Time-sharing System.* AT&T Bell Laboratories Technical Journal 63 No. 6 Part 2, October 1984, pp. 1577-93.

Ritchie, Dennis M. *The Development of the C Language.* 1993, Association for Computing Machinery.

Tanenbaum, A. and A. Woodhull. *Operating Systems: Design and Implementation.* 1997, Prentice Hall, ISBN: 0136386776.

Zorn, Benjamin. *The Measured Cost of Conservative Garbage Collection.* 1992, University of Colorado at Boulder, Technical Report, CU-CS-573-92.

This is the original paper that touts the BDW garbage collector as having "comparable" performance relative to `malloc()` and `free()`. You can crank through the numbers yourself to see what "comparable" means.

Zorn, B. and D. Grunwald. *Empirical Measurements of Six Allocation-Intensive C Programs.* 1992, University of Colorado at Boulder, Technical Report, CU-CS-604-92.

This paper looks at the allocation behavior of Cfraq, Espresso, GhostScript, Gnu Awk, Perl, and Chameleon.

Zorn, B., D. Detlefs, and A. Dosser. *Memory Allocation Costs in Large C and C++ Programs.* 1993, University of Colorado at Boulder, Technical Report, CU-CS-665-93.

This is another paper that looks at the comparable performance of garbage collectors.

Chapter 4

Manual Memory Management

Managing memory in the heap is defined by the requirement that services be provided to allocate and deallocate arbitrary size blocks of memory in an arbitrary order. In other words, the heap is a free-for-all zone, and the heap manager has to be flexible enough to deal with a number of possible requests. There are two ways to manage the heap: manual and automatic memory management. In this chapter, I will take an in-depth look at manual memory management and how it is implemented in practice.

Replacements for `malloc()` and `free()`

Manual memory management dictates that the engineer writing a program must keep track of the memory allocated. This forces all of the bookkeeping to be performed when the program is being designed instead of while the program is running. This can benefit execution speed because the related bookkeeping instructions are not placed in the application itself. However, if a programmer makes an accounting error, they could be faced with a memory leak or a dangling pointer. Nevertheless, properly implemented manual memory management is lighter and faster than the alternatives. I provided evidence of this in the previous chapter.

In ANSI C, manual memory management is provided by the `malloc()` and `free()` standard library calls. There are two other standard library functions (`calloc()` and `realloc()`), but as we saw in Chapter 3, they resolve to calls to `malloc()` and `free()`.

I thought that the best way to illustrate how manual memory management facilities are constructed would be to offer several different implementations of `malloc()` and `free()`. To use these alternative implementations, all you will need to do is include the appropriate source file and then call `newMalloc()` and `newFree()` instead of `malloc()` and `free()`. For example:

```
#include<mallocV1.cpp>

void main()
{
    char *cptr;
    initMemMgr();

    cptr = newMalloc(10);
    if(cptr==NULL){ printf("allocation failed!\n"); }
    newFree(cptr);

    closeMemMgr();
    return;
}
```

The remainder of this chapter will be devoted to describing three different approaches. In each case, I will present the requisite background theory, offer a concrete implementation, provide a test driver, and look at associated trade-offs. Along the way, I will also discuss performance measuring techniques and issues related to program simulation.

System Call Interface and Porting Issues

The C standard library `malloc()` and `free()` functions are procedures that execute in user mode. Inevitably, they rely on native library routines to do the actual dirty work of allocating and releasing memory. The native libraries, in turn, make use of the system call gate to access system calls that reside in kernel mode. This dance step is displayed in Figure 4.1.

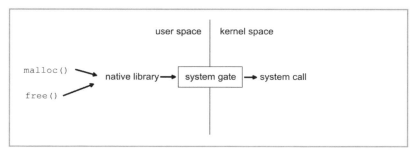

Figure 4.1

The specific native library functions that malloc() and free() invoke will differ from one operating system to the next. On UNIX platforms, malloc() and free() end up invoking the brk() system call through its native library wrapper function, sbrk(). Figure 4.2 shows an example of how this works in MINIX.

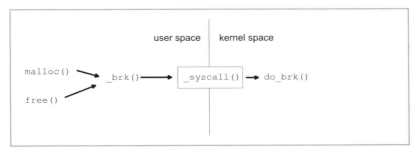

Figure 4.2

Because I am developing on Windows, instead of sbrk() I will be using the Win32 HeapXXX() functions to act as my touch point to the kernel. Here are the specific Win32 routines that I will be invoking:

```
HANDLE GetProcessHeap(VOID);
LPVOID HeapAlloc(HANDLE hHeap, DWORD dwFlags, DWORD dwBytes);
LPVOID HeapReAlloc(HANDLE hHeap, DWORD dwFlags, LPVOID lpMem,
       DWORD dwBytes);
BOOL HeapFree(HANDLE hHeap, DWORD dwFlags, LPVOID lpMem);
```

Here is a short example to give you a feel for how these functions are utilized. In the following example, I allocate a 2MB heap and populate it with the letter "a." Then I increase the size of the heap by 1MB (without moving the original memory block) and repopulate it all with "a."

```
/* --heapDemo.c-- */

#include<stdio.h>
#include<windows.h>

#define MB   1048576
#define U1   unsigned char
#define U4   unsigned long

void main()
{
    HANDLE handle;
    U4 *ptr;
    U1 *cptr;
```

```c
    int i;

    handle = GetProcessHeap();
    if(handle==NULL)
    {
        printf("could not get heap handle\n");
        return;
    }

    /*allocate and fill 2MB with 'a' character----------------*/

    ptr = HeapAlloc(handle,HEAP_ZERO_MEMORY,2*MB);

    if(ptr==NULL)
    {
        printf("HeapAlloc() failed\n");
        return;
    }

    printf("address=%p\n",ptr);
    printf("size=%lu\n",HeapSize(handle,HEAP_NO_SERIALIZE,ptr));

    cptr = (U1*)ptr;

    for(i=0;i<2*MB;i++){ cptr[i] = 'a'; }

    /*increase heap by 1MB but do NOT move and fill with 'a'--*/

    ptr = HeapReAlloc(handle,HEAP_REALLOC_IN_PLACE_ONLY,
        ptr,3*MB);

    if(ptr==NULL)
    {
        printf("HeapAlloc() failed\n");
        return;
    }

    printf("address=%p\n",ptr);
    printf("size=%lu\n",HeapSize(handle,HEAP_NO_SERIALIZE,ptr));

    cptr = (U1*)ptr;

    for(i=0;i<3*MB;i++){ cptr[i] = 'a'; }

    /*set the heap free---------------------------------------*/

    if(HeapFree(handle,HEAP_NO_SERIALIZE,ptr)==0)
    {
        printf("HeapFree() failed\n");
        return;
    }
```

```
    return;
}
```

> **NOTE** I decided on Windows because it is the most accessible platform. Everyone and his brother has at least one Windows box sitting around somewhere. The documentation for Windows is better also. Linux and BSD variants tend to require a little more investment in terms of the learning curve, so I decided on Windows in an effort to keep the audience as broad as possible.

If you value portability above more direct access to the kernel, you could probably get away with using malloc() to allocate yourself a large "heap," though (see Figure 4.3) this would add an extra layer of code between the memory management that I am going to implement and the operating system.

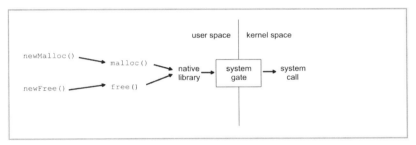

Figure 4.3

Keep It Simple...Stupid!

My goal in this chapter is to help you learn how to implement your own manual memory management code. I could have very easily gotten sidetracked with optimization, and my code would have quickly become very hard to read (if not impossible). If you want to see what I mean, go look at the malloc.c code for the Gnu Compiler Collection. It should keep you occupied for a couple of hours, or maybe a day or two.

Hence, I had to strike a balance between performance and comprehension. I have decided, in the interest of keeping the learning threshold low, that I would keep my source code *as simple as possible*. I will not try to impress you with syntactic acrobatics. Instead, I intend to show you the basic idea so that you can "get it" without seven hours of frustrating rereading. Having perused several malloc() implementations myself, I know how demoralizing it can be to have to decipher optimized code.

I also make the assumption that this chapter's code will be executing in a *single-threaded* environment. I know that some members of the reading audience may be gasping at my negligence. Again, I want to focus on memory management without being distracted by complicated synchronization issues. Once you have a working knowledge under your belt, you can add all the amenities. I will leave it as an exercise to the reader to make everything thread safe.

Measuring Performance

Given that I have decided to error on the side of simplicity, it would be interesting to see what it costs me in terms of performance relative to a commercial implementation of `malloc()` and `free()`. Although marketing people will barrage you with all sorts of obscure metrics when they are trying to sell you something, measuring performance is really not that complicated, as you will see.

The Ultimate Measure: Time

According to John Hennessy and David Patterson in their book *Computer Architecture: A Quantitative Approach*, there is one true measure of performance: *execution time*. In other words, how long did it take for an event to transpire from the moment it started to the moment it completed? Execution time is also known as *wall clock time*, or *response time*.

NOTE There are other measures of performance that you may see in literature, like MIPS (millions of instructions per second) and MFLOPS (million floating-point operations per second), but these are poor metrics that can lead to confusing comparisons. For an explanation of why, see Patterson and Hennessey's book.

Naturally, there are ways to slice and dice execution time. You can measure how much time the processor itself spends executing a program. This may be a pertinent value if you are working on a multitasking operating system. If you are executing a program on a machine that is carrying a heavy load of tasks, the program under observation may appear to run more slowly (via wall clock time) even if it is actually running faster.

You can subdivide processor time into how much time the processor spends executing a task in user mode and how much time the processor spends executing a task in kernel mode. Encryption programs spend most of their time in user space crunching numbers, while I/O-intensive programs spend most of their time in kernel space interacting with the hardware.

NOTE Given that time is such a useful performance metric, what exactly is it? According to Einstein, "Time is that which is measured by a clock." While this is correct, it is not really satisfying. Another possible definition lies in the nature of light; you could define one second as the amount of time it takes a photon in a vacuum to travel 3×10^8 meters. Again, this still may not give you a concise enough definition. There is a story of a foreign student who once asked a professor at Princeton, "Please, sir, what is time?" The professor responded by saying, "I am afraid I can't tell you; I am a physics professor. Maybe you should ask someone in the philosophy department."

Unfortunately, a time measurement in and of itself really doesn't tell you everything. This is because time measurements are context sensitive. Telling someone that a program took 300 milliseconds to execute doesn't give them the entire picture. The execution time of a program is dependent upon many things, including:

- The hardware that the program ran on
- The algorithms that the program used
- The development tools used to build the program
- The distribution of the data that the program operated on

The time measurements that I collected in this chapter were generated by programs running on a 700 MHz Pentium III. All of the programs were built using Visual Studio 6.0. Each implementation uses a different algorithm in conjunction with a data distribution that, I will admit, is slightly artificial. The system that I worked on was a single-user Windows 2000 machine with a bare minimum number of running tasks.

My hope, however, is not that the individual measurements will mean anything by themselves. Rather, I am more interested in seeing how the different algorithms compare to each other. You should notice a time differential between algorithms, as long as the other three independent variables (hardware, tools, data) are held constant. This time differential is what is important.

ANSI and Native Time Routines

In order to determine the execution time of a program, you will need to take advantage of related library calls. There are two standard ANSI C functions declared in the `time.h` header file that can be applied to this end:

```
clock_t clock();
time_t time(time_t *tptr);
```

The `time()` function returns the number of seconds that have occurred since the epoch. The *epoch* is an arbitrary reference point;

in most cases, it is January 1, 1970 (00:00:00). The problem with the `time()` function is that it works with time units that do not possess a fine enough granularity. Most important application events occur on the scale of milliseconds, microseconds, or even nanoseconds.

The `clock()` function returns the number of system clock ticks that have occurred since a process was launched. The number of ticks per second is defined by the `CLOCKS_PER_SEC` macro. This value will vary from one hardware platform to the next, seeing as how it is a processor-specific value.

The Win32 API provides a routine called `GetTickCount()` that returns the number of milliseconds that have passed since the operating system was booted. I decided to use this function to time my code. If you are more interested in writing portable code, you might want to use `clock()`.

Here is a short example that demonstrates how all three of these functions are used in practice:

```c
/* --ansiTime.c-- */

#include<stdio.h>
#include<time.h>
#include<windows.h>

void main()
{
    unsigned long i;
    time_t t1,t2;
    clock_t ticks1,ticks2, dt;
    unsigned long msec1,msec2;

    time(&t1);
    ticks1 = clock();
    msec1 = GetTickCount();

    /*do some work*/
    for(i=0;i<0xFFFFFFFF;i++){}

    time(&t2);
    ticks2 = clock();
    msec2 = GetTickCount();

    printf("number of elapsed seconds = %lu\n",t2-t1);

    dt = ticks2-ticks1;
    printf("number of clock ticks = %lu\n",dt);
    printf("ticks/second = %lu\n",CLOCKS_PER_SEC);
```

```
        printf("number of elapsed seconds = %lu\n",
                dt/CLOCKS_PER_SEC);
        printf("msecs=%lu\n",msec2-msec1);

        return;
}
```

If this program is built and run, the following type of output will be generated:

```
number of elapsed seconds = 31
number of clock ticks = 30980
ticks/second = 1000
number of elapsed seconds = 30
msecs=30960
```

The Data Distribution: Creating Random Variates

To test the performance of my manual memory managers, I will need to run them through a lengthy series of allocations and deallocations. Naturally, I cannot simply allocate memory blocks that all have the same size.

```
#include<stdlib.h>

void main()
{
    unsigned int i,j;
    unsigned int nblocks;
    unsigned int nbytes;
    unsigned char* ptrs[1024];

    nbytes=4096;
    nblocks=1024;

    for(i=0;i<nblocks;i++)
    {
        ptrs[i]=malloc(nbytes);
        for(j=0;j<nbytes;j++)
        {
            char *cptr;
            cptr = ptrs[i];
            cptr[j] = 'a';
        }
    }
    for(i=0;i<nblocks;i++)
    {
        free(ptrs[i]);
    }
    return;
}
```

The previous program does not force a manager to deal with the arbitrary requests that a heap manager normally encounters. This kind of test is unrealistic.

On the other hand, a completely random series of allocations is also not very realistic.

```c
#include<stdlib.h>

void main()
{
    unsigned int i,j;
    unsigned int nblocks;
    unsigned int nbytes;
    unsigned char* ptrs[1024];

    nblocks=1024;

    for(i=0;i<nblocks;i++)
    {
        nbytes=rand();

        ptrs[i]=malloc(nbytes);
        for(j=0;j<nbytes;j++)
        {
            char *cptr;
            cptr = ptrs[i];
            cptr[j] = 'a';
        }
    }
    for(i=0;i<nblocks;i++)
    {
        free(ptrs[i]);
    }
    return;
}
```

NOTE Another problem with both of the previous examples is that memory is released in the exact order in which it is allocated. It would be a bad move to assume that this type of behavior could be expected.

High-grade memory managers usually try to take advantage of regularities that exist in executing programs. If there are patterns, special steps can be instituted to exploit those patterns and benefit overall performance. Random data destroys regularity. This can lead to incorrect performance evaluations because a memory manager that does successfully take advantage of regularities will not be able to flex its muscles. On the same note, a memory manager that does a poor job of exploiting patterns will be able to hide its weakness behind the random allocation stream.

This leads me to a dilemma. I cannot use a series of fixed-sized memory block requests, and I cannot use a random stream of allocation requests. I need to create a synthetic stream of allocation requests and release requests that are reasonably random but still exhibit a basic element of regularity. The caveat is that, although programs can demonstrate regular behavior, there are an infinite number of programs that a manual memory manager might confront. What type of allocation behavior is the most likely?

This is where I threw my hands up and decided to use a stream of allocation requests that followed a specific discrete probability distribution. This allowed me to weight certain types of memory requests, although it also forced me to decide on a certain type of allocation behavior (i.e., one that might not be realistic).

I decided to use the following discrete probability distribution to model allocation requests:

Table 4.1

(x) Size of Allocation in Bytes	(P(x)) Probability
16	$.15 = p_1$
32	$.20 = p_2$
64	$.35 = p_3$
128	$.20 = p_4$
256	$.02 = p_5$
512	$.04 = p_6$
1024	$.02 = p_7$
4096	$.02 = p_8$

Visually, this looks like what is displayed in Figure 4.4.

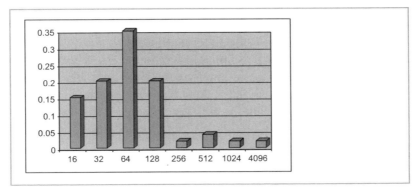

Figure 4.4

I will admit that this distribution is somewhat arbitrary. To actually generate random numbers that obey this distribution, I use an algorithm that is based on what is known as the *inverse transform method*.

1. Generate a uniform random number, U, between 0 and 1.
2. If $U < p_1 = .15$, set allocation to 16 bytes and go to step 10.
3. If $U < p_1+p_2 = .35$, set allocation to 32 bytes and go to step 10.
4. If $U < p_1+p_2+p_3 = .70$, set allocation to 64 bytes and go to step 10.
5. If $U < p_1+p_2+p_3+p_4 = .90$, set allocation to 128 bytes and go to step 10.
6. If $U < p_1+p_2+p_3+p_4+p_5 = .92$, set allocation to 256 bytes and go to step 10.
7. If $U < p_1+p_2+p_3+p_4+p_5+p_6 = .96$, set allocation to 512 bytes and go to step 10.
8. If $U < p_1+p_2+p_3+p_4+p_5+p_6+p_7 = .98$, set allocation to 1024 bytes and go to step 10.
9. Set allocation to 4096 bytes and go to step 10.
10. Stop.

This algorithm is based on being able to generate a uniform random number between 0 and 1. In other words, I must be able to generate a random number that is equally likely to be anywhere between 0 and 1. To do this, I use the following function:

```
double getU()
{
    return(((double)rand())/((double)RAND_MAX));

}/*end getU*/
```

This code invokes the `rand()` function located in the C standard library. The `rand()` function generates what is known as a *pseudorandom* integer in the range 0 to RAND_MAX. A pseudorandom number is one that is generated by a mathematical formula. A well-known formula for creating random integer values is the Linear Congruential Generator (LCG), which makes use of a recursive relationship:

$$x_{n+1} = (ax_n + b) \bmod m \quad \text{for} \quad n = 0, 1, 2, 3, \ldots$$

For example, if we pick $a=5$, $b=3$, $m=16$, and $x_0=3$, we will obtain the following stream of values:

$$x_0 = 3, \; x_1 = 2, \; x_2 = 13, \; x_3 = 4, \; \ldots$$

The value x_0 is known as the *seed*. One thing you should know about LCGs is that they eventually begin to repeat themselves. In general, the constants that are chosen (i.e., a, b, and m) make the difference between a good and a bad LCG. According to Knuth, a good LCG is:

$$(3141592653 x_n + 2718281829) \bmod 2^{35} \qquad x_0 = 0$$

Because the formula allows us to determine what the next number is going to be, the numbers are not truly random. However, the formula guarantees that generated values will be evenly distributed between 0 and RAND_MAX, just like a long series of values that are actually uniformly random. The fact that these formula-based numbers are not really random, in the conventional sense, is what led John Von Neumann to proclaim the following in 1951:

> "Anyone who considers arithmetical methods of producing random digits is, of course, in a state of sin."

NOTE The LCG technique for creating random numbers was discovered by Dick Lehmer in 1949. Lehmer was a prominent figure in the field of computational mathematics during the twentieth century. He was involved with the construction of ENIAC, the first digital computer in the United States, and was also the director of the National Bureau of Standards' Institute for Numerical Analysis.

Testing Methodology

Each memory manager that I implement will be subjected to two tests: a diagnostic test and a performance test.

If you modify any of the source code that I provide, you may want to run the diagnostic test to make sure that everything still operates correctly. The goal of a diagnostic test is to examine the operation of a component, so it will necessarily execute much more slowly than a performance test. Once a memory manager has passed its diagnostic test, it can be barraged with a performance test.

Performance testing will be executed by an instantiation of the `PerformanceTest` class. The class is used as follows:

```
double p[8] = {.15, .20, .35, .20, .02, .04, .02, .02};
unsigned long x[8] = {16,32,64,128,256,512,1024,4096};

struct TestData td;
td.dptr = p;
td.lptr = x;
td.samplesize = 1024;
td.length = 8;
```

```
PerformanceTest pt = PerformanceTest(&td);
printf("milli-seconds=%lu\n",pt.runTest());
```

The `PerformanceTest` class, mentioned in the previous code snippet, has the following implementation:

```
/* --perform.cpp-- */

/*holds setup data to pass to constructor*/

struct TestData
{
    double *dptr;              // probability array
    unsigned long *lptr;       // allocation sizes
    unsigned long samplesize;  // # malloc() calls
    unsigned long length;      // size of arrays
};

class PerformanceTest
{
    public:
    PerformanceTest(struct TestData *tdptr);
    unsigned long runTest();

    private:
    unsigned long nAllocations;  // # of malloc() calls to make
    unsigned long arraySize;     // size of P(x) and x arrays
    double *p;                   // P(x) = probability for X=x
    unsigned long *x;            // X    = # bytes allocated

    double getU();
    unsigned long getRandomVariate();
    void getAllocArray(unsigned long *lptr);
};

PerformanceTest::PerformanceTest(struct TestData *tdptr)
{
    p = (*tdptr).dptr;
    x = (*tdptr).lptr;
    nAllocations = (*tdptr).samplesize;
    arraySize = (*tdptr).length;
    return;

}/*end constructor------------------------------------------------*/


double PerformanceTest::getU()
{
    return(((double)rand())/((double)RAND_MAX));

}/*end getU------------------------------------------------------*/
```

```
unsigned long PerformanceTest::getRandomVariate()
{
    double U;
    unsigned long i;
    double total;

    U = getU();

    for(i=0,total=p[0];i<=arraySize-2;i++)
    {
        if(U<total){ return(x[i]); }
        total = total + p[i+1];
    }

    return(x[arraySize-1]);

    /*
    the above is a cleaner/slower way of doing something like:
    if(U < p[0]){return(x[0]);}
    else if(U <(p[0]+p[1])){return(x[1]);}
    else if(U <(p[0]+p[1]+p[2])){return(x[2]);}
    else if(U <(p[0]+p[1]+p[2]+p[3])){return(x[3]);}
    else if(U <(p[0]+p[1]+p[2]+p[3]+p[4])){return(x[4]);}
    else if(U <(p[0]+p[1]+p[2]+p[3]+p[4]+p[5])){return(x[5]);}
    else if(U <(p[0]+p[1]+p[2]+p[3]+p[4]+p[5]+p[6]))
              {return(x[6]);}
    else{ return(x[7]);}
    */

}/*end getRandomVariate-----------------------------------*/

void PerformanceTest::getAllocArray(unsigned long *lptr)
{
    unsigned long i;

    for(i=0;i<nAllocations;i++)
    {
        lptr[i]=getRandomVariate();
    }

    return;

}/*end getAllocationArray---------------------------------*/

unsigned long PerformanceTest::runTest()
{
    unsigned long *allocs;
    unsigned long i;
    unsigned long ticks1,ticks2;
```

```
    char **addr;      /*pointer to an array of pointers*/

    /*create array of address holders to stockpile
      malloc() returns*/

    addr = (char **)malloc(sizeof(char *)*nAllocations);
    if(addr==NULL)
    {
        printf("could not allocate address repository\n");
        exit(1);
    }

    /*create stream of allocation values*/

    allocs = (unsigned long *)malloc(sizeof(long)*nAllocations);
    if(allocs==NULL)
    {
        printf("could not allocate malloc() request stream\n");
        exit(1);
    }

    getAllocArray(allocs);

    /*start timer and do some work*/

    initMemMgr(1024*1024);

    printf("PerformanceTest::runTest(): time whistle blown\n");

    ticks1 = GetTickCount();

    for(i=0;i<nAllocations;i++)
    {
        addr[i] = (char *)newMalloc(allocs[i]);
        if(addr[i]==NULL)
        {
            printf("mallco()=addr[%lu]=%lu failed\n",i,addr[i]);
            exit(1);
        }
    }

    for(i=0;i<nAllocations;i++)
    {
        newFree(addr[i]);
    }

    ticks2 = GetTickCount();

    printf("PerformanceTest::runTest(): race has ended\n");

    closeMemMgr();
```

```
    free(addr);
    free(allocs);

    return(ticks2-ticks1);

}/*end runTest----------------------------------------------------*/
```

Depending on the source files that I #include, different versions of newMalloc() and newFree() can be used. I can also replace newMalloc()/newFree() with the native malloc()/free() implementations to get a baseline measurement.

You may notice that I defer time measurement until the last possible moment. I don't start measuring clock ticks until the instant directly before the memory allocation calls start occurring. This is because I don't want to include the time that was spent loading the application, constructing input values, and executing shutdown code.

I will admit that my testing code is synthetic, but my crude approach is motivated by a need to keep my discussion limited. You could fill up several books with an explanation and analysis of more sophisticated performance testing methods. Per my initial design goal (keep it simple ... stupid), I have opted for the path of least resistance.

There are a number of industrial-strength benchmark suites that have been built to provide a more accurate picture of how well a processor or application performs. For example, the TOP500 Supercomputer Sites portal (http://www.top500.org) uses the LINPACK Benchmark to rank high-performance installations. The LINPACK Benchmark tests the horsepower of a system by asking it to solve a dense set of linear equations.

SPEC, the Standard Performance Evaluation Corporation, is a nonprofit corporation registered in California that aims to "establish, maintain, and endorse a standardized set of relevant benchmarks that can be applied to the newest generation of high-performance computers" (quoted from SPEC's bylaws; see http://www.spec.org). SPEC basically sells a number of benchmark suites that can be used to collect performance metrics. For example, SPEC sells a CPU2000 V1.2 package that can be used to benchmark processors. SPEC also sells a JVM98 suite to test the performance of Java virtual machines. If you have $1,800 to spare, you can purchase SPEC's MAIL2000 mail server benchmark suite.

Indexing: The General Approach

For the remainder of this chapter, I will introduce three different ways to manage memory with explicit recycling. All of the approaches that I discuss use techniques that fall into the category of indexing schemes, which is to say that they keep track of free and allocated memory using an indexing data structure. What distinguishes the following three techniques is the type of indexing data structure that they use and how they use it. In each case, I will start with an abstract explanation of how the basic mechanism works. Then I will offer a concrete implementation and take it for a test drive. I will end each discussion with an analysis that looks into the benefits and potential disadvantages of each approach.

`malloc()` Version 1: Bitmapped Allocation

Theory

The bit map approach uses an array of bits to keep track of which regions of memory are free and which regions are occupied. Memory is broken up into small plots of real estate, and each bit in the bit map represents one of these plots. This is illustrated in Figure 4.5.

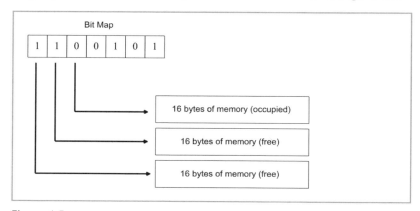

Figure 4.5

The problem with this approach is that the bit map does not indicate how much memory has been allocated for a given region. If you execute a command like

```
my_address = malloc(55);
free(my_address);
```

the bit map will not know how much storage to free because a bit map has no place to record how much storage was allocated. All a bit map can do is tell you which regions of memory are free and which are taken. When you allocate the 55 bytes above, a certain number of bits in the bit map will be cleared. However, once this happens, the bit map cannot tell who owns the region and how much memory they control.

This means that we need to augment the bit map with another data structure that will be able to record how much memory is reserved for each allocation. I decided to use a binary search tree (BST) to serve this purpose. These two data structures — the bit map and the binary search tree — complement each other nicely. The bit map is used during the allocation phase to locate a free memory region, and the BST is used during the release phase to determine how many bits in the bit map to reset.

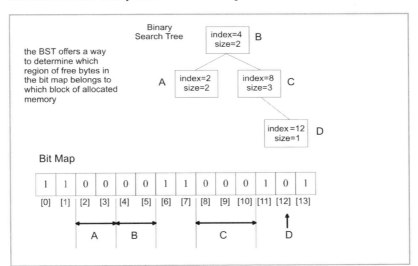

Figure 4.6

NOTE In my implementation, I used a *set* bit (1) to indicate a free region of memory and a *clear* bit (0) to indicate an occupied region of memory. The choice is arbitrary, but it is important to remember this if you are going to understand my bookkeeping.

The best way to prepare you to look at the source is to provide psuedocode for the core memory management algorithms:

```
allocation: ( void * newMalloc(unsigned long size) )
```

1. Translate the number of bytes requested to an equivalent number of bits in the bit map.

2. Look for a run of free bits equal to the value calculated in step 1.
3. If such a run exists, go to step 4; otherwise return NULL.
4. Clear the bits in the bit map to indicate that the associated memory is occupied.
5. Create a BST entry for the allocated memory and insert it into the BST.
6. Return the address of the first byte of the allocated memory.

A *run* of bits in the bit map is just a sequence of consecutively set or clear bits. With regard to allocation, we are interested in runs of bits that are set (i.e., set to 1).

release: (void newFree(void *addr))

1. Take the address supplied and use it to index an entry in the BST.
2. If an entry exists, then go to step 3; otherwise stop.
3. Use the information in the BST entry to set bits in the bit map to the "free" state.

Each BST node represents a region of allocated memory. As such, the nodes contain three vital pieces of information. They store the allocated memory's address in the heap. They also store the allocated memory's starting index in the bit map and the number of bits that are utilized in the bit map. This allows the node to take a call from a function like `newFree()` and map the function's linear address argument to a location in the bit map.

Implementation

The source code implementation of the bit map memory manager is broken up into several files:

Table 4.2

File	Use
driver.cpp	contains `main()`, is the scene of the crime
mallocV1.cpp	`newMalloc()`, `newFree()` wrappers
perform.cpp	implements the `PerformanceTest` class
memmgr.cpp	uses `bitmap.cpp` and `tree.cpp` to institute a policy
bitmap.cpp	implements the bit map
tree.cpp	implements the BST

The `tree.cpp` and `bitmap.cpp` files provide the mechanism side of the memory manager. These files contain fairly neutral implementations of a BST and a bit map. The `MemoryManager` class in `memmgr.cpp` is what brings these two mechanisms together to institute a working policy.

tree.cpp

The BST implementation is fairly generic:

```
/*+++++++++++++++++++++++++++++++++++++++++++++++++++++++++++++++++
+ declarations
+
+++++++++++++++++++++++++++++++++++++++++++++++++++++++++++++++++*/

struct BiNode
{
    unsigned long value;         //linear address
    unsigned long index;         //index into bitmap [0,nbits-1]
    unsigned long nreserved;     //number of bits reserved

    struct BiNode *left;
    struct BiNode *right;
};

class BinarySearchTree
{
    public:
    struct BiNode *root_ptr;

    void insertNode(struct BiNode **link, unsigned long val);
    void insertNode(struct BiNode **link, struct BiNode *ptr);

    struct BiNode* findNode(struct BiNode *link, unsigned
                        long val);

    struct BiNode* deleteSmallestNode(struct BiNode **link);
    void deleteNode(struct BiNode **link, unsigned long val);
    void deleteAll(struct BiNode **link);

    void printTree(struct BiNode *link, int level);
    unsigned long getHeight(struct BiNode *link);

};

/*+++++++++++++++++++++++++++++++++++++++++++++++++++++++++++++++++
+ definitions
+
+++++++++++++++++++++++++++++++++++++++++++++++++++++++++++++++++*/

/*
    given struct Binode **link
```

```
        link  = address of a variable which holds the address
                of the node
        *link  = address of the node
        **link = node
*/

void BinarySearchTree::insertNode(struct BiNode **link,
                                  unsigned long val)
{
    if( *link==NULL )
    {
        (*link) = (struct BiNode*)malloc(sizeof(struct BiNode));
        (*(*link)).value = val;
        (*(*link)).left  = NULL;
        (*(*link)).right = NULL;
        PRINT("insertNode(): inserting %d\n",val);
    }
    else if( val < (*(*link)).value)
    {
        PRINT("insertNode(): moving left\n",val);
        insertNode(&((*(*link)).left),val);
    }
    else
    {
        PRINT("insertNode(): moving right\n",val);
        insertNode(&((*(*link)).right),val);
    }
    return;

}/*end insertNode--------------------------------------------*/

void BinarySearchTree::insertNode(struct BiNode **link, struct
                                  BiNode *ptr)
{
    if( *link==NULL )
    {
        (*link) = (struct BiNode*)malloc(sizeof(struct BiNode));

        (*(*link)).value    = (*ptr).value;
        (*(*link)).index    = (*ptr).index;
        (*(*link)).nreserved = (*ptr).nreserved;

        (*(*link)).left  = NULL;
        (*(*link)).right = NULL;
        PRINT("insertNode(): inserting %d\n",(*ptr).value);
    }
    else if( (*ptr).value < (*(*link)).value)
    {
        PRINT("insertNode(): moving left\n",(*ptr).value);
        insertNode(&((*(*link)).left),ptr);
    }
```

Manual Memory Management

```cpp
    else
    {
        PRINT("insertNode(): moving right\n",(*ptr).value);
        insertNode(&((*(*link)).right),ptr);
    }
    return;

}/*end insertNode-----------------------------------------*/

struct BiNode* BinarySearchTree::findNode
(
    struct BiNode *link,
    unsigned long val
)
{
    if(link==NULL)
    {
        return(NULL);
    }
    else if((*link).value == val)
    {
        return(link);
    }
    else if(val >= (*link).value)
    {
        return(findNode((*link).right,val));
    }
    else
    {
        return(findNode((*link).left,val));
    }

}/*end findNode-------------------------------------------*/

struct BiNode* BinarySearchTree::deleteSmallestNode(struct
              BiNode **link)
{
    if((*(*link)).left != NULL)
    {
        return(deleteSmallestNode(&((*(*link)).left)));
    }
    else
    {
        struct BiNode *temp;
        temp = *link;
        (*link) = (*(*link)).right;
        return(temp);
    }

}/*end deleteSmallestNode---------------------------------*/
```

```
void BinarySearchTree::deleteNode
(
    struct BiNode **link,
    unsigned long val
)
{
    if( (*link)==NULL )
    {
        PRINT("deleteNode(): %d does not exist\n",val);
        return;
    }

    if(val < (*(*link)).value)
    {
        deleteNode(&((*(*link)).left),val);
    }
    else if(val > (*(*link)).value)
    {
        deleteNode(&((*(*link)).right),val);
    }
    else
    {
        /*
        have equality
        3 cases
            i)   node has no children (just delete it)
            ii)  node has one child
            (set parent of current node
              to child of current node, delete current node)
            iii) node has two children/subtrees

            In the third case, get smallest/leftmost node in
            right subtree of current node. Then delete the
            leftmost node and place its value in the current
            node (retain binary tree properties)
        */

        struct BiNode *temp;
        temp = *link;

        if((*(*link)).right==NULL)
        {
            (*link) = (*(*link)).left;
        }
        else if((*(*link)).left==NULL)
        {
            (*link) = (*(*link)).right;
        }
        else
        {
            temp = deleteSmallestNode(&((*(*link)).right));
```

Manual Memory Management

```c
            (*(*link)).value = (*temp).value;
        }

        PRINT("deleteNode(): freeing %d\n",val);
        free(temp);

    }
    return;
}/*end deleteNode-------------------------------------------*/

void BinarySearchTree::deleteAll(struct BiNode **link)
{
    if((*link)==NULL)
    {
        return;
    }
    deleteAll(&((*(*link)).left));
    deleteAll(&((*(*link)).right));

    PRINT("deleteAll(): freeing %d\n",(*(*link)).value);
    free((*link));
    *link=NULL;
    return;

}/*end deleteAll--------------------------------------------*/

void BinarySearchTree::printTree(struct BiNode *link, int level)
{
    int i;
    if(link==NULL)
    {
        return;
    }

    printTree((*link).right,level+1);

    for(i=0;i<level;i++){ printf("-");}
    printf("(%d)\n",(*link).value);

    printTree((*link).left,level+1);
    return;

}/*end printTree--------------------------------------------*/

unsigned long BinarySearchTree::getHeight(struct BiNode *link)
{
    unsigned long u;
    unsigned long v;

    if(link==NULL){ return(-1); }
```

```
        u = getHeight((*link).left);
        v = getHeight((*link).right);

        if(u > v){ return(u+1); }
        else{ return(v+1); }

}/*end getHeight----------------------------------------------*/
```

bitmap.cpp

The `BitMap` class is also fairly straightforward in its implementation and could be reused for something else:

```
/*
1 bitmap bit = 16-byte block of memory
1 bitmap byte (i.e., block) = 128-byte block of memory
*/

#define BYTES_PER_BITMAP_BIT     16
#define BYTES_PER_BITMAP_BYTE    128

/*+++++++++++++++++++++++++++++++++++++++++++++++++++++++++++++++++
+ declarations
+
++++++++++++++++++++++++++++++++++++++++++++++++++++++++++++++++*/

class BitMap
{
    private:
    unsigned char *map;
    unsigned long nbytes;
    unsigned long nbits;

    public:
    BitMap(unsigned long nblocks);
    ~BitMap();
    unsigned long getByteSize();
    void setBits(int val,unsigned long nbits,unsigned long
                 index);
    int getBit(unsigned long index);
    long getBitRun(unsigned long size);
    void printMap();
};


/*+++++++++++++++++++++++++++++++++++++++++++++++++++++++++++++++++
+ definitions
+
++++++++++++++++++++++++++++++++++++++++++++++++++++++++++++++++*/
```

```
BitMap::BitMap(unsigned long nblocks)
{
    unsigned long i;

    map = (unsigned char*)calloc(nblocks,1);
    if(map==NULL)
    {
        printf("BitMap::BitMap():");
        printf("could not allocate bitmap\n");
        exit(1);
    }
    nbytes = nblocks;
    nbits = nbytes*8;

    for(i=0;i<nbytes;i++){ map[i]=0xFF; }

    printf("BitMap::BitMap(): nbytes=%lu",nbytes);
    printf(", nbits=%lu\n",nbits);

    return;

}/*end constructor----------------------------------------------*/

BitMap::~BitMap()
{
    printf("BitMap::~BitMap(): freeing map[%ld]\n",nbytes);
    free(map);
    return;

}/*end destructor-----------------------------------------------*/

unsigned long BitMap::getByteSize()
{
    return(nbytes);

}/*end getByteSize()--------------------------------------------*/

/*
set nbits to val(i.e., 0,1) starting at bit specified by index
*/
void BitMap::setBits
(
    int val,
    unsigned long nbits,
    unsigned long index
)
{
    unsigned long bit;
    unsigned long i,j;
    unsigned char mask;
```

```
    bit=0;

    for(i=0;i<nbytes;i++)
    {
        mask = 1;

        for(j=0;j<8;j++)
        {
            if(bit>=index)
            {
                if(bit==index+nbits){ return; }
                if(val){ map[i]=map[i]|mask; }
                else{ map[i]=map[i]&(~mask); }
            }
            bit++;
            mask = mask*2;
        }
    }
    return;
}/*setBits------------------------------------------------------*/

/*
returns that value of the specified bit (0-nbits-1)
or -1 if index is out of bounds
*/

int BitMap::getBit(unsigned long index)
{
    unsigned long bit;
    unsigned long i,j;
    unsigned char mask;

    bit=0;

    for(i=0;i<nbytes;i++)
    {
        mask = 1;

        for(j=0;j<8;j++)
        {
            if(bit==index)
            {
                if(map[i]&mask){ return(1); }
                else{ return(0); }
            }
            bit++;
            mask = mask*2;
        }
    }
    return(-1);
```

```
}/*getBit----------------------------------------------------*/

/*
returns the index that marks the start of 'size' bits set to 1
or returns -1 if such a run was not found
*/

long BitMap::getBitRun(unsigned long size)
{
    unsigned long current_size;
    unsigned long bit;
    unsigned long i,j;
    unsigned char mask;

    current_size=0;
    bit=0;

    for(i=0;i<nbytes;i++)
    {
        mask = 1;

        for(j=0;j<8;j++)
        {
            if(map[i]&mask)
            {
                current_size++;
                if(current_size==size){ return(bit-size+1); }
            }
            else
            {
                current_size=0;
            }
            bit++;
            mask = mask*2;
        }
    }

    return(-1);

}/*getBitRun--------------------------------------------------*/

void BitMap::printMap()
{
    unsigned long bit;
    unsigned long i,j;
    unsigned char mask;

    bit=0;

    for(i=0;i<nbytes;i++)
```

```
        {
            mask = 1;
            printf("byte[%u]=%x\n",i,map[i]);

            for(j=0;j<8;j++)
            {
                if(map[i]&mask){ printf("1"); }
                else{ printf("0"); }
                bit++;
                mask = mask*2;
            }
            printf("\n\n");
        }
        return;
}/*end printMap----------------------------------------------*/
```

memmgr.cpp

This source file brings the two previous data structures together to form an actual memory manager, known fittingly as the `Memory-Manager` class.

```
/*++++++++++++++++++++++++++++++++++++++++++++++++++++++++++++++
+ declarations
+
++++++++++++++++++++++++++++++++++++++++++++++++++++++++++++++*/

class MemoryManager
{
    private:
    BinarySearchTree bst;
    BitMap *bmap;
    HANDLE handle;              //handle to heap
    unsigned char *mem;         //actual memory to manage
    unsigned long memLength;    //size in bytes of memory

    public:
    MemoryManager(unsigned long totalbytes);
    ~MemoryManager();
    void* allocate(unsigned long nbytes);
    void release(void *ptr);
    void printState();
};


/*++++++++++++++++++++++++++++++++++++++++++++++++++++++++++++++
+ definitions
+
++++++++++++++++++++++++++++++++++++++++++++++++++++++++++++++*/
```

Manual Memory Management

```c
/*
sets the total amount of memory, no re-sizing in this case each
byte in the BitMap represents BYTES_BITMAP_BYTE bytes of memory
*/
MemoryManager::MemoryManager(unsigned long totalbytes)
{
    //init 3 dynamic objects: bmap, bst, mem[]

    bmap = new BitMap((totalbytes/BYTES_PER_BITMAP_BYTE)+1);

    bst.root_ptr=NULL;

    memLength = (*bmap).getByteSize()*BYTES_PER_BITMAP_BYTE;

    handle = GetProcessHeap();
    if(handle==NULL)
    {
        printf("MemoryManager::MemoryManager(): invalid
                handle\n");
        return;
    }

    mem = (unsigned char*)HeapAlloc(handle,HEAP_ZERO_MEMORY,
            memLength);

    //for portability, you could use:
    //mem = (unsigned char*)malloc(memLength);

    if(mem==NULL)
    {
        printf("MemoryManager::MemoryManager():");
        printf("could not alloc memory\n");
        exit(1);
    }
    printf("MemoryManager::MemoryManager():");
    printf("mallloc() mem[%lu]\n",memLength);

    return;

}/*end constructor--------------------------------------------*/

MemoryManager::~MemoryManager()
{
    //release resources for objects: bmap, bst, mem[]

    delete(bmap);

    bst.deleteAll(&(bst.root_ptr));

    if(HeapFree(handle,HEAP_NO_SERIALIZE,mem)==0)
    {
```

```
            printf("MemoryManager::~MemoryManager(): HeapFree()
                    failed\n");
            return;
        }

        //for portability, you could use:
        //free(mem);

        printf("MemoryManager::~MemoryManager():");
        printf("free() mem[%lu]\n",memLength);

        return;

}/*end destructor----------------------------------------------*/

void* MemoryManager::allocate(unsigned long nbytes)
{
        unsigned long run_bits;
        long index;
        struct BiNode node;

        PRINT("MemoryManager::allocate(): request %lu bytes\n",
              nbytes);

        //translate nbytes into # of bits in BitMap

        run_bits = (nbytes/BYTES_PER_BITMAP_BIT)+1;

        PRINT("MemoryManager::allocate(): run_bits=%lu\n",run_bits);

        //look for # of free bits in BitMap

        index = ((*bmap).getBitRun(run_bits));

        PRINT("MemoryManager::allocate(): found run of %lu bits
              ",run_bits);
        PRINT("at %lu\n",index);

        if(index==-1){ return(NULL); }

        //reserved bits in BitMap

        (*bmap).setBits(0,run_bits,index);

        node.value = (unsigned long)(&mem[index*16]);
        node.index = index;
        node.nreserved = run_bits;

        bst.insertNode(&(bst.root_ptr),&node);

        //return memory represented by BitMap bits
```

```
        PRINT("MemoryManager::allocate(): address=%lu\n",&mem
              [index*16]);

        return((void*)&mem[index*16]);
}/*end allocate----------------------------------------------*/

void MemoryManager::release(void *addr)
{
    struct BiNode *ptr;

    ptr = bst.findNode(bst.root_ptr,(unsigned long)addr);
    if(ptr!=NULL)
    {
        PRINT("MemoryManager::release(): addr=%lu\n",(unsigned
              long)addr);
        (*bmap).setBits(1,(*ptr).nreserved,(*ptr).index);
        bst.deleteNode(&(bst.root_ptr),(unsigned long)addr);
    }
    return;

}/*end release-----------------------------------------------*/

void MemoryManager::printState()
{
    printf("------------------------------------------------\n");
    (*bmap).printMap();
    printf("------------------------------------------------\n");
    bst.printTree(bst.root_ptr,0);
    printf("------------------------------------------------\n");
    return;

}/*end printState--------------------------------------------*/
```

mallocV1.cpp

This file supplies wrappers that allow the `MemoryManager` class to be used under the guise of the `newMalloc()` and `newFree()` functions so that existing applications will only have to be slightly modified.

```
#include<stdio.h>
#include<stdlib.h>
#include<windows.h>

// these DEBUG_XXX macros insert printf() statements in the
   final executable
//#define DEBUG_TREE
//#define DEBUG_BITMAP
```

```
//#define DEBUG_MEM_MGR
//#define DEBUG_MALLOCV1

#include<tree.cpp>
#include<bitmap.cpp>
#include<memmgr.cpp>

/*
wrapper functions
*/

MemoryManager *mmptr;

void initMemMgr(unsigned long totalbytes)
{
    mmptr = new MemoryManager(totalbytes);
}

void closeMemMgr()
{
    delete(mmptr);
}

void *newMalloc(unsigned long size)
{
    void *ptr = (*mmptr).allocate(size);

#ifdef DEBUG_MALLOCV1
    (*mmptr).printState();
#endif

    return(ptr);
}

void newFree(void *ptr)
{
    (*mmptr).release(ptr);

#ifdef DEBUG_MALLOCV1
    (*mmptr).printState();
#endif

    return;
}
```

The `DEBUG_XXX` macros, defined at the top of this file insert, activate a set of debugging `printf()` statements in each file. For the performance test run, I commented these macros out so that none of the `printf()` statements made it into the build.

perform.cpp

In addition to the `PerformanceTest` class described earlier, this file also contains the definition of the `PerformanceTestDriver()` function that will be called from `main()`.

```
void PerformanceTestDriver()
{
    double p[8] = {.15, .20, .35, .20, .02, .04, .02, .02};
    unsigned long x[8] = {16,32,64,128,256,512,1024,4096};

    struct TestData td;
    td.dptr = p;
    td.lptr = x;
    td.samplesize = 1024;
    td.length = 8;

    PerformanceTest pt = PerformanceTest(&td);
    printf("msecs=%lu\n",pt.runTest());

    return;
}/*end PerformanceTestDriver----------------------------------*/
```

driver.cpp

This file is where everything comes together. The `main()` function contains a call to `debugTest()` and `PerformanceTestDriver()`. For diagnostic builds, I activate the debug macros in `mallocV1.cpp` and then comment out the `PerformanceTestDriver()` function call. For the build that tests performance, I comment out the debug macros and the `debugTest()` function invocation. The version of `driver.cpp` below is set up to build an executable that runs a performance test.

```
#include<mallocV1.cpp>
#include<perform.cpp>

void debugTest()
{
    void *ptr[10];
    int i;

    initMemMgr(270);

    ptr[0] = newMalloc(8);
    ptr[1] = newMalloc(12);
    ptr[2] = newMalloc(33);
    ptr[3] = newMalloc(1);
    ptr[4] = newMalloc(122);
```

```
    ptr[5] = newMalloc(50);

    for(i=0;i<6;i++){ newFree(ptr[i]); }

    closeMemMgr();
    return;

}/*end debugTest--------------------------------------------------*/

void main()
{
    //for the debug test, should activate debug macros in
    //mallocVx.cpp
    //debugTest();

    //for the performance test, should comment out debug macros
    PerformanceTestDriver();
    return;

}/*end main-------------------------------------------------------*/
```

Tests

I performed two different tests against this memory manager. A debug test was performed to make sure that the manager was doing what it was supposed to do. If you modify my source code, I would suggest running the debug test again to validate your changes. Once I was sure that the memory manager was operational, I turned off debugging features and ran a performance test.

The debug test was performed by executing the code in the `debugTest()` function defined in the `driver.cpp` source file. I keep things fairly simple, but at the same time, I take a good, hard look at what is going on. If you decide to run a debug test, you will want to make sure that the DEBUG_XXX macros in `malloc-V1.cpp` are turned on. You will also want to comment out the `PerformanceTestDriver()` function call in `main()`.

The following output was generated by the debug build of the memory manager. After every allocation and release, I print out the contents of the bit map and the binary search tree. This provides a state snapshot of the memory manager. Also, the bits in each bit map byte read from left to right (which is to say that the lower order bits are on the left-hand side):

```
BitMap::BitMap(): nbytes=3, nbits=24
MemoryManager::MemoryManager():malloc() mem[384]
MemoryManager::allocate(): request 8 bytes
MemoryManager::allocate(): run_bits=1
MemoryManager::allocate(): found run of 1 bits at 0
```

```
insertNode(): inserting 5373964
MemoryManager::allocate(): address=5373964
-----------------------------------------------
byte[0]=fe
01111111
byte[1]=ff
11111111
byte[2]=ff
11111111
-----------------------------------------------
(5373964)
-----------------------------------------------
MemoryManager::allocate(): request 12 bytes
MemoryManager::allocate(): run_bits=1
MemoryManager::allocate(): found run of 1 bits at 1
insertNode(): moving right
insertNode(): inserting 5373980
MemoryManager::allocate(): address=5373980
-----------------------------------------------
byte[0]=fc
00111111
byte[1]=ff
11111111
byte[2]=ff
11111111
-----------------------------------------------
-(5373980)
 (5373964)
-----------------------------------------------
MemoryManager::allocate(): request 33 bytes
MemoryManager::allocate(): run_bits=3
MemoryManager::allocate(): found run of 3 bits at 2
insertNode(): moving right
insertNode(): moving right
insertNode(): inserting 5373996
MemoryManager::allocate(): address=5373996
-----------------------------------------------
byte[0]=e0
00000111
byte[1]=ff
11111111
byte[2]=ff
11111111
-----------------------------------------------
--(5373996)
 -(5373980)
  (5373964)
-----------------------------------------------
MemoryManager::allocate(): request 1 bytes
MemoryManager::allocate(): run_bits=1
MemoryManager::allocate(): found run of 1 bits at 5
```

```
insertNode(): moving right
insertNode(): moving right
insertNode(): moving right
insertNode(): inserting 5374044
MemoryManager::allocate(): address=5374044
------------------------------------------------
byte[0]=c0
00000011
byte[1]=ff
11111111
byte[2]=ff
11111111
------------------------------------------------
---(5374044)
--(5373996)
-(5373980)
(5373964)
------------------------------------------------
MemoryManager::allocate(): request 122 bytes
MemoryManager::allocate(): run_bits=8
MemoryManager::allocate(): found run of 8 bits at 6
insertNode(): moving right
insertNode(): moving right
insertNode(): moving right
insertNode(): moving right
insertNode(): inserting 5374060
MemoryManager::allocate(): address=5374060
------------------------------------------------
byte[0]=0
00000000
byte[1]=c0
00000011
byte[2]=ff
11111111
------------------------------------------------
----(5374060)
---(5374044)
--(5373996)
-(5373980)
(5373964)
------------------------------------------------
MemoryManager::allocate(): request 50 bytes
MemoryManager::allocate(): run_bits=4
MemoryManager::allocate(): found run of 4 bits at 14
insertNode(): moving right
insertNode(): moving right
insertNode(): moving right
insertNode(): moving right
insertNode(): moving right
insertNode(): inserting 5374188
MemoryManager::allocate(): address=5374188
```

```
------------------------------------------
byte[0]=0
00000000
byte[1]=0
00000000
byte[2]=fc
00111111
------------------------------------------
-----(5374188)
----(5374060)
---(5374044)
--(5373996)
-(5373980)
(5373964)
------------------------------------------
MemoryManager::release(): address=5373964
deleteNode(): freeing 5373964
------------------------------------------
byte[0]=1
10000000
byte[1]=0
00000000
byte[2]=fc
00111111
------------------------------------------
----(5374188)
---(5374060)
--(5374044)
-(5373996)
(5373980)
------------------------------------------
MemoryManager::release(): address=5373980
deleteNode(): freeing 5373980
------------------------------------------
byte[0]=3
11000000
byte[1]=0
00000000
byte[2]=fc
00111111
------------------------------------------
---(5374188)
--(5374060)
-(5374044)
(5373996)
------------------------------------------
MemoryManager::release(): address=5373996
deleteNode(): freeing 5373996
------------------------------------------
byte[0]=1f
11111000
```

```
byte[1]=0
0000C000
byte[2]=fc
00111111
-------------------------------------------------
--(5374188)
-(5374060)
(5374044)
-------------------------------------------------
MemoryManager::release(): address=5374044
deleteNode(): freeing 5374044
-------------------------------------------------
byte[0]=3f
11111100
byte[1]=0
00000000
byte[2]=fc
00111111
-------------------------------------------------
-(5374188)
(5374060)
-------------------------------------------------
MemoryManager::release(): address=5374060
deleteNode(): freeing 5374060
-------------------------------------------------
byte[0]=ff
11111111
byte[1]=3f
11111100
byte[2]=fc
00111111
-------------------------------------------------
(5374188)
-------------------------------------------------
MemoryManager::release(): address=5374188
deleteNode(): freeing 5374188
-------------------------------------------------
byte[0]=ff
11111111
byte[1]=ff
11111111
byte[2]=ff
11111111
-------------------------------------------------
-------------------------------------------------
BitMap::~BitMap(): freeing map[3]
MemoryManager::~MemoryManager():free() mem[384]
```

The performance test was nowhere near as extended with regard to the output that it produced. This was primarily because all the debug `printf()` statements had been precluded from the build. Here is the output generated by the performance test build:

```
BitMap::BitMap(): nbytes=8193, nbits=65544
MemoryManager::MemoryManager():malloc() mem[1048704]
PerformanceTest::runTest(): time whistle blown
PerformanceTest::runTest(): race has ended
BitMap::~BitMap(): freeing map[8193]
MemoryManager::~MemoryManager():free() mem[1048704]
msecs=856
```

The most important value is located on the last line of the output. The bitmapped memory manager took 856 milliseconds to allocate and free 1024 regions of memory. This will not mean much until we look at the other memory managers.

Trade-Offs

Bit mapped memory managers have the benefit of providing a straightforward way to organize memory that, depending on the bit-to-memory ratio, can minimize internal fragmentation. Many early operating systems used bit maps to help manage memory because bit maps are fixed in size and thus can be placed outside of the chaos of the kernel's dynamic memory pools. For example, if each bit in a bit map represents 16 bytes of memory, a 512KB bit map will be needed to manage 64MB of memory. Although this doesn't include the storage needed for the associated BST, you can see that the overhead isn't that bad.

On the other hand, finding a run of free bits in a bit map means that you may have to traverse the entire set of bits to find what you are looking for (assuming that you do find it). This mandatory searching makes allocation very expensive in terms of execution time.

If I had to improve this code, I would replace the binary search tree with a tree data structure that is guaranteed to be well-balanced. As you can see from the debug output, the binary tree that was formed was worst-case unbalanced (and that's an understatement). This is more a function of the request stream than of anything else.

I would also tackle the code in the `BitMap` class that traverses the bit map data structure. Most of my `BitMap` member function implementations are based on brute force iteration. There are some circumstances where I could skip needless iteration by being a little more skillful with implied starting points. For example, it is obvious that the 18th bit will be in the third byte of the bit map, so there is no need to cycle through the first two bytes of the map.

Finally, another weak point of my implementation is that it cannot grow. The memory manager described in this section starts off with a fixed amount of heap memory, and that is all that it gets. A production-quality memory manager would be able to increase its pool of storage by making a request to the underlying operating system.

malloc() Version 2: Sequential Fit

Back in the early 1990s, I was experimenting with DOS in an effort to see how malloc() and free() were implemented by Borland's Turbo C libraries.

Here is the program that I used:

```
#include<stdio.h>
#include<stdlib.h>

void main()
{
    void *ptr[5];
    int i;
    for(i=0;i<5;i++)
    {
        ptr[i]=malloc(32);
        printf("%p\n",ptr[i]);
    }
    for(i=0;i<5;i++)
    {
        free(ptr[i]);
    }
    return;
}
```

I compiled this using the following command line: C:\dos> tcc -mh dmalloc.c.

I specified a "huge" memory model (via the -mh option) so that addresses would be specified in the segment:offset real mode format.

This program produced the following output while running on DOS:

```
193B:0004    ( physical address 193B4 )
193E:0004    ( physical address 193E4 )
1941:0004    ( physical address 19414 )
1944:0004    ( physical address 19444 )
1947:0004    ( physical address 19474 )
```

As you can see, the libraries give each allocation its own 48-bit block. It is more than likely that the extra 16 bytes is used by the

Turbo C `malloc()` and `free()` libraries to link the regions of memory together into a linked list. This is a key feature of the sequential fit approach to memory management.

Theory

The sequential fit technique organizes memory into a linear linked list of free and reserved regions (see Figure 4.7). When an allocation request occurs, the memory manager moves sequentially through the list until it finds a free block of memory that can service/fit the request (hence the name "sequential fit").

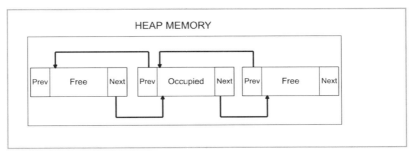

Figure 4.7

Typically, an external data structure is not needed because portions of the allocated memory are reserved so that the memory being managed can index itself. Logically, the blocks of memory are arranged as in Figure 4.7. However, the actual organization of each block, be it free or reserved, in my implementation is specified by Figure 4.8.

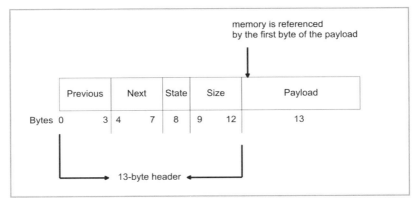

Figure 4.8

The scheme for allocation is pretty simple; the memory manager simply traverses the linked list of memory blocks until it reaches a free block that is big enough to satisfy the request. If the free block is much larger than the memory request, it will split the free block into two pieces. One part of the split block will be used to service the request, and the other part will remain free to service other requests for memory (see Figure 4.9).

Figure 4.9

The algorithm for releasing blocks of memory requires adjacent blocks of free memory to be merged. This is where the real work occurs. For a block situated between two other blocks, there are basically four different scenarios that are possible (see Figure 4.10).

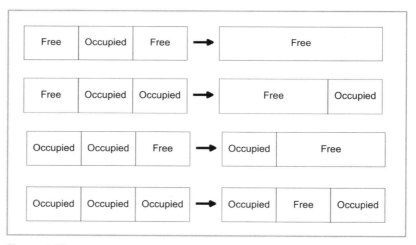

Figure 4.10

The trick is to be able to reassign the NEXT and PREVIOUS pointers, shown in Figure 4.7, correctly. If both blocks on either side of a freed block are occupied, no pointer manipulation needs to be performed. However, if one or both of the adjacent blocks is free, blocks of memory will need to be merged.

The best way to understand this is visually. Figure 4.11 shows an example of the pointer manipulation that needs to be performed in order to merge two adjacent blocks.

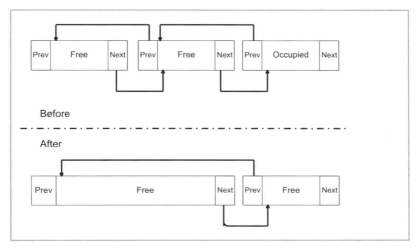

Figure 4.11

For a rigorous explanation of how memory block merging works, read the source code of the `SequentialFitMemoryManager` class.

Implementation

Because storage space in the heap is used to help organize heap memory, the sequential fit memory manager implementation is not as prolific as the bit map-based manager. My implementation requires only four files:

Table 4.3

File	Use
`driver.cpp`	contains `main()`, is the scene of the crime
`mallocV2.cpp`	`newMalloc()`, `newFree()` wrappers (2nd version)
`perform.cpp`	implements the `PerformanceTest` class
`memmgr.cpp`	implements the `SequentialFitMemoryManager` class

memmgr.cpp

The majority of the real work is performed by the class defined in this file. The `SequentialFitMemoryManager` class takes care of allocating heap storage from Windows and managing it. Both the allocation and release functions have secondary private helper routines. The allocation function uses a helper function to split free blocks. The release function calls a helper function to perform the actual merging of free memory blocks.

```c
#ifdef   DEBUG_SF_MEM_MGR
#define MSG0(arg);              printf(arg);
#define MSG1(arg1,arg2);        printf(arg1,arg2);
#else
#define MSG0(arg);
#define MSG1(arg1,arg2);
#endif

#define U1 unsigned char
#define U4 unsigned long

/*
    list element format
                |0   3||4   7||  8  ||9 12||13 .. n|
                [PREV][NEXT][STATE][SIZE][payload]
                  U4    U4    U1     U4     ?

    byte allocated/freed is address of first byte of payload
    header = 13 bytes

    byte[0] is occupied by header data, so is always used, thus
            first link has prev=0 ( 0 indicates not used )
            last link has next=0
*/

#define PREV(i)         (*((U4*)(&ram[i-13])))
#define NEXT(i)         (*((U4*)(&ram[i-9])))
#define STATE(i)        (*((U1*)(&ram[i-5])))   /*FREE,OCCUPIED*/
#define SIZE(i)         (*((U4*)(&ram[i-4])))

#define FREE            0
#define OCCUPIED        1
char *stateStr[3]={"FREE","OCCUPIED"};

#define START       13      /*address of first payload*/
#define SZ_HEADER   13

class SequentialFitMemoryManager
{
    private:
    HANDLE handle;
    U1  *ram;    /*memory storage*/
    U4  size;

    void split(U4 addr,U4 nbytes);
    void merge(U4 prev,U4 current,U4 next);

    public:

    SequentialFitMemoryManager(U4 nbytes);
    ~SequentialFitMemoryManager();
```

```
    void*allocate(U4 nbytes);
    void release(void* addr);
    void printState();
};

SequentialFitMemoryManager::SequentialFitMemoryManager(U4
          nbytes)
{
    handle = GetProcessHeap();
    if(handle==NULL)
    {
        printf("SequentialFitMemoryManager::");
        printf("SequentialFitMemoryManager():");
        printf("invalid handle\n");
        exit(1);
    }

    ram = (U1*)HeapAlloc(handle,HEAP_ZERO_MEMORY,nbytes);

    //for portability, you could use:
    //ram = (unsigned char*)malloc(nbytes);


    size = nbytes;

    if(size<=SZ_HEADER)
    {
        printf("SequentialFitMemoryManager::");
        printf("SequentialFitMemoryManager():");
        printf("not enough memory fed to constructor\n");
        exit(1);
    }

    PREV(START)=0;
    NEXT(START)=0;
    STATE(START)=FREE;
    SIZE(START)=size-SZ_HEADER;

    MSG0("SequentialFitMemoryManager::");
    MSG1("SequentialFitMemoryManager(%lu)\n",nbytes);

    return;

}/*end constructor----------------------------------------------*/

SequentialFitMemoryManager::~SequentialFitMemoryManager()
{
    if(HeapFree(handle,HEAP_NO_SERIALIZE,ram)==0)
    {
        printf("SequentialFitMemoryManager::");
```

```
        printf("~SequentialFitMemoryManager():");
        printf("could not free heap storage\n");
        return;
    }

    //for portability, you could use:
    //free(ram);

    MSG0("SequentialFitMemoryManager::");
    MSG0("~SequentialFitMemoryManager()");
    MSG1("free ram[%lu]\n",size);
    return;

}/*end destructor----------------------------------------------*/

/*
U4 nbytes    -    number of bytes required
returns address of first byte of memory region allocated
( or NULL if cannot allocate a large enough block )
*/

void* SequentialFitMemoryManager::allocate(U4 nbytes)
{
    U4 current;

    MSG0("SequentialFitMemoryManager::");
    MSG1("allocate(%lu)\n",nbytes);

    if(nbytes==0)
    {
        MSG0("SequentialFitMemoryManager::");
        MSG0("allocate(): zero bytes requested\n");
        return(NULL);
    }

    //traverse the linked list, starting with first element

    current = START;
    while(NEXT(current)!=0)
    {
        if((SIZE(current)>=nbytes)&&(STATE(current)==FREE))
        {
            split(current,nbytes);
            return((void*)&ram[current]);
        }
        current = NEXT(current);
    }

    //handle the last block ( which has NEXT(current)=0 )

    if((SIZE(current)>=nbytes)&&(STATE(current)==FREE))
```

Manual Memory Management

```
    {
        split(current,nbytes);
        return((void*)&ram[current]);
    }

    return(NULL);

}/*end allocation-------------------------------------------*/

/*
breaks [free] region into [alloc][free] pair, if possible
*/

void SequentialFitMemoryManager::split(U4 addr, U4 nbytes)
{
    /*
    want payload to have enough room for
    nbytes = size of request
    SZ_HEADER = header for new region
    SZ_HEADER = payload for new region (arbitrary 13 bytes)
    */

    if(SIZE(addr)>= nbytes+SZ_HEADER+SZ_HEADER)
    {
        U4 oldnext;
        U4 oldprev;
        U4 oldsize;

        U4 newaddr;

        MSG0("SequentialFitMemoryManager::");
        MSG0("split(): split=YES\n");

        oldnext=NEXT(addr);
        oldprev=PREV(addr);
        oldsize=SIZE(addr);

        newaddr = addr + nbytes + SZ_HEADER;

        NEXT(addr)=newaddr;
        PREV(addr)=oldprev;
        STATE(addr)=OCCUPIED;
        SIZE(addr)=nbytes;

        NEXT(newaddr)=oldnext;
        PREV(newaddr)=addr;
        STATE(newaddr)=FREE;
        SIZE(newaddr)=oldsize-nbytes-SZ_HEADER;
    }
    else
    {
```

```
            MSG0("SequentialFitMemoryManager::");
            MSG0("split(): split=NO\n");
            STATE(addr)=OCCUPIED;
        }
        return;

}/*end split-------------------------------------------------*/

void SequentialFitMemoryManager::release(void *addr)
{
    U4 free;     //index into ram[]

    if(addr==NULL)
    {
        MSG0("SequentialFitMemoryManager::");
        MSG0("release(): cannot release NULL pointer\n");
        return;
    }

    MSG0("SequentialFitMemoryManager::");
    MSG1("release(%lu)\n",addr);

    //perform sanity check to make sure address is kosher

    if( (addr>= (void*)&ram[size]) || (addr< (void*)&ram[0]) )
    {
        MSG0("SequentialFitMemoryManager::");
        MSG0("release(): address out of bounds\n");
        return;
    }

    //translate void* addr to index in ram[]

    free = (U4)( ((U1*)addr) - &ram[0] );

    MSG0("SequentialFitMemoryManager::");
    MSG1("address resolves to index %lu\n",free);

    //a header always occupies first 13 bytes of storage

    if(free<13)
    {
        MSG0("SequentialFitMemoryManager::");
        MSG0("release(): address in first 13 bytes\n");
        return;
    }

    //yet more sanity checks

    if((STATE(free)!=OCCUPIED)      ||   //region if free
```

```
        (PREV(free)>=free)   ||   //previous element not previous
        (NEXT(free)>=size)   ||   //next is beyond the end
        (SIZE(free)>=size)   ||   //size region greater than whole
        (SIZE(free)==0))          //no size at all
    {
        MSG0("SequentialFitMemoryManager::");
        MSG0("release(): referencing invalid region\n");
        return;
    }

    merge(PREV(free),free,NEXT(free));

    return;

}/*end release----------------------------------------------------*/

/*
        4 cases ( F=free O=occupied )
            FOF -> [F]
            OOF -> O[F]
            FOO -> [F]O
            OOO -> OFO
*/

void SequentialFitMemoryManager::merge(U4 prev,U4 current,U4
            next)
{
    /*
    first handle special cases of region at end(s)
    prev=0                          low end
    next=0                          high end
    prev=0 and next=0       only 1 list element
    */

    if(prev==0)
    {
        if(next==0)
        {
            STATE(current)=FREE;
        }
        else if(STATE(next)==OCCUPIED)
        {
            STATE(current)=FREE;
        }
        else if(STATE(next)==FREE)
        {
            U4 temp;

            MSG0("SequentialFitMemoryManager::merge():");
            MSG0("merging to NEXT\n");
```

```cpp
            STATE(current)=FREE;
            SIZE(current)=SIZE(current)+SIZE(next)+SZ_HEADER;
            NEXT(current)=NEXT(next);

            temp = NEXT(next);
            PREV(temp)=current;
        }
    }
    else if(next==0)
    {
        if(STATE(prev)==OCCUPIED)
        {
            STATE(current)=FREE;
        }
        else if(STATE(prev)==FREE)
        {
            MSG0("SequentialFitMemoryManager::merge():");
            MSG0("merging to PREV\n");
            SIZE(prev)=SIZE(prev)+SIZE(current)+SZ_HEADER;
            NEXT(prev)=NEXT(current);
        }
    }

    /* now we handle 4 cases */

    else if((STATE(prev)==OCCUPIED)&&(STATE(next)==OCCUPIED))
    {
        STATE(current)=FREE;
    }
    else if((STATE(prev)==OCCUPIED)&&(STATE(next)==FREE))
    {
        U4 temp;

        MSG0("SequentialFitMemoryManager::merge():");
        MSG0("merging to NEXT\n");
        STATE(current)=FREE;
        SIZE(current)=SIZE(current)+SIZE(next)+SZ_HEADER;
        NEXT(current)=NEXT(next);

        temp = NEXT(next);
        if(temp!=0){ PREV(temp)=current; }
    }
    else if((STATE(prev)==FREE)&&(STATE(next)==OCCUPIED))
    {
        MSG0("SequentialFitMemoryManager::merge():");
        MSG0("merging to PREV\n");
        SIZE(prev)=SIZE(prev)+SIZE(current)+SZ_HEADER;
        NEXT(prev)=NEXT(current);
        PREV(next)=prev;
    }
    else if((STATE(prev)==FREE)&&(STATE(next)==FREE))
```

```
    {
        U4 temp;

        MSG0("SequentialFitMemoryManager::merge():");
        MSG0("merging with both sides\n");
        SIZE(prev)=SIZE(prev)+
                    SIZE(current)+SZ_HEADER+
                    SIZE(next)+SZ_HEADER;
        NEXT(prev)=NEXT(next);

        temp = NEXT(next);
        if(temp!=0){ PREV(temp)=prev; }
    }

    return;

}/*end merge---------------------------------------------------------*/

void SequentialFitMemoryManager::printState()
{
    U4 i;
    U4 current;

    i=0;
    current=START;

    while(NEXT(current)!=0)
    {
        printf("%lu) [P=%lu]",i,PREV(current));
        printf("[addr=%lu]",current);
        printf("[St=%s]",stateStr[STATE(current)]);
        printf("[Sz=%lu]",SIZE(current));
        printf("[N=%lu]\n",NEXT(current));
        current = NEXT(current);
        i++;
    }

    //print the last list element

    printf("%lu) [P=%lu]",i,PREV(current));
    printf("[addr=%lu]",current);
    printf("[St=%s]",stateStr[STATE(current)]);
    printf("[Sz=%lu]",SIZE(current));
    printf("[N=%lu]\n",NEXT(current));

    return;

}/*end printState----------------------------------------------------*/
```

mallocV2.cpp

There were several minor alterations to this file, most notably the presence of a different set of debugging macros. To activate debugging code, uncomment the macros and compile a new build.

```cpp
#include<stdio.h>
#include<stdlib.h>
#include<windows.h>

//#define DEBUG_SF_MEM_MGR
//#define DEBUG_MALLOCV2

#include<memmgr.cpp>

/*
wrapper functions
*/

SequentialFitMemoryManager *mmptr;

void initMemMgr(unsigned long totalbytes)
{
    mmptr = new SequentialFitMemoryManager(totalbytes);
}

void closeMemMgr()
{
    delete(mmptr);
}

void *newMalloc(unsigned long size)
{
    void *ptr = (*mmptr).allocate(size);

#ifdef DEBUG_MALLOCV2
    (*mmptr).printState();
#endif

    return(ptr);
}
void newFree(void *ptr)
{
    (*mmptr).release(ptr);

#ifdef DEBUG_MALLOCV2
    (*mmptr).printState();
#endif

    return;
}
```

driver.cpp

As in the last example, this file contains the main() function definition that invokes the testing code. The debugTest() was completely rewritten for this implementation. The PerformanceTestDriver() function, defined in perform.cpp that makes use of the PerformanceTest class, has been left untouched.

```cpp
#include<mallocV2.cpp>
#include<perform.cpp>

void debugTest()
{
    void *ptr[6];
    unsigned long allocs[6]={8,12,33,1,122,50};
    int i;

    initMemMgr(270);

    for(i=0;i<6;i++)
    {
        ptr[i] = newMalloc(allocs[i]);
        if(ptr[i]==NULL){ printf("ptr[%lu]==NULL!\n",i); }
    }

    printf("\n\nFREE MEMORY-------------------------------\n\n");

    newFree(ptr[0]);     //8
    newFree(ptr[3]);     //1
    newFree(ptr[4]);     //122
    newFree(ptr[2]);     //33
    newFree(ptr[1]);     //12
    newFree(ptr[5]);     //50

    closeMemMgr();
    return;
}/*end debugTest----------------------------------------*/

void main()
{
    //for the debug test, should activate debug macros in
      mallocVx.cpp
    //debugTest();
    //for the performance test, should comment out debug macros
    PerformanceTestDriver();
    return;
}/*end main--------------------------------------------*/
```

Tests

If you look at the main() function defined in driver.cpp, you will see that I performed both a debug test and a performance test. I performed a debug test to make sure that the manager was doing what it was supposed to do. If you modify my source code, I would suggest running the debug test again to validate your changes. Once I was sure that the memory manager was operational, I turned off debugging features and ran a performance test.

The debug test is fairly simple, but at the same time, I would take a good, hard look at what is going on. If you decide to run a debug test, you will want to make sure that the DEBUG_XXX macros in mallocV2.cpp are turned on. You will also want to comment out the PerformanceTestDriver() function call in main().

The following output was generated by the debug build of the memory manager:

```
SequentialFitMemoryManager::SequentialFitMemoryManager(270)
SequentialFitMemoryManager::allocate(8)
SequentialFitMemoryManager::split(): split=YES
0)  [P=0][addr=13][St=OCCUPIED][Sz=8][N=34]
1)  [P=13][addr=34][St=FREE][Sz=236][N=0]
SequentialFitMemoryManager::allocate(12)
SequentialFitMemoryManager::split(): split=YES
0)  [P=0][addr=13][St=OCCUPIED][Sz=8][N=34]
1)  [P=13][addr=34][St=OCCUPIED][Sz=12][N=59]
2)  [P=34][addr=59][St=FREE][Sz=211][N=0]
SequentialFitMemoryManager::allocate(33)
SequentialFitMemoryManager::split(): split=YES
0)  [P=0][addr=13][St=OCCUPIED][Sz=8][N=34]
1)  [P=13][addr=34][St=OCCUPIED][Sz=12][N=59]
2)  [P=34][addr=59][St=OCCUPIED][Sz=33][N=105]
3)  [P=59][addr=105][St=FREE][Sz=165][N=0]
SequentialFitMemoryManager::allocate(1)
SequentialFitMemoryManager::split(): split=YES
0)  [P=0][addr=13][St=OCCUPIED][Sz=8][N=34]
1)  [P=13][addr=34][St=OCCUPIED][Sz=12][N=59]
2)  [P=34][addr=59][St=OCCUPIED][Sz=33][N=105]
3)  [P=59][addr=105][St=OCCUPIED][Sz=1][N=119]
4)  [P=105][addr=119][St=FREE][Sz=151][N=0]
SequentialFitMemoryManager::allocate(122)
SequentialFitMemoryManager::split(): split=YES
0)  [P=0][addr=13][St=OCCUPIED][Sz=8][N=34]
1)  [P=13][addr=34][St=OCCUPIED][Sz=12][N=59]
2)  [P=34][addr=59][St=OCCUPIED][Sz=33][N=105]
3)  [P=59][addr=105][St=OCCUPIED][Sz=1][N=119]
4)  [P=105][addr=119][St=OCCUPIED][Sz=122][N=254]
5)  [P=119][addr=254][St=FREE][Sz=16][N=0]
SequentialFitMemoryManager::allocate(50)
```

```
0)  [P=0][addr=13][St=OCCUPIED][Sz=8][N=34]
1)  [P=13][addr=34][St=OCCUPIED][Sz=12][N=59]
2)  [P=34][addr=59][St=OCCUPIED][Sz=33][N=105]
3)  [P=59][addr=105][St=OCCUPIED][Sz=1][N=119]
4)  [P=105][addr=119][St=OCCUPIED][Sz=122][N=254]
5)  [P=119][addr=254][St=FREE][Sz=16][N=0]
ptr[5]==NULL!


FREE MEMORY--------------------------------------

SequentialFitMemoryManager::release(5439513)
SequentialFitMemoryManager::address resolves to index 13
0)  [P=0][addr=13][St=FREE][Sz=8][N=34]
1)  [P=13][addr=34][St=OCCUPIED][Sz=12][N=59]
2)  [P=34][addr=59][St=OCCUPIED][Sz=33][N=105]
3)  [P=59][addr=105][St=OCCUPIED][Sz=1][N=119]
4)  [P=105][addr=119][St=OCCUPIED][Sz=122][N=254]
5)  [P=119][addr=254][St=FREE][Sz=16][N=0]
SequentialFitMemoryManager::release(5439605)
SequentialFitMemoryManager::address resolves to index 105
0)  [P=0][addr=13][St=FREE][Sz=8][N=34]
1)  [P=13][addr=34][St=OCCUPIED][Sz=12][N=59]
2)  [P=34][addr=59][St=OCCUPIED][Sz=33][N=105]
3)  [P=59][addr=105][St=FREE][Sz=1][N=119]
4)  [P=105][addr=119][St=OCCUPIED][Sz=122][N=254]
5)  [P=119][addr=254][St=FREE][Sz=16][N=0]
SequentialFitMemoryManager::release(5439619)
SequentialFitMemoryManager::address resolves to index 119
SequentialFitMemoryManager::merge():merging with both sides
0)  [P=0][addr=13][St=FREE][Sz=8][N=34]
1)  [P=13][addr=34][St=OCCUPIED][Sz=12][N=59]
2)  [P=34][addr=59][St=OCCUPIED][Sz=33][N=105]
3)  [P=59][addr=105][St=FREE][Sz=165][N=0]
SequentialFitMemoryManager::release(5439559)
SequentialFitMemoryManager::address resolves to index 59
SequentialFitMemoryManager::merge():merging to NEXT
0)  [P=0][addr=13][St=FREE][Sz=8][N=34]
1)  [P=13][addr=34][St=OCCUPIED][Sz=12][N=59]
2)  [P=34][addr=59][St=FREE][Sz=211][N=0]
SequentialFitMemoryManager::release(5439534)
SequentialFitMemoryManager::address resolves to index 34
SequentialFitMemoryManager::merge():merging with both sides
0)  [P=0][addr=13][St=FREE][Sz=257][N=0]
SequentialFitMemoryManager::release(): cannot release NULL
pointer
0)  [P=0][addr=13][St=FREE][Sz=257][N=0]
SequentialFitMemoryManager::~SequentialFitMemoryManager()free
ram[270]
```

Although it may seem a tad tedious, it will help you tremendously to read the `debugTest()` function and then step through the previous output. It will give you an insight into what the code is doing and how the particulars are implemented.

The performance test was conducted by commenting out `debugTest()` and the debug macros in `mallocV2.cpp`, and then enabling the `PerformanceTestDriver()` function. The results of the performance run were interesting:

```
PerformanceTest::runTest(): time whistle blown
PerformanceTest::runTest(): race has ended
msecs=35
```

As you can see, the performance increase is dramatic.

Trade-Offs

The sequential fit approach solves many of the problems that plagued the bitmapped approach by using an indexing scheme that decreased redundant effort. Instead of manually sifting through each bit in a bit map, we were able to use a series of pointers to find what we needed much more quickly.

While the sequential fit technique did exhibit far better performance than the bit map technique, we were only using a 270-byte heap. For much larger heaps, such as a 15MB heap, the amount of time needed to traverse a sequential linked list from beginning to end can hurt performance. Thus, the sequential fit method is not exactly a scalable solution.

In terms of choosing a memory block to allocate, I use what is known as the *first-fit policy*, which is to say that my implementation uses the first satisfactory block of memory that it finds. There are other policies, like next-fit, best-fit, and worst-fit.

The first-fit policy tends to cause the blocks of memory at the start of the linked list to splinter into a number of smaller blocks. Given that the sequential fit algorithm traverses the list starting from the beginning during an allocation, this can hurt execution time.

The *next-fit* policy is like the first-fit policy, but the memory manager keeps track of the position of the last allocation. When the next allocation request is processed, the manager will start traversing the linked list from the point of the last allocation. This is done in an attempt to avoid re-traversing the beginning of the list.

The *best-fit* policy traverses the linked list of memory blocks and uses the smallest possible block that will satisfy an allocation request. The best-fit approach does not waste memory and minimizes internal fragmentation. In doing so, however, the policy tends to generate significant external fragmentation. The search for a "best" block can also be expensive in terms of execution time because several possible blocks may have to be located and compared.

The *worst-fit* policy is instituted by having the memory manager allocate the largest possible memory block for a given request. This policy aims at minimizing external fragmentation. It also does a good job of eliminating large memory blocks so that the memory manager will fail when a request for a large block is submitted.

`malloc()` **Version 3: Segregated Lists**

Theory

With the sequential fit approach, we spent a lot of effort in terms of splitting and merging blocks of memory. The segregated lists approach attempts to sidestep this problem by keeping several lists of fixed-sized memory blocks. In other words, the heap storage is segregated into groups of blocks based on their size. If you need a 32-byte block, query the appropriate list for free space instead of traversing the entire heap.

In my segregated list implementation, I break memory into 6,136-byte rows, where each row consists of eight different blocks of memory. This is illustrated in Figure 4.12. The size of the first element in each row is 16 bytes, and the size of the last element in each row is 4,096 bytes.

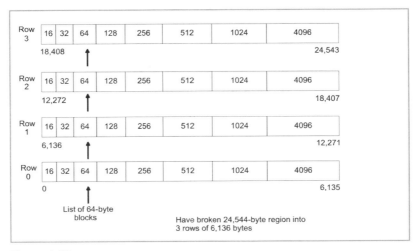

Figure 4.12

Because the list elements are fixed in size, and their positions are known, we do not need the PREVIOUS, FREE, and SIZE header fields that were used in the sequential fit scheme. However, we do need the STATE header field. This causes every plot of real estate in memory to be prefixed by a header that is a single byte in size.

Each 6,136-byte row of memory contains eight memory blocks that increase in size (see Figure 4.13). Given that rows are stacked on top of each other in memory, as displayed in Figure 4.12, to get to the next element of a specific size, take the index of a given element and add 6,136 to it.

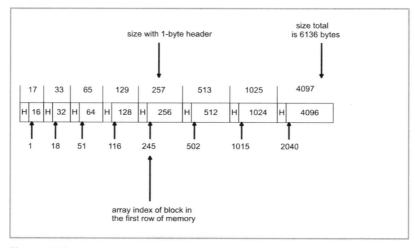

Figure 4.13

Implementation

The implementation of the segregated memory manager closely mirrors the implementation of the sequential fit manager:

Table 4.4

File	Use
driver.cpp	contains main(), is the scene of the crime
mallocV3.cpp	newMalloc(), newFree() wrappers (3rd version)
perform.cpp	implements the PerformanceTest class
memmgr.cpp	implements the SegregatedMemoryManager class

The only files that I had to modify were the mallocV3.cpp file and the memmgr.cpp file.

memmgr.cpp

The majority of the real work is performed by the class defined in this file. The `SegregatedMemoryManager` class takes care of allocating heap storage from Windows and managing it. The allocation function uses a helper function to search through the free lists. The release function does everything by itself.

```
#ifdef   DEBUG_SL_MEM_MGR
#define MSG0(arg);              printf(arg);
#define MSG1(arg1,arg2);        printf(arg1,arg2);
#else
#define MSG0(arg);
#define MSG1(arg1,arg2);
#endif

#define U1 unsigned char
#define U4 unsigned long

/*
    list element format
                |0|   |1 .. n|
             [STATE][payload]
                U1      ?

    byte allocated/freed is address of first byte of payload
    header = 1 bytes
*/

#define STATE(i)     (*((U1*)(&ram[i-1])))    /*FREE,OCCUPIED*/

#define FREE                    0
#define OCCUPIED                1
char *stateStr[3]={"FREE","OCCUPIED"};

#define STATE16      1        /*index of first 16-byte payload*/
#define START32      18       /*index of first 16-byte payload*/
#define START64      51       /*index of first 16-byte payload*/
#define START128     116      /*index of first 16-byte payload*/
#define START256     245      /*index of first 16-byte payload*/
#define START512     502      /*index of first 16-byte payload*/
#define START1024    1015     /*index of first 16-byte payload*/
#define START4096    2040     /*index of first 16-byte payload*/

#define SZ_ROW       6136     /*size of a row of entries in table*/


class SegregatedMemoryManager
{
    private:
```

```
    HANDLE handle;
    U1   *ram;          /*memory storage*/
    U4   size;          /*# bytes*/
    U4   nrows;         /*# of 6136 byte rows*/

    void initColumn(U4 index);
    U4 searchColumn(U4 index);
    void printColumn(U4 index);

    public:

    SegregatedMemoryManager(U4 nbytes);
    ~SegregatedMemoryManager();

    void*allocate(U4 nbytes);
    void release(void* addr);
    void printState();
};

SegregatedMemoryManager::SegregatedMemoryManager(U4 nbytes)
{
    handle = GetProcessHeap();
    if(handle==NULL)
    {
        printf("SegregatedMemoryManager::");
        printf("SegregatedMemoryManager():");
        printf("invalid handle\n");
        exit(1);
    }

    ram = (U1*)HeapAlloc(handle,HEAP_ZERO_MEMORY,nbytes);

    //for portability, you could use:
    //ram = (unsigned char*)malloc(nbytes);


    size = nbytes;

    if(size<SZ_ROW)
    {
        printf("SegregatedMemoryManager::");
        printf("SegregatedMemoryManager():");
        printf("not enough memory fed to constructor\n");
        exit(1);
    }

    nrows = size/SZ_ROW;

    initColumn(START16);
    initColumn(START32);
    initColumn(START64);
```

```
    initColumn(START128);
    initColumn(START256);
    initColumn(START512);
    initColumn(START1024);
    initColumn(START4096);

    MSG0("SegregatedMemoryManager::");
    MSG1("SegregatedMemoryManager(%lu)\n",nbytes);

    return;

}/*end constructor-----------------------------------------*/

void SegregatedMemoryManager::initColumn(U4 index)
{
    U4 i;
    for(i=0;i<nrows;i++)
    {
        STATE(index)=FREE;
        index = index + SZ_ROW;
    }
    return;

}/*end initColumn------------------------------------------*/

SegregatedMemoryManager::~SegregatedMemoryManager()
{
    if(HeapFree(handle,HEAP_NO_SERIALIZE,ram)==0)
    {
        printf("SegregatedMemoryManager::");
        printf("~SegregatedMemoryManager():");
        printf("could not free heap storage\n");
        return;
    }

    //for portability, you could use:
    //free(ram);

    MSG0("SegregatedMemoryManager::");
    MSG0("~SegregatedFitMemoryManager()");
    MSG1("free ram[%lu]\n",size);
    return;

}/*end destructor------------------------------------------*/
/*
U4 nbytes    -    number of bytes required
returns address of first byte of memory region allocated
( or NULL if cannot allocate a large enough block )
*/
```

```
void* SegregatedMemoryManager::allocate(U4 nbytes)
{
    U4 index;

    MSG0("SegregatedMemoryManager::");
    MSG1("allocate(%lu)\n",nbytes);

    if(nbytes==0)
    {
        MSG0("SegregatedMemoryManager::");
        MSG0("allocate(): zero bytes requested\n");
        return(NULL);
    }

    if(nbytes<=16)
    {
        index = searchColumn(START16);
        if(index){ return((void*)&ram[index]); }
        index = searchColumn(START32);
        if(index){ return((void*)&ram[index]); }
        index = searchColumn(START64);
        if(index){ return((void*)&ram[index]); }
        index = searchColumn(START128);
        if(index){ return((void*)&ram[index]); }
        index = searchColumn(START256);
        if(index){ return((void*)&ram[index]); }
        index = searchColumn(START512);
        if(index){ return((void*)&ram[index]); }
        index = searchColumn(START1024);
        if(index){ return((void*)&ram[index]); }
        index = searchColumn(START4096);
        if(index){ return((void*)&ram[index]); }
    }
    else if(nbytes<=32)
    {
        index = searchColumn(START32);
        if(index){ return((void*)&ram[index]); }
        index = searchColumn(START64);
        if(index){ return((void*)&ram[index]); }
        index = searchColumn(START128);
        if(index){ return((void*)&ram[index]); }
        index = searchColumn(START256);
        if(index){ return((void*)&ram[index]); }
        index = searchColumn(START512);
        if(index){ return((void*)&ram[index]); }
        index = searchColumn(START1024);
        if(index){ return((void*)&ram[index]); }
        index = searchColumn(START4096);
        if(index){ return((void*)&ram[index]); }
    }
    else if(nbytes<=64)
```

Manual Memory Management

```
    {
        index = searchColumn(START64);
        if(index){ return((void*)&ram[index]); }
        index = searchColumn(START128);
        if(index){ return((void*)&ram[index]); }
        index = searchColumn(START256);
        if(index){ return((void*)&ram[index]); }
        index = searchColumn(START512);
        if(index){ return((void*)&ram[index]); }
        index = searchColumn(START1024);
        if(index){ return((void*)&ram[index]); }
        index = searchColumn(START4096);
        if(index){ return((void*)&ram[index]); }
    }
    else if(nbytes<=128)
    {
        index = searchColumn(START128);
        if(index){ return((void*)&ram[index]); }
        index = searchColumn(START256);
        if(index){ return((void*)&ram[index]); }
        index = searchColumn(START512);
        if(index){ return((void*)&ram[index]); }
        index = searchColumn(START1024);
        if(index){ return((void*)&ram[index]); }
        index = searchColumn(START4096);
        if(index){ return((void*)&ram[index]); }
    }
    else if(nbytes<=256)
    {
        index = searchColumn(START256);
        if(index){ return((void*)&ram[index]); }
        index = searchColumn(START512);
        if(index){ return((void*)&ram[index]); }
        index = searchColumn(START1024);
        if(index){ return((void*)&ram[index]); }
        index = searchColumn(START4096);
        if(index){ return((void*)&ram[index]); }
    }
    else if(nbytes<=512)
    {
        index = searchColumn(START512);
        if(index){ return((void*)&ram[index]); }
        index = searchColumn(START1024);
        if(index){ return((void*)&ram[index]); }
        index = searchColumn(START4096);
        if(index){ return((void*)&ram[index]); }
    }
    else if(nbytes<=1024)
    {
        index = searchColumn(START1024);
        if(index){ return((void*)&ram[index]); }
```

```
        index = searchColumn(START4096);
        if(index){ return((void*)&ram[index]); }
    }
    else if(nbytes<=4096)
    {
        index = searchColumn(START4096);
        if(index){ return((void*)&ram[index]); }
    }

    return(NULL);

}/*end allocation-----------------------------------------------*/

/*
search a given size range for a free element
return index
or zero if no available memory
*/

U4 SegregatedMemoryManager::searchColumn(U4 index)
{
    U4 i;
    for(i=0;i<nrows;i++)
    {
        if(STATE(index)==FREE)
        {
            MSG0("SegregatedMemoryManager::");
            MSG1("searchColumn(): free at index %lu, ",index);
            MSG1("address=%p\n",&ram[index]);
            STATE(index)=OCCUPIED;
            return(index);
        }
        index = index + SZ_ROW;
    }
    return(0);

}/*end searchColumn---------------------------------------------*/

void SegregatedMemoryManager::release(void *addr)
{
    U4 free;    //index into ram[]

    if(addr==NULL)
    {
        MSG0("SegregatedMemoryManager::");
        MSG0("release(): cannot release NULL pointer\n");
        return;
    }

    MSG0("SegregatedMemoryManager::");
    MSG1("release(%p)\n",addr);
```

Manual Memory Management

```cpp
    //perform sanity check to make sure address is kosher

    if( (addr>= (void*)&ram[size]) || (addr< (void*)&ram[0]) )
    {
        MSG0("SegregatedMemoryManager::");
        MSG0("release(): address out of bounds\n");
        return;
    }

    //translate void* addr to index in ram[]

    free = (U4)( ((U1*)addr) - &ram[0] );

    MSG0("SegregatedMemoryManager::");
    MSG1("address resolves to index %lu\n",free);

    //a header always occupies first 13 bytes of storage

    if(free==0)
    {
        MSG0("SegregatedMemoryManager::");
        MSG0("release(): address in first 1st byte\n");
        return;
    }

    //yet more sanity checks

    if(STATE(free)!=OCCUPIED)
    {
        MSG0("SegregatedMemoryManager::");
        MSG0("release(): referencing invalid region\n");
        return;
    }

    STATE(free)=FREE;

    return;

}/*end release----------------------------------------------*/

void SegregatedMemoryManager::printState()
{
    printf("[16 bytes]");
    printColumn(START16);

    printf("[32 bytes]");
    printColumn(START32);

    printf("[64 bytes]");
    printColumn(START64);
```

```
        printf("[128 bytes]");
        printColumn(START128);

        printf("[256 bytes]");
        printColumn(START256);

        printf("[512 bytes]");
        printColumn(START512);

        printf("[1024 bytes]");
        printColumn(START1024);

        printf("[4096 bytes]");
        printColumn(START4096);

        return;
}/*end printState---------------------------------------------*/

void SegregatedMemoryManager::printColumn(U4 index)
{
    U4 i;
    for(i=0;i<nrows;i++)
    {
        if(STATE(index)==OCCUPIED)
        {
            printf("[%p] ",&ram[index]);
        }
        index = index + SZ_ROW;
    }
    printf("\n");
    return;

}/*end printColumn--------------------------------------------*/
```

mallocV3.cpp

There were several minor alterations to this file, most notably the presence of a different set of debugging macros. To activate debugging code, uncomment the macros and compile a new build.

```
#include<stdio.h>
#include<stdlib.h>
#include<windows.h>

//#define DEBUG_SL_MEM_MGR
//#define DEBUG_MALLOCV3

#include<memmgr.cpp>
```

```
/*
wrapper functions
*/

SegregatedMemoryManager *mmptr;

void initMemMgr(unsigned long totalbytes)
{
    mmptr = new SegregatedMemoryManager(totalbytes);
}

void closeMemMgr()
{
    delete(mmptr);
}

void *newMalloc(unsigned long size)
{
    void *ptr = (*mmptr).allocate(size);

#ifdef DEBUG_MALLOCV3
    (*mmptr).printState();
#endif

    return(ptr);
}

void newFree(void *ptr)
{
    (*mmptr).release(ptr);

#ifdef DEBUG_MALLOCV3
    (*mmptr).printState();
#endif

    return;
}
```

Tests

If you look at the main() function defined in driver.cpp, you will see that I performed both a debug test and a performance test. I performed a debug test to make sure the manager was doing what it was supposed to do. If you modify my source code, I would suggest running the debug test again to validate your changes. Once I was sure that the memory manager was operational, I turned off debugging features and ran a performance test.

The debug test is fairly simple, but at the same time, I would take a good, hard look at what is going on. If you decide to run a debug test, you will want to make sure that the DEBUG_XXX macros in mallocV3.cpp are turned on. You will also want to comment out the PerformanceTestDriver() function call in main().

The following output was generated by the debug build of the memory manager:

```
SegregatedMemoryManager::SegregatedMemoryManager(1048576)
SegregatedMemoryManager::allocate(8)
SegregatedMemoryManager::searchColumn(): free at index 1, address=00B8000D
[16 bytes][00B8000D]
[32 bytes]
[64 bytes]
[128 bytes]
[256 bytes]
[512 bytes]
[1024 bytes]
[4096 bytes]
SegregatedMemoryManager::allocate(12)
SegregatedMemoryManager::searchColumn(): free at index 6137, address=00B81805
[16 bytes][00B8000D] [00B81805]
[32 bytes]
[64 bytes]
[128 bytes]
[256 bytes]
[512 bytes]
[1024 bytes]
[4096 bytes]
SegregatedMemoryManager::allocate(33)
SegregatedMemoryManager::searchColumn(): free at index 51, address=00B8003F
[16 bytes][00B8000D] [00B81805]
[32 bytes]
[64 bytes][00B8003F]
[128 bytes]
[256 bytes]
[512 bytes]
[1024 bytes]
[4096 bytes]
SegregatedMemoryManager::allocate(1)
SegregatedMemoryManager::searchColumn(): free at index 12273, address=00B82FFD
[16 bytes][00B8000D] [00B81805] [00B82FFD]
[32 bytes]
[64 bytes][00B8003F]
[128 bytes]
[256 bytes]
[512 bytes]
[1024 bytes]
```

```
[4096 bytes]
SegregatedMemoryManager::allocate(122)
SegregatedMemoryManager::searchColumn(): free at index 116,
address=00B80080
[16 bytes][00B8000D] [00B81805] [00B82FFD]
[32 bytes]
[64 bytes][00B8003F]
[128 bytes][00B80080]
[256 bytes]
[512 bytes]
[1024 bytes]
[4096 bytes]
SegregatedMemoryManager::allocate(50)
SegregatedMemoryManager::searchColumn(): free at index 6187,
address=00B81837
[16 bytes][00B8000D] [00B81805] [00B82FFD]
[32 bytes]
[64 bytes][00B8003F] [00B81837]
[128 bytes][00B80080]
[256 bytes]
[512 bytes]
[1024 bytes]
[4096 bytes]

FREE MEMORY--------------------------------------

SegregatedMemoryManager::release(00B8000D)
SegregatedMemoryManager::address resolves to index 1
[16 bytes][00B81805] [00B82FFD]
[32 bytes]
[64 bytes][00B8003F] [00B81837]
[128 bytes][00B80080]
[256 bytes]
[512 bytes]
[1024 bytes]
[4096 bytes]
SegregatedMemoryManager::release(00B82FFD)
SegregatedMemoryManager::address resolves to index 12273
[16 bytes][00B81805]
[32 bytes]
[64 bytes][00B8003F] [00B81837]
[128 bytes][00B80080]
[256 bytes]
[512 bytes]
[1024 bytes]
[4096 bytes]
SegregatedMemoryManager::release(00B80080)
SegregatedMemoryManager::address resolves to index 116
[16 bytes][00B81805]
[32 bytes]
[64 bytes][00B8003F] [00B81837]
```

```
[128 bytes]
[256 bytes]
[512 bytes]
[1024 bytes]
[4096 bytes]
SegregatedMemoryManager::release(00B8003F)
SegregatedMemoryManager::address resolves to index 51
[16 bytes][00B81805]
[32 bytes]
[64 bytes][00B81837]
[128 bytes]
[256 bytes]
[512 bytes]
[1024 bytes]
[4096 bytes]
SegregatedMemoryManager::release(00B81805)
SegregatedMemoryManager::address resolves to index 6137
[16 bytes]
[32 bytes]
[64 bytes][00B81837]
[128 bytes]
[256 bytes]
[512 bytes]
[1024 bytes]
[4096 bytes]
SegregatedMemoryManager::release(00B81837)
SegregatedMemoryManager::address resolves to index 6187
[16 bytes]
[32 bytes]
[64 bytes]
[128 bytes]
[256 bytes]
[512 bytes]
[1024 bytes]
[4096 bytes]
SegregatedMemoryManager::~SegregatedFitMemoryManager()free
ram.[1048576]
```

Although it may seem a tad tedious, it will help you tremendously to read the `debugTest()` function and then step through the previous output. It will give you an insight into what the code is doing and how the particulars are implemented.

The performance test was conducted by commenting out `debugTest()` and the debug macros in `mallocV3.cpp`, and then enabling the `PerformanceTestDriver()` function. The results of the performance run were:

```
PerformanceTest::runTest(): time whistle blown
PerformanceTest::runTest(): race has ended
msecs=5
```

Trade-Offs

Compared to the sequential fit technique, the segregated list implementation is blazing fast. However, this does not come without a cost. The segregated list approach demands a large initial down payment of memory. The fact that only certain block sizes are provided can also lead to severe internal fragmentation. For example, a 1,024-byte block could end up being used to service a 32-byte request.

Another issue resulting from fixed block sizes is that there is a distinct ceiling placed on the size of the memory region that can be allocated. In my implementation, you cannot allocate a block larger than 4,096 bytes. If, for some reason, you need a 4,097-byte block of memory, you are plain out of luck. There are variations of my segregated list approach, such as the *buddy system*, that allow certain forms of splitting and merging to deal with this size-limit problem.

Performance Comparison

Let us revisit all three of the previous implementations. In each of the performance tests, the resident memory manager was given 1MB of storage and was asked to service 1,024 consecutive memory allocation/release operations. The score card is provided in Table 4.5.

Table 4.5

Manager	Milliseconds
bitmapped	856
sequential fit	35
segregated list	5

By a long shot, the bitmapped memory manager was the worst. Now you know why almost nobody uses it. The segregated memory manager outperformed the sequential fit memory manager. However, there are significant trade-offs that might make the sequential fit method preferable to the segregated list method.

One common theme you will see in your journey through computer science is the *storage-versus-speed* trade-off. If you increase the amount of available memory storage, you can usually make something run faster.

Here is an example: If you rewrite all of the functions in a program as inline macros, you can increase the speed at which the program executes. This is because the processor doesn't have to waste time jumping around to different memory locations. In addition, because execution will not frequently jump to a nonlocal spot in memory, the processor will be able to spend much of its time executing code in the cache.

Likewise, you can make a program smaller by isolating every bit of redundant code and placing it in its own function. While this will decrease the total number of machine instructions, this tactic will make a program slower because not only does the processor spend most of its time jumping around memory, but the processor's cache will also need to be constantly refreshed.

This is the type of situation that we face with the segregated list and sequential fit approaches. The segregated list approach is much faster, but it also wastes a lot of memory. The sequential fit algorithm, on the other hand, decreases the amount of wasted storage at the expense of execution time. This leads me to think that the segregated list approach would be useful for embedded systems that do not typically have much memory to spend. The segregated storage approach might be suited for large enterprise servers that are running high-performance transaction processing software.

Chapter 5

Automatic Memory Management

Automatic memory managers keep track of the memory that is allocated from the heap so that the programmer is absolved of the responsibility. This makes life easier for the programmer. In fact, not only does it make the programmer's job easier, but it also eliminates other nasty problems, like memory leaks and dangling pointers. The downside is that automatic memory managers are much more difficult to build because they must incorporate all the extra bookkeeping functionality.

NOTE Automatic memory managers are often referred to as *garbage collectors*. This is because blocks of memory in the heap that were allocated by a program, but which are no longer referenced by the program, are known as *garbage*. It is the responsibility of a garbage collector to monitor the heap and free garbage so that it can be recycled for other allocation requests.

Garbage Collection Taxonomy

Taking out the trash is a dance with two steps:

1. Identifying garbage in the heap
2. Recycling garbage once it is found

The different garbage collection algorithms are distinguished in terms of the mechanisms that they use to implement these two steps. For example, garbage can be identified by *reference counting* or by *tracing*. Most garbage collectors can be categorized into one of these two types.

Reference counting collectors identify garbage by maintaining a running tally of the number of pointers that reference each block of allocated memory. When the number of references to a particular block of memory reaches zero, the memory is viewed as garbage and reclaimed. There are a number of types of reference counting algorithms, each one implementing its own variation of the counting mechanism (i.e., simple reference counting, deferred reference counting, 1-bit reference counting, etc.).

Tracing garbage collectors traverse the application run-time environment (i.e., registers, stack, heap, data section) in search of pointers to memory in the heap. Think of tracing collectors as pointer hunter-gatherers. If a pointer is found somewhere in the run-time environment, the heap memory that is pointed to is assumed to be "alive" and is not recycled. Otherwise, the allocated memory is reclaimed. There are several subspecies of tracing garbage collectors, including mark-sweep, mark-compact, and copying garbage collectors.

An outline of different automatic memory management approaches is provided in Figure 5.1.

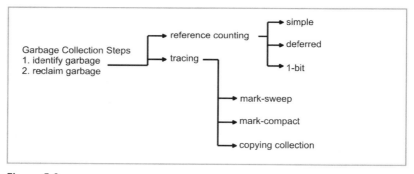

Figure 5.1

In this chapter I am going to examine a couple of garbage collection algorithms and offer sample implementations. Specifically, I will implement a garbage collector that uses reference counting and another that uses tracing. As in the previous chapter, I will present these memory managers as drop-in replacements for the C standard library `malloc()` and `free()` routines.

In an attempt to keep the learning threshold low, I will forego extensive optimization and performance enhancements in favor of keeping my source code simple. I am not interested in impressing you with elaborate syntax kung fu; my underlying motivation is to make it easy for you to pick up my ideas and internalize them. If you are interested in taking things to the next level, you can follow up on some of the suggestions and ideas that I discuss at the end of the chapter.

`malloc()` Version 4: Reference Counting

Theory

The reference count approach keeps track of the number of pointers that hold the address of a given block of memory. The reference count of a block of memory is incremented every time that its address is assigned or copied to another pointer. The reference count of a memory block is decremented when a pointer holding its address is overwritten, goes out of scope, or is recycled. When the reference count reaches a value of zero, the corresponding memory is reclaimed.

Consider the following short program:

```c
#include<stdlib.h>

void main()
{
    char *cptr1;
    char *cptr2;
    char *cptr3;

    cptr1 = (char*)malloc(16);   //increment memory_block_1

    cptr2 = cptr1;               //increment memory_block_1

    cptr3 = (char*)malloc(16);   //increment memory_block_2

    cptr2 = cptr3;       //increment memory_block_2,
                         //decrement memory_block_1

    //decrement memory_block_2 (cptr3 out of scope)
    //decrement memory_block_2 (cptr2 out of scope)
    //decrement memory_block_1 (cptr1 out of scope)

    return;
}
```

Each reference increment and decrement has been marked with a comment to give you an idea of what would need to be done behind the scenes.

The one line:

```
cptr2 = cptr3;
```

increments the reference count to `memory_block_2` because its address is being copied into `cptr2`. On the other hand, the reference count to `memory_block_1` is decremented because its address in `cptr2` is being overwritten.

Reference counting is a technique that requires the cooperation of the compiler. Specifically, the compiler will need to recognize when it is necessary to increment or decrement a reference count and emit special code to do the job. For example, normally, the native code generated for:

```
cptr2 = cptr1;
```

would resemble something like:

```
mov     eax, DWORD PTR _cptr1$[ebp]
mov     DWORD PTR _cptr2$[ebp], eax
```

However, because the reference count to memory_block_1 needs to be maintained, the compiler will need to generate something like:

```
mov     eax, DWORD PTR _cptr1$[ebp]
mov     DWORD PTR _cptr2$[ebp], eax
mov     ecx, DWORD PTR _cptr1$[ebp]
push    ecx
call    _increment
add     esp, 4
```

Likewise, when a pointer goes out of scope or is overwritten, the compiler will need to emit something that looks like:

```
mov     ecx, DWORD PTR _cptr3$[ebp]
push    ecx
call    _decrement
add     esp, 4
```

NOTE The alternative to emitting extra instructions to perform the reference counting is to use an interpreter, or virtual machine, which can keep pointer tallies without help from the compiler.

Implementation

I decided to implement a reference counting garbage collector by modifying the sequential fit implementation in Chapter 4. As with the sequential fit approach, memory is arranged as a series of blocks where each block is prefixed by a 16-byte header (see Figure 5.2).

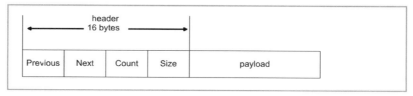

Figure 5.2

The STATE field, which was a byte in the sequential fit implementation, has been replaced by a 32-bit field called COUNT. This COUNT field keeps track of the number of references to a block of memory.

My implementation of the reference counting memory manager required four files:

Table 5.1

File	Use
driver.cpp	contains main(), is the scene of the crime
mallocV4.cpp	newMalloc(), newFree() wrappers (4th version)
perform.cpp	implements the PerformanceTest class
memmgr.cpp	implements the RefCountMemoryManager class

driver.cpp

This file contains the main() entry point. You can build my implementation to execute a diagnostic test or a performance test. To build the diagnostic version, you will need to comment out the PerformanceTestDriver() invocation and uncomment the debugTest() invocation. You will also need to activate the DEBUG_XXX macros in the mallocV4.cpp file.

Because the compiler that I used has not been engineered to emit the extra instructions needed to support reference counting, I had to manually insert the code. Throughout debugTest(), I added inc() and dec() function calls. I also added comments indicating that these calls should have been generated by the compiler.

```
#include<mallocV4.cpp>
#include<perform.cpp>

/*
not using a modified compiler, so will need to insert
reference counting code manually
*/

void debugTest()
{
    void *ptr[6];
    void *ptr1;
    void *ptr2;
    void *ptr3;

    unsigned long allocs[6]={8,12,33,1,122,50};
    int i;

    initMemMgr(270);
```

```
    for(i=0;i<6;i++)
    {
        ptr[i] = newMalloc(allocs[i]);
        if(ptr[i]==NULL){ printf("ptr[%lu]==NULL!\n",i); }
    }

    //copying addresses

    printf("copying ptr[0]\n");
    ptr1 = ptr[0];
    (*mmptr).inc(ptr[0]);      //compiler insert

    printf("copying ptr[1]\n");
    ptr3 = ptr[1];
    (*mmptr).inc(ptr[1]);      //compiler insert

    printf("copying ptr1\n");
    ptr2 = ptr1;
    (*mmptr).inc(ptr1);        //compiler insert

    //overwritting

    printf("overwriting ptr1 with ptr3\n");
    (*mmptr).dec(ptr2);        //compiler insert
    ptr2 = ptr3;
    (*mmptr).inc(ptr3);        //compiler insert

    //locals going out of scope, need to decrement

    printf("leaving scope\n");
    for(i=0;i<6;i++)
    {
        (*mmptr).dec(ptr[i]);  //compiler insert
    }
    (*mmptr).dec(ptr1);        //compiler insert
    (*mmptr).dec(ptr2);        //compiler insert
    (*mmptr).dec(ptr3);        //compiler insert

    closeMemMgr();
    return;

}/*end debugTest----------------------------------------------*/

void main()
{
    //for the debug test, should activate debug macros in
      mallocVx.cpp
    //debugTest();

    //for the performance test, should comment out debug macros
```

```
        PerformanceTestDriver();
        return;
    }
}/*end main----------------------------------------------------*/
```

mallocV4.cpp

Because we are now in the domain of automatic memory management, I disabled the newFree() function that has traditionally been defined in this file. The newMalloc() function is still operational, albeit using a different underlying object. If you wish to perform a debug/diagnostic test, you will need to activate the DEBUG_XXX macros.

```
#include<stdio.h>
#include<stdlib.h>
#include<windows.h>

//#define DEBUG_RC_MEM_MGR
//#define DEBUG_MALLOCV4

#include<memmgr.cpp>

/*
wrapper functions
*/

RefCountMemoryManager *mmptr;

void initMemMgr(unsigned long totalbytes)
{
    mmptr = new RefCountMemoryManager(totalbytes);
}

void closeMemMgr()
{
    delete(mmptr);
}

void *newMalloc(unsigned long size)
{
    void *ptr = (*mmptr).allocate(size);

#ifdef DEBUG_MALLOCV4
    (*mmptr).printState();
#endif

    return(ptr);
}
```

```
void newFree(void *ptr)
{
    printf("newFree(): cannot free %p\n",ptr);
    printf("newFree(): not implemented, using garbage
                       collector\n");
    return;
}
```

perform.cpp

The `PerformanceTest` class defined in this file has not been modified very much. The only thing that changed was the implementation of the `runTest()` member function. Specifically, I had to remove the calls to `newFree()`, which are no longer valid, and add in the `dec()` invocations that the compiler should normally emit.

```
unsigned long PerformanceTest::runTest()
{
    unsigned long *allocs;
    unsigned long i;
    unsigned long ticks1,ticks2;

    char **addr;     /*pointer to an array of pointers*/

    /*create array of address holders to stockpile malloc()
     returns*/

    addr = (char **)malloc(sizeof(char *)*nAllocations);
    if(addr==NULL)
    {
        printf("could not allocate address repository\n");
        exit(1);
    }

    /*create stream of allocation values*/

    allocs = (unsigned long *)malloc(sizeof(long)*nAllocations);
    if(allocs==NULL)
    {
        printf("could not allocate malloc() request stream\n");
        exit(1);
    }

    getAllocArray(allocs);

    /*start timer and do some work*/

    initMemMgr(1024*1024);
```

```
    printf("PerformanceTest::runTest(): time whistle blown\n");

    ticks1 = GetTickCount();

    for(i=0;i<nAllocations;i++)
    {
        //printf("%lu\n",allocs[i]);
        addr[i] = (char *)newMalloc(allocs[i]);
        if(addr[i]==NULL)
        {
            printf("mallco()=addr[%lu]=%lu failed\n",i,addr[i]);
            exit(1);
        }
    }

    //array goes out of scope
    for(i=0;i<nAllocations;i++)
    {
        (*mmptr).dec(addr[i]);
    }

    ticks2 = GetTickCount();

    printf("PerformanceTest::runTest(): race has ended\n");

    closeMemMgr();

    free(addr);
    free(allocs);

    return(ticks2-ticks1);
}/*end runTest--------------------------------------------------*/
```

memmgr.cpp

The `RefCountMemoryManager` class defined in this file is basically an extended version of the `SequentialFitMemory-Manager`. To give you an idea of how this class operates, I have enumerated the possible paths of execution for this class in Figure 5.3 (on the following page).

Most of the action happens as a result of the `allocate()` or `dec()` functions being called. Both the `inc()` and `dec()` functions perform a series of sanity checks before they modify the heap block list. The `inc()` function increments the reference count of a memory block, and the `dec()` function decrements the reference count of a memory block. As you can see from Figure 5.3, the `release()` function has been made subservient to the `dec()` function.

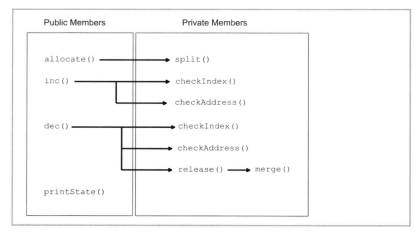

Figure 5.3

```
#ifdef   DEBUG_RC_MEM_MGR
#define MSG0(arg);              printf(arg);
#define MSG1(arg1,arg2);        printf(arg1,arg2);
#else
#define MSG0(arg);
#define MSG1(arg1,arg2);
#endif

#define U1 unsigned char
#define U4 unsigned long

/*
    list element format
                |0   3||4   7||8   11||12   15||16 .. n|
                [PREV][NEXT][COUNT][ SIZE ][payload]
                  U4    U4    U4      U4         ?

    byte allocated/freed is address of first byte of payload
    header = 16 bytes

    byte[0] is occupied by header data, so is always used, thus
           first link has prev=0 ( 0 indicates not used )
           last link has next=0
*/

#define PREV(i)         (*((U4*)(&ram[i-16])))
#define NEXT(i)         (*((U4*)(&ram[i-12])))
#define COUNT(i)        (*((U1*)(&ram[i-8])))    /*# references*/
#define SIZE(i)         (*((U4*)(&ram[i-4])))

#define FREE       0    /*free blocks have COUNT=0*/
```

Automatic Memory Management

```cpp
#define START        16      /*address of first payload*/
#define SZ_HEADER    16

class RefCountMemoryManager
{
    private:
    HANDLE handle;
    U1  *ram;    /*memory storage*/
    U4  size;

    int checkAddress(void *addr);
    int checkIndex(U4 free);
    void release(U4 free);

    void split(U4 addr,U4 nbytes);
    void merge(U4 prev,U4 current,U4 next);

    public:

    RefCountMemoryManager(U4 nbytes);
    ~RefCountMemoryManager();

    void*allocate(U4 nbytes);
    void inc(void *addr);
    void dec(void *addr);
    void printState();
};

RefCountMemoryManager::RefCountMemoryManager(U4 nbytes)
{
    handle = GetProcessHeap();
    if(handle==NULL)
    {
        printf("RefCountMemoryManager::");
        printf("RefCountMemoryManager():");
        printf("invalid handle\n");
        exit(1);
    }

    ram = (U1*)HeapAlloc(handle,HEAP_ZERO_MEMORY,nbytes);

    //for portability, you could use:
    //ram = (unsigned char*)malloc(nbytes);

    size = nbytes;

    if(size<=SZ_HEADER)
    {
        printf("RefCountMemoryManager::");
        printf("RefCountMemoryManager():");
        printf("not enough memory fed to constructor\n");
```

Chapter 5

```
        exit(1);
    }

    PREV(START)=0;
    NEXT(START)=0;
    COUNT(START)=0;
    SIZE(START)=size-SZ_HEADER;

    MSG0("RefCountMemoryManager::");
    MSG1("RefCountMemoryManager(%lu)\n",nbytes);

    return;

}/*end constructor----------------------------------------------*/

RefCountMemoryManager::~RefCountMemoryManager()
{
    if(HeapFree(handle,HEAP_NO_SERIALIZE,ram)==0)
    {
        printf("RefCountMemoryManager::");
        printf("~RefCountMemoryManager():");
        printf("could not free heap storage\n");
        return;
    }

    //for portability, you could use:
    //free(ram);

    MSG0("RefCountMemoryManager::");
    MSG0("~RefCountMemoryManager()");
    MSG1("free ram[%lu]\n",size);
    return;

}/*end destructor-----------------------------------------------*/

/*
U4 nbytes    -    number of bytes required
returns address of first byte of memory region allocated
( or NULL if cannot allocate a large enough block )
*/

void* RefCountMemoryManager::allocate(U4 nbytes)
{
    U4 current;

    MSG0("RefCountMemoryManager::");
    MSG1("allocate(%lu)\n",nbytes);

    if(nbytes==0)
    {
        MSG0("RefCountMemoryManager::");
```

Automatic Memory Management

```
        MSG0("allocate(): zero bytes requested\n");
        return(NULL);
    }

    //traverse the linked list, starting with first element

    current = START;
    while(NEXT(current)!=0)
    {
        if((SIZE(current)>=nbytes)&&(COUNT(current)==FREE))
        {
            split(current,nbytes);
            return((void*)&ram[current]);
        }
        current = NEXT(current);
    }

    //handle the last block ( which has NEXT(current)=0 )

    if((SIZE(current)>=nbytes)&&(COUNT(current)==FREE))
    {
        split(current,nbytes);
        return((void*)&ram[current]);
    }

    return(NULL);

}/*end allocation----------------------------------------------*/

/*
breaks [free] region into [alloc][free] pair, if possible
*/

void RefCountMemoryManager::split(U4 addr, U4 nbytes)
{
    /*
    want payload to have enough room for
    nbytes = size of request
    SZ_HEADER = header for new region
    SZ_HEADER = payload for new region (arbitrary 16 bytes)
    */

    if(SIZE(addr)>= nbytes+SZ_HEADER+SZ_HEADER)
    {
        U4 oldnext;
        U4 oldprev;
        U4 oldsize;

        U4 newaddr;

        MSG0("RefCountMemoryManager::");
```

```
        MSG0("split(): split=YES\n");

        oldnext=NEXT(addr);
        oldprev=PREV(addr);
        oldsize=SIZE(addr);

        newaddr = addr + nbytes + SZ_HEADER;

        NEXT(addr)=newaddr;
        PREV(addr)=oldprev;
        COUNT(addr)=1;
        SIZE(addr)=nbytes;

        NEXT(newaddr)=oldnext;
        PREV(newaddr)=addr;
        COUNT(newaddr)=FREE;
        SIZE(newaddr)=oldsize-nbytes-SZ_HEADER;
    }
    else
    {
        MSG0("RefCountMemoryManager::");
        MSG0("split(): split=NO\n");
        COUNT(addr)=1;
    }
    return;

}/*end split------------------------------------------------------*/

int RefCountMemoryManager::checkAddress(void *addr)
{
    if(addr==NULL)
    {
        MSG0("RefCountMemoryManager::");
        MSG0("checkAddress(): cannot release NULL pointer\n");
        return(FALSE);
    }

    MSG0("RefCountMemoryManager::");
    MSG1("checkAddress(%lu)\n",addr);

    //perform sanity check to make sure address is kosher

    if( (addr>= (void*)&ram[size]) || (addr< (void*)&ram[0]) )
    {
        MSG0("RefCountMemoryManager::");
        MSG0("checkAddress(): address out of bounds\n");
        return(FALSE);
    }

    return(TRUE);
```

Automatic Memory Management

```
}/*end checkAddress----------------------------------------*/

int RefCountMemoryManager::checkIndex(U4 free)
{
    //a header always occupies first SZ_HEADER bytes of storage

    if(free<SZ_HEADER)
    {
        MSG0("RefCountMemoryManager::");
        MSG0("checkIndex(): address in first 16 bytes\n");
        return(FALSE);
    }

    //more sanity checks

    if((COUNT(free)==FREE)    ||    //region if free
       (PREV(free)>=free)     ||    //previous element not previous
       (NEXT(free)>=size)     ||    //next is beyond the end
       (SIZE(free)>=size)     ||    //size greater than whole
       (SIZE(free)==0))             //no size at all
    {
        MSG0("RefCountMemoryManager::");
        MSG0("checkIndex(): referencing invalid region\n");
        return(FALSE);
    }

    return(TRUE);

}/*end checkIndex------------------------------------------*/

void RefCountMemoryManager::inc(void *addr)
{
    U4 free;    //index into ram[]

    if(checkAddress(addr)==FALSE){ return; }

    //translate void* addr to index in ram[]

    free = (U4)( ((U1*)addr) - &ram[0] );
    MSG0("RefCountMemoryManager::");
    MSG1("inc(): address resolves to index %lu\n",free);

    if(checkIndex(free)==FALSE){ return; }

    COUNT(free) = COUNT(free)+1;
    MSG0("RefCountMemoryManager::");
    MSG1("inc(): incrementing ram[%lu] ",free);
    MSG1("to %lu\n",COUNT(free));

    return;
```

```
}/*end inc-------------------------------------------------------*/

void RefCountMemoryManager::dec(void *addr)
{
    U4 free;     //index into ram[]

    if(checkAddress(addr)==FALSE){ return; }

    //translate void* addr to index in ram[]

    free = (U4)( ((U1*)addr) - &ram[0] );

    MSG0("RefCountMemoryManager::");
    MSG1("dec(): address resolves to index %lu\n",free);

    if(checkIndex(free)==FALSE){ return; }

    COUNT(free) = COUNT(free)-1;
    MSG0("RefCountMemoryManager::");
    MSG1("dec(): decrementing ram[%lu] ",free);
    MSG1("to %lu\n",COUNT(free));

    if(COUNT(free)==FREE)
    {
        MSG0("RefCountMemoryManager::");
        MSG1("dec(): releasing ram[%lu]\n",free);
        release(free);
    }

    return;

}/*end dec-------------------------------------------------------*/

void RefCountMemoryManager::release(U4 free)
{
    merge(PREV(free),free,NEXT(free));

#ifdef  DEBUG_RC_MEM_MGR
    printState();
#endif
    return;

}/*end release---------------------------------------------------*/

/*
        4 cases ( F=free O=occupied )
            FOF -> [F]
            OOF -> O[F]
            FOO -> [F]O
            OOO -> OFO
*/
```

Automatic Memory Management

```
void RefCountMemoryManager::merge(U4 prev,U4 current,U4 next)
{
    /*
    first handle special cases of region at end(s)
    prev=0                      low end
    next=0                      high end
    prev=0 and next=0           only 1 list element
    */

    if(prev==0)
    {
        if(next==0)
        {
            COUNT(current)=FREE;
        }
        else if(COUNT(next)!=FREE)
        {
            COUNT(current)=FREE;
        }
        else if(COUNT(next)==FREE)
        {
            U4 temp;

            MSG0("RefCountMemoryManager::merge():");
            MSG0("merging to NEXT\n");

            COUNT(current)=FREE;
            SIZE(current)=SIZE(current)+SIZE(next)+SZ_HEADER;
            NEXT(current)=NEXT(next);

            temp = NEXT(next);
            if(temp!=0){ PREV(temp)=current; }
        }
    }
    else if(next==0)
    {
        if(COUNT(prev)!=FREE)
        {
            COUNT(current)=FREE;
        }
        else if(COUNT(prev)==FREE)
        {
            MSG0("RefCountMemoryManager::merge():");
            MSG0("merging to PREV\n");
            SIZE(prev)=SIZE(prev)+SIZE(current)+SZ_HEADER;
            NEXT(prev)=NEXT(current);
        }
    }

    /* now we handle 4 cases */
```

```cpp
    else if((COUNT(prev)!=FREE)&&(COUNT(next)!=FREE))
    {
        COUNT(current)=FREE;
    }
    else if((COUNT(prev)!=FREE)&&(COUNT(next)==FREE))
    {
        U4 temp;

        MSG0("RefCountMemoryManager::merge():");
        MSG0("merging to NEXT\n");
        COUNT(current)=FREE;
        SIZE(current)=SIZE(current)+SIZE(next)+SZ_HEADER;
        NEXT(current)=NEXT(next);

        temp = NEXT(next);
        if(temp!=0){ PREV(temp)=current; }
    }
    else if((COUNT(prev)==FREE)&&(COUNT(next)!=FREE))
    {
        MSG0("RefCountMemoryManager::merge():");
        MSG0("merging to PREV\n");
        SIZE(prev)=SIZE(prev)+SIZE(current)+SZ_HEADER;
        NEXT(prev)=NEXT(current);
        PREV(next)=prev;
    }
    else if((COUNT(prev)==FREE)&&(COUNT(next)==FREE))
    {
        U4 temp;

        MSG0("RefCountMemoryManager::merge():");
        MSG0("merging with both sides\n");
        SIZE(prev)=SIZE(prev)+
                   SIZE(current)+SZ_HEADER+
                   SIZE(next)+SZ_HEADER;
        NEXT(prev)=NEXT(next);

        temp = NEXT(next);
        if(temp!=0){ PREV(temp)=prev; }
    }

    return;

}/*end merge-----------------------------------------------*/

void RefCountMemoryManager::printState()
{
    U4 i;
    U4 current;

    i=0;
```

```
    current=START;

    while(NEXT(current)!=0)
    {
        printf("%lu)  [P=%lu]",i,PREV(current));
        printf("[addr=%lu]",current);
        if(COUNT(current)==FREE){ printf("[FREE]"); }
        else{ printf("[Ct=%lu]",COUNT(current)); }
        printf("[Sz=%lu]",SIZE(current));
        printf("[N=%lu]\n",NEXT(current));
        current = NEXT(current);
        i++;
    }

    //print the last list element

    printf("%lu)  [P=%lu]",i,PREV(current));
    printf("[addr=%lu]",current);
    if(COUNT(current)==FREE){ printf("[FREE]"); }
    else{ printf("[Ct=%lu]",COUNT(current)); }
    printf("[Sz=%lu]",SIZE(current));
    printf("[N=%lu]\n",NEXT(current));

    return;

}/*end printState---------------------------------------------*/
```

Tests

I performed two different tests against this memory manager. A debug test was performed to make sure that the manager was doing what it was supposed to do. If you modify my source code, I would suggest running the debug test again to validate your changes. Once I was sure that the memory manager was operational, I turned off debugging features and ran a performance test.

The debug test was performed by executing the code in the `debugTest()` function defined in the `driver.cpp` source file. I keep things fairly simple, but at the same time, I take a good, hard look at what is going on. If you decide to run a debug test, you will want to make sure that the DEBUG_XXX macros in `mallocV4.cpp` are turned on. You will also want to comment out the `PerformanceTestDriver()` function call in `main()`.

The following output was generated by the debug build of the memory manager:

```
RefCountMemoryManager::RefCountMemoryManager(270)
RefCountMemoryManager::allocate(8)
RefCountMemoryManager::split(): split=YES
```

```
0) [P=0][addr=16][Ct=1][Sz=8][N=40]
1) [P=16][addr=40][FREE][Sz=230][N=0]
RefCountMemoryManager::allocate(12)
RefCountMemoryManager::split(): split=YES
0) [P=0][addr=16][Ct=1][Sz=8][N=40]
1) [P=16][addr=40][Ct=1][Sz=12][N=68]
2) [P=40][addr=68][FREE][Sz=202][N=0]
RefCountMemoryManager::allocate(33)
RefCountMemoryManager::split(): split=YES
0) [P=0][addr=16][Ct=1][Sz=8][N=40]
1) [P=16][addr=40][Ct=1][Sz=12][N=68]
2) [P=40][addr=68][Ct=1][Sz=33][N=117]
3) [P=68][addr=117][FREE][Sz=153][N=0]
RefCountMemoryManager::allocate(1)
RefCountMemoryManager::split(): split=YES
0) [P=0][addr=16][Ct=1][Sz=8][N=40]
1) [P=16][addr=40][Ct=1][Sz=12][N=68]
2) [P=40][addr=68][Ct=1][Sz=33][N=117]
3) [P=68][addr=117][Ct=1][Sz=1][N=134]
4) [P=117][addr=134][FREE][Sz=136][N=0]
RefCountMemoryManager::allocate(122)
RefCountMemoryManager::split(): split=NO
0) [P=0][addr=16][Ct=1][Sz=8][N=40]
1) [P=16][addr=40][Ct=1][Sz=12][N=68]
2) [P=40][addr=68][Ct=1][Sz=33][N=117]
3) [P=68][addr=117][Ct=1][Sz=1][N=134]
4) [P=117][addr=134][Ct=1][Sz=136][N=0]
RefCountMemoryManager::allocate(50)
0) [P=0][addr=16][Ct=1][Sz=8][N=40]
1) [P=16][addr=40][Ct=1][Sz=12][N=68]
2) [P=40][addr=68][Ct=1][Sz=33][N=117]
3) [P=68][addr=117][Ct=1][Sz=1][N=134]
4) [P=117][addr=134][Ct=1][Sz=136][N=0]
ptr[5]==NULL!
copying ptr[0]
RefCountMemoryManager::checkAddress(5439516)
RefCountMemoryManager::inc(): address resolves to index 16
RefCountMemoryManager::inc(): incrementing ram[16] to 2
copying ptr[1]
RefCountMemoryManager::checkAddress(5439540)
RefCountMemoryManager::inc(): address resolves to index 40
RefCountMemoryManager::inc(): incrementing ram[40] to 2
copying ptr1
RefCountMemoryManager::checkAddress(5439516)
RefCountMemoryManager::inc(): address resolves to index 16
RefCountMemoryManager::inc(): incrementing ram[16] to 3
overwriting ptr1 with ptr3
RefCountMemoryManager::checkAddress(5439516)
RefCountMemoryManager::dec(): address resolves to index 16
RefCountMemoryManager::dec(): decrementing ram[16] to 2
RefCountMemoryManager::checkAddress(5439540)
```

```
RefCountMemoryManager::inc(): address resolves to index 40
RefCountMemoryManager::inc(): incrementing ram[40] to 3
leaving scope
RefCountMemoryManager::checkAddress(5439516)
RefCountMemoryManager::dec(): address resolves to index 16
RefCountMemoryManager::dec(): decrementing ram[16] to 1
RefCountMemoryManager::checkAddress(5439540)
RefCountMemoryManager::dec(): address resolves to index 40
RefCountMemoryManager::dec(): decrementing ram[40] to 2
RefCountMemoryManager::checkAddress(5439568)
RefCountMemoryManager::dec(): address resolves to index 68
RefCountMemoryManager::dec(): decrementing ram[68] to 0
RefCountMemoryManager::dec(): releasing ram[68]
0) [P=0][addr=16][Ct=1][Sz=8][N=40]
1) [P=16][addr=40][Ct=2][Sz=12][N=68]
2) [P=40][addr=68][FREE][Sz=33][N=117]
3) [P=68][addr=117][Ct=1][Sz=1][N=134]
4) [P=117][addr=134][Ct=1][Sz=136][N=0]
RefCountMemoryManager::checkAddress(5439617)
RefCountMemoryManager::dec(): address resolves to index 117
RefCountMemoryManager::dec(): decrementing ram[117] to 0
RefCountMemoryManager::dec(): releasing ram[117]
RefCountMemoryManager::merge():merging to PREV
0) [P=0][addr=16][Ct=1][Sz=8][N=40]
1) [P=16][addr=40][Ct=2][Sz=12][N=68]
2) [P=40][addr=68][FREE][Sz=50][N=134]
3) [P=68][addr=134][Ct=1][Sz=136][N=0]
RefCountMemoryManager::checkAddress(5439634)
RefCountMemoryManager::dec(): address resolves to index 134
RefCountMemoryManager::dec(): decrementing ram[134] to 0
RefCountMemoryManager::dec(): releasing ram[134]
RefCountMemoryManager::merge():merging to PREV
0) [P=0][addr=16][Ct=1][Sz=8][N=40]
1) [P=16][addr=40][Ct=2][Sz=12][N=68]
2) [P=40][addr=68][FREE][Sz=202][N=0]
RefCountMemoryManager::checkAddress(): cannot release NULL
pointer
RefCountMemoryManager::checkAddress(5439516)
RefCountMemoryManager::dec(): address resolves to index 16
RefCountMemoryManager::dec(): decrementing ram[16] to 0
RefCountMemoryManager::dec(): releasing ram[16]
0) [P=0][addr=16][FREE][Sz=8][N=40]
1) [P=16][addr=40][Ct=2][Sz=12][N=68]
2) [P=40][addr=68][FREE][Sz=202][N=0]
RefCountMemoryManager::checkAddress(5439540)
RefCountMemoryManager::dec(): address resolves to index 40
RefCountMemoryManager::dec(): decrementing ram[40] to 1
RefCountMemoryManager::checkAddress(5439540)
RefCountMemoryManager::dec(): address resolves to index 40
RefCountMemoryManager::dec(): decrementing ram[40] to 0
RefCountMemoryManager::dec(): releasing ram[40]
```

```
RefCountMemoryManager::merge():merging with both sides
0) [P=0][addr=16][FREE][Sz=254][N=0]
RefCountMemoryManager::~RefCountMemoryManager()free ram[270]
```

The performance test was conducted by commenting out `debugTest()` and the debug macros in `mallocV4.cpp`, and then enabling the `PerformanceTestDriver()` function. The results of the performance run were, well, surprising:

```
PerformanceTest::runTest(): time whistle blown
PerformanceTest::runTest(): race has ended
msecs=30
```

Not bad.

Trade-Offs

The reference counting approach to garbage collection is convenient because it offers a type of collection that is *incremental*, which is to say that the bookkeeping needed to reclaim garbage is done in short, bite-sized bursts. This allows the memory manager to do its jobs without introducing a significant time delay into the program's critical path. Some garbage collectors wait to do everything at once so that users may experience a noticeable pause while a program runs.

While the reference counting approach is fast, it also suffers from some serious problems. For example, reference counting garbage collectors cannot reclaim objects that reference each other. This is known as a *cycle* (see Figure 5.4).

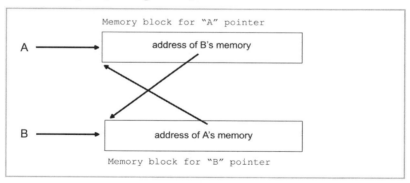

Figure 5.4

Let us assume that we have two heap-allocated variables, A and B, which reference one another. For example:

```
#include<stdlib.h>
#include<stdio.h>
```

```
void function()
{
    void **A;      //points to value storing an address
    void **B;

    //create 2 blocks in heap that can store addresses

    A = (void*)malloc(sizeof(void*));
    B = (void*)malloc(sizeof(void*));

    // A's reference count = 1
    // B's reference count = 1

    (*A) = B;      //set A's heap value to the address of B
    (*B) = A;      //set B's heap value to the address of A

    // A's reference count = 2
    // B's reference count = 2

    printf("address A=%p\t",A);
    printf("value in A=%p\n\n",*A);

    printf("address B=%p\t",B);
    printf("value in B=%p\n",*B);

    //decrement A's reference count to 1 ( A goes out of scope )
    //decrement B's reference count to 1 ( B goes out of scope )

    return;
}

void main()
{
    function();
    return;
}
```

If the variable A goes out of scope, its heap storage will still not be reclaimed. This is because B still references it so that its reference count is 1. The same holds true for B. Because of the pointer tomfoolery performed, and because of the nature of reference counting, neither of these blocks of memory will ever have their storage reclaimed because their reference counts will never be able to reach zero.

NOTE The ugly truth is that the inability to handle cyclic references is what allows reference counting schemes to develop memory leaks. This is one reason why most run-time systems, like the Java virtual machine, avoid reference counting garbage collection.

Another problem with reference counting schemes is that functions with a lot of local variables can cause the memory manager to perform an excessive amount of reference count incrementing and decrementing.

One solution is to use *deferred reference counting*, where the memory manager does not include local variables when it maintains reference counts. The problem with this is that you cannot be sure if a memory block can be reclaimed when its reference count is zero. This is because there might still be one or more local variables referencing the memory block. If you reclaim too early, you will end up with a bunch of dangling pointers! This is why most memory managers that implement deferred reference counting will use it in conjunction with a tracing algorithm that can survey the stack for local variable pointers.

Another reference counting technique is to use a COUNT field that is a single bit in size. This is known as *1-bit reference counting*. The gist of this technique is that the number of references to a block of memory is always zero, one, or many. So the 1-bit COUNT field will be zero or one. When it is one, there may be one or more references. In many cases, there is only a single reference and garbage collection is very quick. However, there also may be many references, which is why the 1-bit reference counting technique is usually used with another tracing garbage collector.

`malloc()` Version 5: Mark-Sweep

Theory

The operation of automatic memory managers consists of two phases: locating memory garbage and reclaiming that garbage. The mark-sweep approach to garbage collection is named after how it implements these two phases. The mark-sweep technique belongs to the tracing school of garbage collection. This means that a mark-sweep collector takes an active role in ferreting out memory references instead of relying on the compiler to do all the work.

The mark phase involves taking all the currently occupied memory blocks and marking them as "testing" because, for the moment, we do not know which memory blocks are genuinely occupied and which memory blocks are garbage. Next, the mark-sweep collector looks through the application's memory space searching for pointers to the heap. Any memory blocks that still have pointers referencing them are allowed to return to "occupied" status.

The remaining "testing" blocks are assumed to be garbage and collected. The sweep phase involves moving through the heap and releasing these "testing" blocks. In other words, the memory manager sweeps all of the garbage back into the "free" bucket.

The basic mark-sweep dance steps are displayed in Figure 5.5.

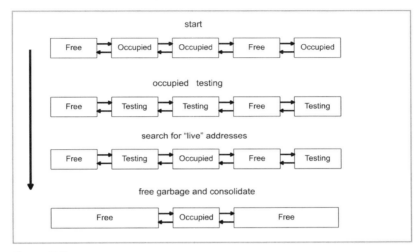

Figure 5.5

As mentioned in Chapter 3, most applications have four types of sections: code sections, data sections, stack sections, and one or more heaps. Because code sections tend to be designated as execute-only memory areas, only the stack, heap, and data section of an application can be scanned for pointers (see Figure 5.6). In my implementation, I scan only the heap and the stack.

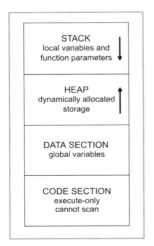

Figure 5.6

QUESTION

OK, so if the manager looks for pointers, what does a pointer look like?

ANSWER

Some compilers add a special tag to pointers. The problem with this approach is that the tag consumes part of a pointer's storage space and prevents a pointer from being capable of referencing the full address space. I decided that in my implementation, I would use a *conservative garbage collection* approach and consider any 32-bit value to be a potential pointer. This basically means that I have to scan memory byte-by-byte to enumerate every possible 32-bit value (see Figure 5.7).

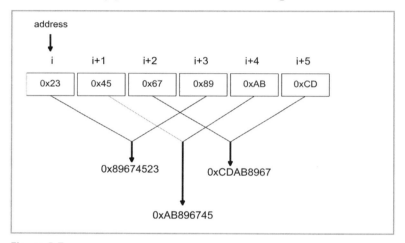

Figure 5.7

In my implementation, each memory block header has a STATE field. This field is 8 bits in size and may be in one of three states: Free, Occupied, Testing. The remaining fields are similar to those used by the sequential fit manual memory manager (see Figure 5.8).

There are a couple of policy decisions that a mark-sweep collector has to make. Specifically, a mark-sweep memory manager has to decide which parts of memory it is going to monitor and when it is going sweep them to reclaim garbage.

I decided in my implementation that I would search for pointers in the heap and the stack. This would allow me to search through an application's local variables and dynamically allocated storage. As far as deciding when to garbage collect, I decided to use a counter variable called tick that would invoke the garbage collection algorithm after reaching a certain value (stored in a variable called period).

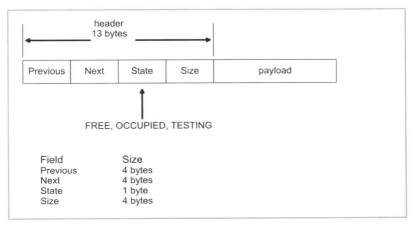

Figure 5.8

The programmer can configure the value of period so that they may control how often garbage collection occurs.

I also provide a forceCollection() function that can be used to force the memory manager to perform a sweep of memory.

NOTE This function does not suggest that garbage collection occur; it demands that garbage collection occur.

Implementation

I decided to implement a mark-sweep garbage collector by modifying the sequential fit implementation in Chapter 4. My implementation of the reference counting memory manager required four files:

Table 5.2

File	Use
driver.cpp	contains main(), is the scene of the crime
mallocV5.cpp	newMalloc(), newFree() wrappers (5th version)
perform.cpp	implements the PerformanceTest class
memmgr.cpp	implements the MarkSweepMemoryManager class

driver.cpp

This file contains the main() entry point. You can build my implementation to execute a diagnostic test or a performance test. To build the diagnostic version, you will need to comment out the PerformanceTestDriver() invocation and uncomment the debugTest() invocation. You will also need to activate the DEBUG_XXX macros in the mallocV4.cpp file.

```
#include<mallocV5.cpp>
#include<perform.cpp>

void debugTest()
{
    void *ptr;
    void *ptr1;
    void *ptr2;
    unsigned long *lptr;
    unsigned long allocs[6]={8,12,33,1,122,50};

    printf("address of ptr  = %p\n",&ptr);
    printf("address of ptr1 = %p\n",&ptr1);
    printf("address of ptr2 = %p\n",&ptr2);
    printf("address of lptr = %p\n",&lptr);
    printf("address of allocs = %p\n",allocs);

    initMemMgr(270,4);

    //8
    ptr = newMalloc(allocs[0]); if(ptr==NULL){ printf
          ("ptr==NULL!\n"); }

    //12
    ptr = newMalloc(allocs[1]); if(ptr==NULL){ printf
          ("ptr==NULL!\n"); }
    ptr2=ptr;

    //33
    ptr = newMalloc(allocs[2]); if(ptr==NULL){ printf
          ("ptr==NULL!\n"); }
    lptr=(unsigned long*)ptr;
    *lptr =(unsigned long)ptr;
    lptr=NULL;

    //1
    //first garbage collection here

    ptr = newMalloc(allocs[3]); if(ptr==NULL){ printf
          ("ptr==NULL!\n"); }
    ptr2=ptr;

    //122
    ptr = newMalloc(allocs[4]); if(ptr==NULL){ printf
          ("ptr==NULL!\n"); }
    ptr1=ptr;

    //50, should fail
    ptr = newMalloc(allocs[5]); if(ptr==NULL){ printf
          ("ptr==NULL!\n"); }
```

```
    forceCollection();

    closeMemMgr();
    return;

}/*end debugTest---------------------------------------------------*/

void main()
{
    //need this for mark-sweep
    getTOS();

    //for the debug test, should activate debug macros in
      mallocVx.cpp
    //debugTest();

    //for the performance test, should comment out debug macros
    PerformanceTestDriver();
    return;

}/*end main-------------------------------------------------------*/
```

You might notice a weird-looking function called `getTOS()`, which is invoked in `main()`. This is the first statement in `main()`, and it resolves to a macro defined in `memmgr.cpp`. This macro, which stands for get Top Of the Stack, obtains the value of `EBP` register so that my code knows where to stop its scan of the stack while looking for pointers. The `main()` function, like other C functions, has a prologue that sets up the `EBP` register as a stack frame pointer.

```
_main PROC NEAR
      push ebp
      mov  ebp, esp
```

By saving the value of `EBP` as soon as `main()` begins, I ensure that I can scan as much of the stack as legally possible.

mallocV5.cpp

Because we are now in the domain of automatic memory management, I disabled the `newFree()` function that has traditionally been defined in this file. The `newMalloc()` function is still operational, albeit using a different underlying object. If you wish to perform a debug/diagnostic test, you will need to activate the `DEBUG_XXX` macros.

You also might want to keep in mind that I have included a `forceCollection()` wrapper function that allows you to invoke the garbage collector.

```c
#include<stdio.h>
#include<stdlib.h>
#include<windows.h>

//#define DEBUG_MS_MEM_MGR
//#define DEBUG_MALLOCV5

#include<memmgr.cpp>

/*
wrapper functions
*/

MarkSweepMemoryManager *mmptr;

void initMemMgr(unsigned long totalbytes,unsigned char period)
{
    mmptr = new MarkSweepMemoryManager(totalbytes,period);
}

void closeMemMgr()
{
    delete(mmptr);
}

void *newMalloc(unsigned long size)
{
    void *ptr = (*mmptr).allocate(size);

#ifdef DEBUG_MALLOCV5
    (*mmptr).printState();
#endif

    return(ptr);
}

void forceCollection()
{
    (*mmptr).forceCollection();
    return;
}

void newFree(void *ptr)
{
    printf("newFree(): cannot free %p\n",ptr);
    printf("newFree(): not implemented, using garbage
            collector\n");
    return;
}
```

perform.cpp

The `PerformanceTest` class defined in this file has not been modified very much. The only thing that changed was the implementation of the `runTest()` member function. Specifically, I had to remove the calls to `newFree()`, which are no longer valid. I also replaced the array of `void*addr[]` pointers with a single `addr` pointer so that I could overwrite its contents and produce garbage.

```
unsigned long PerformanceTest::runTest()
{
    unsigned long *allocs;
    unsigned long i;
    unsigned long ticks1,ticks2;

    void *addr;

    /*create stream of allocation values*/

    allocs = (unsigned long *)malloc(sizeof(long)*nAllocations);
    if(allocs==NULL)
    {
        printf("could not allocate malloc() request stream\n");
        exit(1);
    }

    getAllocArray(allocs);

    /*start timer and do some work*/

    initMemMgr(1024*1024,200);

    printf("PerformanceTest::runTest(): time whistle blown\n");

    ticks1 = GetTickCount();

    for(i=0;i<nAllocations;i++)
    {
        addr = (char *)newMalloc(allocs[i]);
        if(addr==NULL)
        {
            printf("mallco()=addr[%lu]=%lu failed\n",i,addr);
            exit(1);
        }
    }

    forceCollection();

    ticks2 = GetTickCount();
```

```
    printf("PerformanceTest::runTest(): race has ended\n");

    closeMemMgr();

    free(allocs);

    return(ticks2-ticks1);
}/*end runTest----------------------------------------------------*/
```

memmgr.cpp

The `MarkSweepMemoryManager` class defined in this file is basically an extended version of the `SequentialFitMemoryManager`. To give you an idea of how this class operates, I have enumerated the possible paths of execution for this class in Figure 5.9.

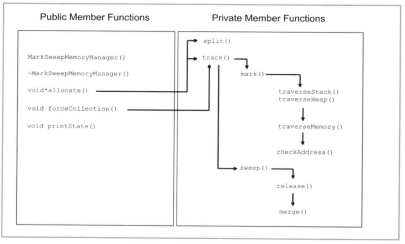

Figure 5.9

Most of what happens is performed as a result of invoking the `allocate()` function. Normally, `allocate()` will reserve storage and split free blocks. However, if the `ticks` variable has hit its `period` value, the garbage collector will kick into action via the `trace()` function.

```
#ifdef   DEBUG_MS_MEM_MGR
#define  MSG0(arg);              printf(arg);
#define  MSG1(arg1,arg2);        printf(arg1,arg2);
#else
#define  MSG0(arg);
#define  MSG1(arg1,arg2);
```

```
#endif

#define U1 unsigned char
#define U4 unsigned long

/*
    list element format
                |0   3||4   7|| 8  ||9  12||13 .. n|
                [PREV][NEXT][STATE][SIZE][payload]
                  U4   U4    U1     U4      ?

    byte allocated/freed is address of first byte of payload
    header = 13 bytes

    byte[0] is occupied by header data, so is always used, thus
            first link has prev=0 ( 0 indicates not used )
            last link has next=0
*/

#define PREV(i)         (*((U4*)(&ram[i-13])))
#define NEXT(i)         (*((U4*)(&ram[i-9])))
#define STATE(i)        (*((U1*)(&ram[i-5])))
/*FREE,OCCUPIED,TESTING*/
#define SIZE(i)         (*((U4*)(&ram[i-4])))

#define FREE                0
#define OCCUPIED            1
#define TESTING             2
char *stateStr[3]={"FREE","OCCUPIED","TESTING"};

#define START       13      /*address of first payload*/
#define SZ_HEADER   13

U4 stackFrameBase;

#define getTOS()    _asm{ MOV stackFrameBase, EBP}

class MarkSweepMemoryManager
{
    private:
    HANDLE handle;
    U1 *ram;        //pointer to memory storage
    U4 size;        //nbytes in storage
    U1 ticks;       //used to trigger collection
    U1 period;      //# ticks before collect

    void split(U4 addr,U4 nbytes);

    void trace();
    void mark();
    void traverseStack();
```

```cpp
    void traverseHeap();
    void traverseMemory(U1 *addr,U4 nbytes);
    int checkAddress(void *addr);
    void sweep();

    void release(U4 index);
    void merge(U4 prev,U4 current,U4 next);

    public:

    MarkSweepMemoryManager(U4 nbytes,U1 maxticks);
    ~MarkSweepMemoryManager();

    void*allocate(U4 nbytes);
    void forceCollection();
    void printState();
};

MarkSweepMemoryManager::MarkSweepMemoryManager(U4 nbytes,U1
        maxticks)
{
    handle = GetProcessHeap();
    if(handle==NULL)
    {
        printf("MarkSweepMemoryManager::");
        printf("MarkSweepMemoryManager():");
        printf("invalid handle\n");
        exit(1);
    }

    ram = (U1*)HeapAlloc(handle,HEAP_ZERO_MEMORY,nbytes);

    //for portability, you could use:
    //ram = (unsigned char*)malloc(nbytes);

    size = nbytes;

    if(size<=SZ_HEADER)
    {
        printf("MarkSweepMemoryManager::");
        printf("MarkSweepMemoryManager():");
        printf("not enough memory fed to constructor\n");
        exit(1);
    }

    PREV(START)=0;
    NEXT(START)=0;
    STATE(START)=FREE;
    SIZE(START)=size-SZ_HEADER;

    MSG0("MarkSweepMemoryManager::");
```

```cpp
    MSG1("MarkSweepMemoryManager(): ram[%lu], ",nbytes);

    ticks = 0;
    period = maxticks;

    MSG1("ticks=%u, ",ticks);
    MSG1("period=%u\n",period);

    return;
}/*end constructor----------------------------------------*/

MarkSweepMemoryManager::~MarkSweepMemoryManager()
{
    if(HeapFree(handle,HEAP_NO_SERIALIZE,ram)==0)
    {
        printf("MarkSweepMemoryManager::");
        printf("~MarkSweepMemoryManager():");
        printf("could not free heap storage\n");
        return;
    }

    //for portability, you could use:
    //free(ram);

    MSG0("MarkSweepMemoryManager::");
    MSG0("~MarkSweepMemoryManager()");
    MSG1("free ram[%lu]\n",size);
    return;

}/*end destructor-----------------------------------------*/

/*
U4 nbytes    -    number of bytes required
returns address of first byte of memory region allocated
( or NULL if cannot allocate a large enough block )
*/

void* MarkSweepMemoryManager::allocate(U4 nbytes)
{
    U4 current;

    MSG0("MarkSweepMemoryManager::");
    MSG1("allocate(%lu)\n",nbytes);

    if(nbytes==0)
    {
        MSG0("MarkSweepMemoryManager::");
        MSG0("allocate(): zero bytes requested\n");
        return(NULL);
    }
```

```
    //before we start, garbage collect if the time has arrived

    ticks++;
    MSG0("MarkSweepMemoryManager::");
    MSG1("allocate(): gc check -> [ticks,period]=[%u,",ticks);
    MSG1("%u]\n",period);
    if(ticks==period)
    {
        trace();
        ticks=0;
    }

    //traverse the linked list, starting with first element

    current = START;
    while(NEXT(current)!=0)
    {
        if((SIZE(current)>=nbytes)&&(STATE(current)==FREE))
        {
            split(current,nbytes);
            return((void*)&ram[current]);
        }
        current = NEXT(current);
    }

    //handle the last block ( which has NEXT(current)=0 )

    if((SIZE(current)>=nbytes)&&(STATE(current)==FREE))
    {
        split(current,nbytes);
        return((void*)&ram[current]);
    }

    return(NULL);

}/*end allocation----------------------------------------------*/
/*
breaks [free] region into [alloc][free] pair, if possible
*/

void MarkSweepMemoryManager::split(U4 addr, U4 nbytes)
{
    /*
    want payload to have enough room for
    nbytes = size of request
    SZ_HEADER = header for new region
    SZ_HEADER = payload for new region (arbitrary 13 bytes)
    */
```

Automatic Memory Management

```cpp
    if(SIZE(addr)>= nbytes+SZ_HEADER+SZ_HEADER)
    {
        U4 oldnext;
        U4 oldprev;
        U4 oldsize;

        U4 newaddr;

        MSG0("MarkSweepMemoryManager::");
        MSG0("split(): split=YES\n");

        oldnext=NEXT(addr);
        oldprev=PREV(addr);
        oldsize=SIZE(addr);

        newaddr = addr + nbytes + SZ_HEADER;

        NEXT(addr)=newaddr;
        PREV(addr)=oldprev;
        STATE(addr)=OCCUPIED;
        SIZE(addr)=nbytes;

        NEXT(newaddr)=oldnext;
        PREV(newaddr)=addr;
        STATE(newaddr)=FREE;
        SIZE(newaddr)=oldsize-nbytes-SZ_HEADER;
    }
    else
    {
        MSG0("MarkSweepMemoryManager::");
        MSG0("split(): split=NO\n");
        STATE(addr)=OCCUPIED;
    }
    return;

}/*end split----------------------------------------------------*/

void MarkSweepMemoryManager::forceCollection()
{
    MSG0("MarkSweepMemoryManager::");
    MSG0("forceCollection(): forcing collection\n");
    trace();
    return;

}/*end forceCollection------------------------------------------*/

void MarkSweepMemoryManager::trace()
{
    MSG0("MarkSweepMemoryManager::");
    MSG0("trace(): initiating mark-sweep\n");
    mark();
```

```
        sweep();
        return;

}/*end trace-------------------------------------------------*/

void MarkSweepMemoryManager::mark()
{
    U4 i;
    U4 current;

    //set all OCCUPIED blocks to TESTING

    i=0;
    current=START;

    while(NEXT(current)!=0)
    {
        if(STATE(current)==OCCUPIED)
        {
            STATE(current)=TESTING;
        }
        current = NEXT(current);
        i++;
    }

    if(STATE(current)==OCCUPIED)
    {
        STATE(current)=TESTING;
    }

#ifdef  DEBUG_MS_MEM_MGR
    MSG0("MarkSweepMemoryManager::");
    MSG0("mark(): toggle OCCUPIED to TESTING\n");
    printState();
#endif

    //traverse the stack and heap
    //if find address to TESTING block, set to OCCUPIED

    MSG0("MarkSweepMemoryManager::");
    MSG0("mark(): initiating stack and heap traversals\n");
    traverseStack();
    traverseHeap();
    return;

}/*end mark--------------------------------------------------*/

void MarkSweepMemoryManager::traverseStack()
{
    U4 currentAddr;
```

```
    _asm{ MOV currentAddr,ESP };

    MSG0("MarkSweepMemoryManager::traverseStack():");
    MSG1("EBP=%p\t",stackFrameBase);
    MSG1("ESP=%p\n",currentAddr);

    //basically traverse stack from current pointer to base
     (Lo->Hi)

traverseMemory((U1*)currentAddr,(stackFrameBase-currentAddr));
    return;

}/*end traverseStack----------------------------------------*/

void MarkSweepMemoryManager::traverseHeap()
{
    MSG0("MarkSweepMemoryManager::traverseHeap(): looking at
          heap\n");
    traverseMemory(ram,size);
    return;

}/*end traverseHeap-----------------------------------------*/

void MarkSweepMemoryManager::traverseMemory(U1 *addr,U4 nbytes)
{
    U4 i;
    U4 start,end;
    U4 *iptr;

    start = (U4)addr;
    end   = start + nbytes -1;

    MSG0("MarkSweepMemoryManager::traverseMemory(): ");
    MSG1("[start=%lx,",start);
    MSG1(" end=%lx]\n",end);

    //address = 4 bytes, so stop 4 bytes from end

    for(i=start;i<=end-3;i++)
    {
        //point to integer value at memory address i
        iptr = (U4*)i;

        //check integer value to see if it is a heap address
        if( checkAddress((void *)(*iptr))==TRUE)
        {
            MSG0("MarkSweepMemoryManager::traverseMemory(): ");
            MSG1("value source address=%p\n",iptr);
        }
    }
```

```
        return;
}/*end traverseMemory----------------------------------------*/

int MarkSweepMemoryManager::checkAddress(void *addr)
{
    U4 index;

    if(addr==NULL){ return(FALSE); }

    //check to see if address is out of heap bounds

    if( (addr>= (void*)&ram[size]) || (addr< (void*)&ram[0]) )
    {
        return(FALSE);
    }

    //translate addr into index

    index = (U4)( ((U1*)addr) - &ram[0] );

    //now check index to see if reference an actual block
    //a header always occupies first SZ_HEADER bytes of storage

    if(index<SZ_HEADER){ return(FALSE); }

    //more sanity checks

    if((STATE(index)!=TESTING)|| //region if free
       (PREV(index)>=index)   || //previous element not previous
       (NEXT(index)>=size)    || //next is beyond the end
       (SIZE(index)>=size)    || //size of region greater
                                 //than whole
       (SIZE(index)==0))         //no size at all
    {

        MSG0("MarkSweepMemoryManager::checkAddress(): ");
        MSG1("failed sanity chk (already found) addr=%p ",addr);
        return(FALSE);
    }

    MSG0("MarkSweepMemoryManager::checkAddress(): ");
    MSG1("live memory block at addr=%p ",addr);
    MSG1("index=%lu\n",index);

    STATE(index)=OCCUPIED;

    return(TRUE);

}/*end checkAddress-------------------------------------------*/
```

```
void MarkSweepMemoryManager::sweep()
{
    U4 i;
    U4 current;

    MSG0("MarkSweepMemoryManager::");
    MSG0("sweep(): link sweep intiated\n");

    //recycle all the TESTING blocks

    i=0;
    current=START;

    while(NEXT(current)!=0)
    {
        if(STATE(current)==TESTING)
        {
            MSG0("MarkSweepMemoryManager::");
            MSG1("sweep(): garbage found at index=%lu\n",
                 current);
            release(current);
        }
        current = NEXT(current);
        i++;
    }

    if(STATE(current)==TESTING)
    {
        MSG0("MarkSweepMemoryManager::");
        MSG1("sweep(): garbage found at index=%lu\n",current);
        release(current);
    }

    return;

}/*end sweep--------------------------------------------------*/

void MarkSweepMemoryManager::release(U4 index)
{

    //a header always occupies first 13 bytes of storage

    if(index<SZ_HEADER)
    {
        MSG0("MarkSweepMemoryManager::");
        MSG0("release(): address in first 13 bytes\n");
        return;
    }

    //yet more sanity checks
```

```
    if((STATE(index)==FREE)    || //region if free
       (PREV(index)>=index)    || //previous element not previous
       (NEXT(index)>=size)     || //next is beyond the end
       (SIZE(index)>=size)     || //size region greater than whole
       (SIZE(index)==0))          //no size at all
    {
        MSG0("MarkSweepMemoryManager::");
        MSG0("release(): referencing invalid region\n");
        return;
    }

    merge(PREV(index),index,NEXT(index));

#ifdef  DEBUG_MS_MEM_MGR
    MSG0("MarkSweepMemoryManager::");
    MSG0("release(): post merge layout\n");
    printState();
#endif

    return;

}/*end release-------------------------------------------------*/

void MarkSweepMemoryManager::merge(U4 prev,U4 current,U4 next)
{
    /*
    first handle special cases of region at end(s)
    prev=0                     low end
    next=0                     high end
    prev=0 and next=0          only 1 list element
    */

    if(prev==0)
    {
        if(next==0)
        {
            STATE(current)=FREE;
        }
        else if((STATE(next)==OCCUPIED)||(STATE(next)==TESTING))
        {
            STATE(current)=FREE;
        }
        else if(STATE(next)==FREE)
        {
            U4 temp;

            MSG0("MarkSweepMemoryManager::merge():");
            MSG0("merging to NEXT\n");

            STATE(current)=FREE;
```

```
            SIZE(current)=SIZE(current)+SIZE(next)+SZ_HEADER;
            NEXT(current)=NEXT(next);

            temp = NEXT(next);
            if(temp!=0){ PREV(temp)=current; }
        }
    }
    else if(next==0)
    {
        if((STATE(prev)==OCCUPIED)||(STATE(prev)==TESTING))
        {
            STATE(current)=FREE;
        }
        else if(STATE(prev)==FREE)
        {
            MSG0("MarkSweepMemoryManager::merge():");
            MSG0("merging to PREV\n");
            SIZE(prev)=SIZE(prev)+SIZE(current)+SZ_HEADER;
            NEXT(prev)=NEXT(current);
        }
    }

    /*
        cases:
                OTO     ->      OFO
                TTT             TFT
                TTO             TFO
                OTT             OFT

                OTF             O[F]
                TTF             T[F]
                FTO             [F]O
                FTT             [F]T
                FTF             [F]
    */

    else if((STATE(prev)==OCCUPIED)&&(STATE(next)==OCCUPIED))
    {
        STATE(current)=FREE;
    }
    else if((STATE(prev)==TESTING)&&(STATE(next)==TESTING))
    {
        STATE(current)=FREE;
    }
    else if((STATE(prev)==TESTING)&&(STATE(next)==OCCUPIED))
    {
        STATE(current)=FREE;
    }
    else if((STATE(prev)==OCCUPIED)&&(STATE(next)==TESTING))
    {
        STATE(current)=FREE;
```

```
    }
    else if((STATE(prev)==OCCUPIED)&&(STATE(next)==FREE))
    {
        U4 temp;

        MSG0("MarkSweepMemoryManager::merge():");
        MSG0("merging to NEXT\n");
        STATE(current)=FREE;
        SIZE(current)=SIZE(current)+SIZE(next)+SZ_HEADER;
        NEXT(current)=NEXT(next);

        temp = NEXT(next);
        if(temp!=0){ PREV(temp)=current; }
    }
    else if((STATE(prev)==TESTING)&&(STATE(next)==FREE))
    {
        U4 temp;

        MSG0("MarkSweepMemoryManager::merge():");
        MSG0("merging to NEXT\n");
        STATE(current)=FREE;
        SIZE(current)=SIZE(current)+SIZE(next)+SZ_HEADER;
        NEXT(current)=NEXT(next);

        temp = NEXT(next);
        if(temp!=0){ PREV(temp)=current; }
    }
    else if((STATE(prev)==FREE)&&(STATE(next)==OCCUPIED))
    {
        MSG0("MarkSweepMemoryManager::merge():");
        MSG0("merging to PREV\n");
        SIZE(prev)=SIZE(prev)+SIZE(current)+SZ_HEADER;
        NEXT(prev)=NEXT(current);
        PREV(next)=prev;
    }
    else if((STATE(prev)==FREE)&&(STATE(next)==TESTING))
    {
        MSG0("MarkSweepMemoryManager::merge():");
        MSG0("merging to PREV\n");
        SIZE(prev)=SIZE(prev)+SIZE(current)+SZ_HEADER;
        NEXT(prev)=NEXT(current);
        PREV(next)=prev;
    }
    else if((STATE(prev)==FREE)&&(STATE(next)==FREE))
    {
        U4 temp;

        MSG0("MarkSweepMemoryManager::merge():");
        MSG0("merging with both sides\n");
        SIZE(prev)=SIZE(prev)+
```

```
                        SIZE(current)+SZ_HEADER+
                        SIZE(next)+SZ_HEADER;
        NEXT(prev)=NEXT(next);

        temp = NEXT(next);
        if(temp!=0){ PREV(temp)=prev; }
    }

    return;

}/*end merge-----------------------------------------------------------*/

void MarkSweepMemoryManager::printState()
{
    U4 i;
    U4 current;

    i=0;
    current=START;

    while(NEXT(current)!=0)
    {
        printf("%lu) [P=%lu]",i,PREV(current));
        printf("[addr=%lu]",current);
        printf("[St=%s]",stateStr[STATE(current)]);
        printf("[Sz=%lu]",SIZE(current));
        printf("[N=%lu]\n",NEXT(current));
        current = NEXT(current);
        i++;
    }

    //print the last list element

    printf("%lu) [P=%lu]",i,PREV(current));
    printf("[addr=%lu]",current);
    printf("[St=%s]",stateStr[STATE(current)]);
    printf("[Sz=%lu]",SIZE(current));
    printf("[N=%lu]\n",NEXT(current));

    return;

}/*end printState------------------------------------------------------*/
```

Tests

I performed two different tests against this memory manager. A debug test was performed to make sure that the manager was doing what it was supposed to do. If you modify my source code, I would suggest running the debug test again to validate your changes. Once

I was sure that the memory manager was operational, I turned off debugging features and ran a performance test.

The debug test was performed by executing the code in the `debugTest()` function defined in the `driver.cpp` source file. I keep things fairly simple, but at the same time, I take a good, hard look at what is going on. If you decide to run a debug test, you will want to make sure that the `DEBUG_XXX` macros in `mallocV4.cpp` are turned on. You will also want to comment out the `PerformanceTestDriver()` function call in `main()`.

The following output was generated by the debug build of the memory manager:

```
address of ptr   = 0065FDE0
address of ptr1  = 0065FDC0
address of ptr2  = 0065FDBC
address of lptr  = 0065FDC4
address of allocs = 0065FDC8
MarkSweepMemoryManager::MarkSweepMemoryManager(): ram[270],
ticks=0, period=4
MarkSweepMemoryManager::allocate(8)
MarkSweepMemoryManager::allocate(): gc check ->
[ticks,period]=[1,4]
MarkSweepMemoryManager::split(): split=YES
0) [P=0] [addr=13] [St=OCCUPIED] [Sz=8] [N=34]
1) [P=13] [addr=34] [St=FREE] [Sz=236] [N=0]
MarkSweepMemoryManager::allocate(12)
MarkSweepMemoryManager::allocate(): gc check ->
[ticks,period]=[2,4]
MarkSweepMemoryManager::split(): split=YES
0) [P=0] [addr=13] [St=OCCUPIED] [Sz=8] [N=34]
1) [P=13] [addr=34] [St=OCCUPIED] [Sz=12] [N=59]
2) [P=34] [addr=59] [St=FREE] [Sz=211] [N=0]
MarkSweepMemoryManager::allocate(33)
MarkSweepMemoryManager::allocate(): gc check ->
[ticks,period]=[3,4]
MarkSweepMemoryManager::split(): split=YES
0) [P=0] [addr=13] [St=OCCUPIED] [Sz=8] [N=34]
1) [P=13] [addr=34] [St=OCCUPIED] [Sz=12] [N=59]
2) [P=34] [addr=59] [St=OCCUPIED] [Sz=33] [N=105]
3) [P=59] [addr=105] [St=FREE] [Sz=165] [N=0]
MarkSweepMemoryManager::allocate(1)
MarkSweepMemoryManager::allocate(): gc check ->
[ticks,period]=[4,4]
MarkSweepMemoryManager::trace(): initiating mark-sweep
MarkSweepMemoryManager::mark(): toggle OCCUPIED to TESTING
0) [P=0] [addr=13] [St=TESTING] [Sz=8] [N=34]
1) [P=13] [addr=34] [St=TESTING] [Sz=12] [N=59]
2) [P=34] [addr=59] [St=TESTING] [Sz=33] [N=105]
3) [P=59] [addr=105] [St=FREE] [Sz=165] [N=0]
```

```
MarkSweepMemoryManager::mark(): initiating stack and heap
traversals
MarkSweepMemoryManager::traverseStack():EBP=0065FDF8
ESP=0065FD5C
MarkSweepMemoryManager::traverseMemory(): [start=65fd5c,
end=65fdf7]
MarkSweepMemoryManager::checkAddress(): live memory block at
addr=00530047 index=59
MarkSweepMemoryManager::traverseMemory(): value source
address=0065FDAC
MarkSweepMemoryManager::checkAddress(): live memory block at
addr=0053002E index=34
MarkSweepMemoryManager::traverseMemory(): value source
address=0065FDBC
MarkSweepMemoryManager::checkAddress(): failed sanity chk
(already found) addr=00530047
MarkSweepMemoryManager::traverseHeap(): looking at heap
MarkSweepMemoryManager::traverseMemory(): [start=53000c,
end=530119]
MarkSweepMemoryManager::checkAddress(): failed sanity chk
(already found) addr=00530047 MarkSweepMemoryManager::sweep():
link sweep intiated
MarkSweepMemoryManager::sweep(): garbage found at index=13
MarkSweepMemoryManager::release(): post merge layout
0) [P=0][addr=13][St=FREE][Sz=8][N=34]
1) [P=13][addr=34][St=OCCUPIED][Sz=12][N=59]
2) [P=34][addr=59][St=OCCUPIED][Sz=33][N=105]
3) [P=59][addr=105][St=FREE][Sz=165][N=0]
MarkSweepMemoryManager::split(): split=NO
0) [P=0][addr=13][St=OCCUPIED][Sz=8][N=34]
1) [P=13][addr=34][St=OCCUPIED][Sz=12][N=59]
2) [P=34][addr=59][St=OCCUPIED][Sz=33][N=105]
3) [P=59][addr=105][St=FREE][Sz=165][N=0]
MarkSweepMemoryManager::allocate(122)
MarkSweepMemoryManager::allocate(): gc check ->
[ticks,period]=[1,4]
MarkSweepMemoryManager::split(): split=YES
0) [P=0][addr=13][St=OCCUPIED][Sz=8][N=34]
1) [P=13][addr=34][St=OCCUPIED][Sz=12][N=59]
2) [P=34][addr=59][St=OCCUPIED][Sz=33][N=105]
3) [P=59][addr=105][St=OCCUPIED][Sz=122][N=240]
4) [P=105][addr=240][St=FREE][Sz=30][N=0]
MarkSweepMemoryManager::allocate(50)
MarkSweepMemoryManager::allocate(): gc check ->
[ticks,period]=[2,4]
0) [P=0][addr=13][St=OCCUPIED][Sz=8][N=34]
1) [P=13][addr=34][St=OCCUPIED][Sz=12][N=59]
2) [P=34][addr=59][St=OCCUPIED][Sz=33][N=105]
3) [P=59][addr=105][St=OCCUPIED][Sz=122][N=240]
4) [P=105][addr=240][St=FREE][Sz=30][N=0]
ptr==NULL!
```

```
MarkSweepMemoryManager::forceCollection(): forcing collection
MarkSweepMemoryManager::trace(): initiating mark-sweep
MarkSweepMemoryManager::mark(): toggle OCCUPIED to TESTING
0) [P=0][addr=13][St=TESTING][Sz=8][N=34]
1) [P=13][addr=34][St=TESTING][Sz=12][N=59]
2) [P=34][addr=59][St=TESTING][Sz=33][N=105]
3) [P=59][addr=105][St=TESTING][Sz=122][N=240]
4) [P=105][addr=240][St=FREE][Sz=30][N=0]
MarkSweepMemoryManager::mark(): initiating stack and heap
traversals
MarkSweepMemoryManager::traverseStack():EBP=0065FDF8
ESP=0065FD6C
MarkSweepMemoryManager::traverseMemory(): [start=65fd6c,
end=65fdf7]
MarkSweepMemoryManager::checkAddress(): live memory block at
addr=00530019 index=13
MarkSweepMemoryManager::traverseMemory(): value source
address=0065FDBC
MarkSweepMemoryManager::checkAddress(): live memory block at
addr=00530075 index=105
MarkSweepMemoryManager::traverseMemory(): value source
address=0065FDC0
MarkSweepMemoryManager::traverseHeap(): looking at heap
MarkSweepMemoryManager::traverseMemory(): [start=53000c,
end=530119]
MarkSweepMemoryManager::checkAddress(): live memory block at
addr=00530047 index=59
MarkSweepMemoryManager::traverseMemory(): value source
address=00530047
MarkSweepMemoryManager::sweep(): link sweep intiated
MarkSweepMemoryManager::sweep(): garbage found at index=34
MarkSweepMemoryManager::release(): post merge layout
0) [P=0][addr=13][St=OCCUPIED][Sz=8][N=34]
1) [P=13][addr=34][St=FREE][Sz=12][N=59]
2) [P=34][addr=59][St=OCCUPIED][Sz=33][N=105]
3) [P=59][addr=105][St=OCCUPIED][Sz=122][N=240]
4) [P=105][addr=240][St=FREE][Sz=30][N=0]
MarkSweepMemoryManager::~MarkSweepMemoryManager()free ram[270]
```

The debug test code is a little involved, so I am going to provide a blow-by-blow account of what happens. Let's start by looking at a snippet of code from `debugTest()`:

```
//8
ptr = newMalloc(allocs[0]); if(ptr==NULL){ printf
            ("ptr==NULL!\n"); }

//12
ptr = newMalloc(allocs[1]); if(ptr==NULL){ printf
            ("ptr==NULL!\n"); }
ptr2=ptr;
```

```
//33
ptr = newMalloc(allocs[2]); if(ptr==NULL){ printf
            ("ptr==NULL!\n"); }
lptr=(unsigned long*)ptr;
*lptr =(unsigned long)ptr;
lptr=NULL;

//1
//first garbage collection here

ptr = newMalloc(allocs[3]); if(ptr==NULL){ printf
            ("ptr==NULL!\n"); }
ptr2=ptr;
```

By the time the `newMalloc(allocs[3])` call has been made, the local variables of `debugTest()` have the following values:

Table 5.3

Variable	ram[ ] index	Size of Block Referenced
ptr	59	33
ptr1	-	-
ptr2	34	12
lptr	NULL	-
heap variable	59	33

The `ptr` variable has overwritten itself several times and will point to the most recent heap allocation. In addition, a variable in the heap, initially pointed to by `lptr`, stores an address belonging to the heap.

When the `newMalloc(allocs[3])` code has been reached, the `ticks` variable will be equal to 4, and garbage collection will occur. This will cause the 8-byte block that was allocated first to be reclaimed. All the other allocated heap blocks still have "live" pointers.

Once garbage collection has occurred, the following code will execute:

```
//122
ptr = newMalloc(allocs[4]);
if(ptr==NULL){ printf("ptr==NULL!\n"); }
ptr1=ptr;

//50, should fail
ptr = newMalloc(allocs[5]);
if(ptr==NULL){ printf("ptr==NULL!\n"); }

forceCollection();
```

This will cause the local variables of `debugTest()` to assume the following values:

Table 5.4

Variable	ram[ ] index	Size of Block Referenced
ptr	NULL	-
ptr1	105	122
ptr2	13	8
lptr	NULL	-
heap variable	59	33

The last allocation call cannot be serviced, so NULL is returned into `ptr`. This leaves us with three "live" pointers. If you look at the debug output, you will see that there are three `OCCUPIED` regions of memory in the heap after garbage collection occurs.

The performance test was conducted by commenting out `debugTest()` and the debug macros in `mallocV5.cpp`, and then enabling the `PerformanceTestDriver()` function. The results of the performance run were initially disappointing:

```
PerformanceTest::runTest(): time whistle blown
PerformanceTest::runTest(): race has ended
msecs=9615
```

Whoa. After changing the value of `period` from 4 to 200, the performance was more acceptable:

```
PerformanceTest::runTest(): time whistle blown
PerformanceTest::runTest(): race has ended
msecs=430
```

This is a far cry from the 35 milliseconds that was necessary for the sequential fit implementation to do its job. As I mentioned earlier, extra bookkeeping is the cost of automatic memory management, and this translates into additional execution time.

Trade-Offs

While my mark-sweep collector does not exactly compete with the reference counting version, it does successfully handle the cyclic-reference problem that caused a memory leak in the previous implementation. With a little refinement, I could probably whittle down the performance time to less than 100 milliseconds. I will present some suggestions for improvement at the end of this chapter.

Besides performance, two additional problems are created through use of the mark-sweep collector: latency and external fragmentation. Not only does my implementation lead to scattered groups of free and reserved blocks, but it would be possible for two related blocks of memory to be located at opposite ends of the heap.

The *copying garbage collector* is a variation of the mark-sweep collector that attempts to deal with these two problems. The copying garbage collector copies "live" memory blocks to the low end of memory so that all the allocated storage ends up concentrated in one region of the heap, leaving the rest of the heap to service allocation requests. Not only does this solve the latency problem, but it also allows memory requests for larger blocks to be serviced. This is illustrated in Figure 5.10.

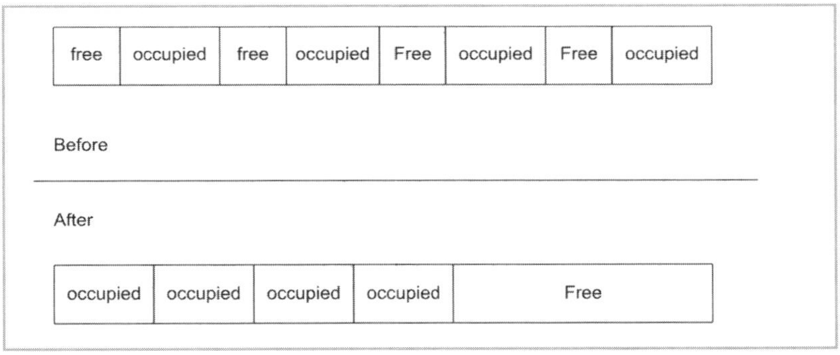

free	occupied	free	occupied	Free	occupied	Free	occupied

Before

After

occupied	occupied	occupied	occupied	Free

Figure 5.10

Because all the "live" pointers on the stack, in the heap, and in the data segment need to be updated with new values when the memory blocks that they point to are relocated, copying collection can be difficult. Not only does this add complexity, but these extra steps also hurt execution time. In addition, extra storage space is needed in order to copy allocated blocks of memory on the heap from one location to another. Depending on the size of the memory block being moved, this can be a significant amount of storage (perhaps even the amount of heap space initially allocated to the garbage collector).

Performance Comparison

At this point, it might be enlightening to gather all of the statistics from the past two chapters together:

Table 5.5

Algorithm	Time to Service 1,024 Requests
bit map	856 milliseconds
sequential fit	35 milliseconds
segregated lists	5 milliseconds
reference counting	30 milliseconds
mark-sweep	430 milliseconds

Hands down, the segregated list approach is the quickest. It also wastes memory like nobody's business. It would be very easy (with the segregated list approach) to end up reserving 1,024 bytes for an 8-byte allocation request. This leaves the sequential fit algorithm as the most attractive implementation with regard to the manual memory managers presented in Chapter 2.

While the reference counting approach is actually faster than two of the manual memory managers, it also has the nasty habit of developing memory leaks when confronted with cyclic pointer references. The whole point of using a garbage collector is to avoid memory leaks, so this problem kicks reference counting out of the race. This leaves us with the mark-sweep garbage collector, which has obvious performance issues.

I will spend the remainder of this book suggesting various ways to augment the mark-sweep collector's execution time and functionality. I will leave it as an exercise to the reader to augment the mark-sweep collector with these additional features.

Potential Additions

The mark-sweep garbage collector that I provided in this chapter was a bare-bones implementation (and that is an understatement). I deliberately kept things as simple as I could so that you could grasp the big picture without being bogged down with details. Seeing as how my mark-sweep collector had only the minimum set of features, I thought it might be wise to point out a few of the features that could be added to round out the functionality of the mark-sweep collector.

Object Format Assumptions

So far, I have referred to regions in the heap as "memory blocks." I have done this intentionally so that I could keep the discussion as general as possible. In the end, everything on the heap is merely a block of memory. Depending on what that block of memory represents, however, it may require additional steps when the block of memory is allocated and reclaimed.

For example, objects have both constructors and destructors. When an object is created, its constructor must be called. When an object's storage is reclaimed, its destructor needs to be invoked.

When an object is created off the heap, the compiler will typically pass the object to its constructor. Consider this code:

```
BluePrint *ptr;
ptr = new BluePrint(15);
```

In addition to requesting storage from the heap via the new operator, most compilers will also emit the code necessary to pass the new object to its constructor:

```
; invoke the new operator, allocate 12 bytes
push    12              ; 0000000cH
call    ??2@YAPAXI@Z    ; operator new
add     esp, 4
; pass allocated memory (the object) to the constructor
push    15              ; 0000000fH
mov     ecx, DWORD PTR $T196[ebp]
call    ??0BluePrint@@QAE@H@Z   ; BluePrint::BluePrint
mov     DWORD PTR -36+[ebp], eax
```

If manual memory management is being used, the programmer will include source code that will take care of reclaiming the object's storage in the heap.

```
delete(ptr);
```

As before, not only will the compiler emit the instructions necessary to reclaim the object, but it will also emit the instructions necessary to call the object's destructor before reclamation occurs:

```
push    1
mov     ecx, DWORD PTR $T200[ebp]
call    ??_GBluePrint@@QAEPAXI@Z    ; BluePrint::'scalar
        deleting destructor'
mov     DWORD PTR -40+[ebp], eax
```

If a garbage collector is being used to manage reclamation, the programmer will never issue a call to delete(). This means that the garbage collector will have to do this behind the scenes. In order to obey this protocol, a memory manager will need to know which blocks are objects. If a given memory block represents an object, the memory manager will also need to know what type of object it is dealing with.

To institute this type of functionality with my mark-sweep collector, you might want to consider adding another field to the memory block header (see Figure 5.11).

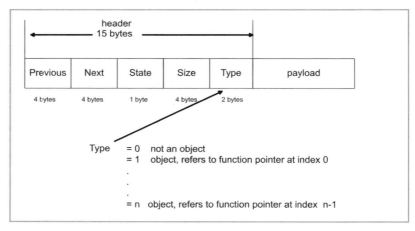

Figure 5.11

This new field, which we'll call TYPE, indicates if the memory block is an object, and if it is, then it indexes an element in an array of function pointers. These function pointers store the addresses of destructor functions. This setup is displayed in Figure 5.12.

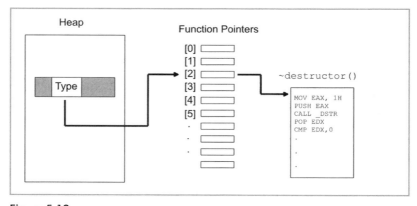

Figure 5.12

When a memory block is about to be reclaimed, the garbage collector will check to see if the memory block represents an object. If the memory block is an object, the collector will invoke the object's destructor before it reclaims the memory block's storage.

Naturally, there are many more details to consider than I've mentioned, such as setting up the table of function pointers and handling nested objects that call different destructors. You will have to experiment with a number of different approaches. Nevertheless, I hope to have guided you in the right direction.

Variable Heap Size

In all of my implementations, the amount of storage space that the memory manager has to work with is fixed in size. This means that if the manager runs out of memory, it will not be able to service additional requests. To provide greater flexibility, you could allow a memory manager to request more memory from the underlying operating system. This way, when a manager runs out of storage, it simply expands its space by calling the operating system for help.

There are problems related to doing this. For example, if you use an ANSI function, like `realloc()`, to increase the memory manager's storage space, you cannot be sure if the resized memory region will be relocated. Relocation basically invalidates all of an application's existing pointers because the memory regions that they referenced have been moved.

Microsoft's `HeapReAlloc()` Win32 call allows you to specify a special flag value:

```
newptr = HeapReAlloc( heapHandle,
                      HEAP_REALLOC_IN_PLACE_ONLY,
                      oldptr,
                      1024*1024*10);
```

This requires that the reallocated memory not be moved.

Indirect Addressing

During the discussion of copying collection and memory reallocation, you have seen how moving memory can make life difficult for an application. The only solution that seems halfway tractable is to traverse the application's stack, heap, and data segment and update the pointer values to reference new locations.

There is, however, a different approach. Rather than have pointers reference actual memory, you can have them store handles. A handle could be implemented simply by a structure that maps an integer handle value to a physical address:

```
struct MemHandle
{
    unsigned long value;
    void *ptr;
};
```

This would allow you to change the address of a memory block (i.e., `void *ptr`) without having to change the value stored by pointers in the application (i.e., `unsigned long value`). When an address change does occur, all you need to update is a single `MemHandle` structure instead of potentially dozens of application variables. This type of relationship is displayed in Figure 5.13.

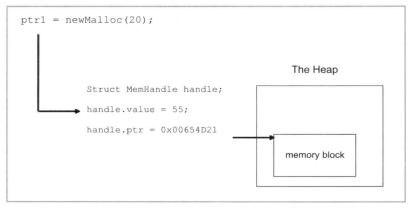

Figure 5.13

For example, consider the following code:

```
void *ptr1;
ptr1 = newMalloc(20);   //assume returns handle value=55
printf("%lu\n",ptr);    //prints out 55
forceCollection();      //memory blocks may shift
printf("%lu\n",ptr);    //still prints out 55
```

When I initially call `newmalloc()`, the value stored in `ptr1` is a handle value instead of an actual address. When I call `force-Collection()` to initiate garbage collection, memory blocks in the heap may end up being rearranged. However, the handle value will not change, even if its associated address does.

Some garbage collectors use handles in conjunction with a stack allocation scheme. Memory is allocated in a fashion similar to a stack. There is a pointer (`SP`) that keeps track of the top of the stack. Allocation requests cause the stack pointer to increment. This is a very fast scheme in practice (even faster than the segregated list approach).

When the stack hits its limit, the garbage collector kicks in and reclaims garbage. To minimize fragmentation, the occupied blocks are all shifted down to the bottom of the heap. Because handles are being used instead of actual pointers, all the collector has to do when it makes this shift is update all the handles. The application variables can remain untouched.

This process is illustrated in Figure 5.14.

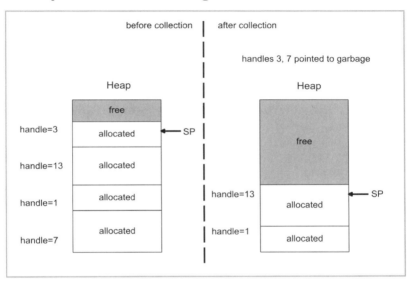

Figure 5.14

Real-Time Behavior

With my mark-sweep collector, there was a noticeable decrease in execution time when the frequency of garbage collection was decreased. This might lead you to think that the best way to speed up a garbage collector is to delay collection until the last possible moment. As it turns out, this approach isn't a good idea because it can force a garbage collector to perform reclamation when the application urgently needs allocation the most. A memory-starved application can be forced to wait for storage space, which it desperately needs, while the garbage collector chugs away.

At the other end of the spectrum, there is the idea that you could speed a garbage collector up by allowing it to do a small amount of work during each allocation. This tactic is known as *incremental garbage collection*, and you got a taste of it when you observed the reference counting collector.

Incremental garbage collection works very nicely in practice because the constant heap maintenance that an incremental manager performs provides enough breathing room for requests to be satisfied in real time.

I like to think of garbage collection as the inspection of a Marine Corps barracks at Parris Island. If you wait until the last minute to clean things up, break out some jelly because you are toast. The drill instructor is going to come storming in and read you the riot act for all of the details that you couldn't possibly have attended to in the 30 minutes you had to get your bunk in order. On the other hand, if you constantly keep your area neat and clean, it will be much easier to deal with the drill instructor when he arrives.

Garbage collection is the same way. Demanding allocations tend to occur when the memory manager can least afford to service them. It is Murphy's Law, plain and simple. By keeping the heap relatively organized at all times, those expensive allocation requests will not hurt as much. It will also allow the memory manager to guarantee service pauses within a certain time range.

Life Span Characteristics

Most applications have a set of objects that exist for the life span of an application and another set of temporal objects that blink in and out of existence. It makes sense, then, to have different storage areas and algorithms to deal with memory blocks that have different life spans. This tactic is known as *generational garbage collection*.

A generational memory manager breaks the heap into regions based on life span, known as *generations* (see Figure 5.15). The memory manager begins by allocating memory from the youngest generation.

When the youngest generation is exhausted, the memory manager will initiate garbage collection. Those memory blocks that survive collection over the course of several iterations will be moved to the next older generation. As this process continues, the memory blocks that survive will be filtered up to the older generations. Each time a generation's storage space is exhausted, the memory manager will garbage collect that generation and all the younger generations.

Most of the garbage collection and allocation activity ends up occurring in the younger storage areas of the heap. This leaves the older memory blocks in relative tranquility. It's like a college physics department: The young guys do all the work, and the old guys hang out and polish their awards.

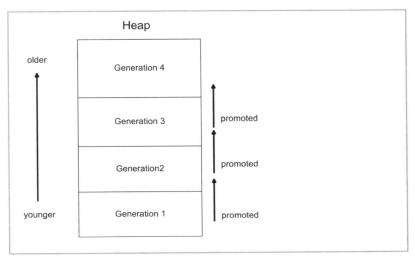

Figure 5.15

This means that because activity in the older generations is limited, slower algorithms that waste less memory can be used to track memory blocks in the older generations. On the other hand, speed should be the determining factor when choosing an algorithm to allocate and track memory in the younger generations.

Multithreaded Support

All the implementations presented in this book have been single-threaded; this was a conscious decision on my part in order to keep things simple so that you could focus on the main ideas. The handicap of using a single-threaded garbage collection scheme is that reclamation is done on the critical path of execution.

I think that most garbage collection implementations assume a multithreaded environment where there will be plenty of CPU cycles off the critical path. This allows the garbage collector to supposedly do its thing as a background thread while the rest of the program chugs merrily along. If you are interested in building a commercial-quality garbage collector, I would recommend that you consider a multithreaded approach.

There are two sides to every coin; such is the case with using threads. The first sacrifice you will typically make is portability. Every vendor seems to supply their own specially tweaked version, and you can expect to dedicate a significant portion of your development time porting your code to work on different operating systems.

Another pitfall of using threads is that it does not necessarily guarantee high performance. For example, let us assume you have a thread-enabled operating system that can perform thread switches at the kernel level so that each process table entry has fields to support one or more threads. Let us also assume that there are 100 processes running, and each process has five active threads (see Figure 5.16).

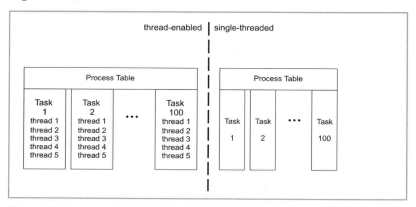

Figure 5.16

This places us in a situation where there are 500 distinct executing threads. Now imagine an operating system, which is not thread-enabled, that just has 100 running processes. On the thread-enabled operating system, a thread will have to potentially wait in line behind 499 other threads before it gets its chance to execute. On the thread-disabled machine, a process only has to share the processor with 99 other tasks, and each execution path will get a larger share of the processor's attention.

Is the thread-enabled system necessarily faster, or does it just give a programmer the ability to load down the operating system so that each thread actually gets less processor time?

NOTE I will admit that this is a somewhat stilted scenario. A fair comparison would be to compare an operating system scheduling 500 threads against an operating system scheduling 500 single-threaded tasks. In this scenario, the thread-enabled operating system would offer better performance.

My point is not that multithreading hurts performance. In fact, using threads can usually boost performance due to the lower relative overhead of the associated context switch. My point is that multithreading does not *guarantee* high performance (ha ha — always read the fine print). In a production environment, actual performance often has more to do with the hardware that an application is deployed on and the current load of tasks that the kernel is servicing than the architecture of a particular application. Performance has many independent variables, and an application's thread model is just one of those variables.

Chapter 6

Miscellaneous Topics

Suballocators

Normally, memory managers have to suffer through the slings and arrows of not knowing when or how much memory will be requested by an application. There are, however, some circumstances where you will know in advance how large an application's memory requests will be or how many there will be. If this is the case, you can construct a dedicated memory manager known as a *suballocator* to handle memory requests and reap tremendous performance gains.

A suballocator is an allocator that is built on top of another allocator. An example of where suballocators could be utilized is in a compiler. Specifically, one of the primary duties of a compiler is to build a *symbol table*. Symbol tables are memory-resident databases that serve as a repository for application data. They are typically built using a set of fixed-size structures. The fact that a symbol table's components are all fixed in size makes a compiler fertile ground for the inclusion of a suballocator. Instead of calling `malloc()` to allocate symbol table objects, you can allocate a large pool of memory and use a suballocator to allocate symbol table objects from that pool.

NOTE In a sense, all of the memory management implementations in this book are suballocators because they are built on top of the Window's `HeapAlloc()` function. Traditionally, however, when someone is talking about a suballocator, they are talking about a special-purpose application component that is implemented by the programmer and based on existing services provided by application libraries (like `malloc()` and `free()`).

To give you an example of how well suballocators function, I am going to offer a brief example. The following `SubAllocator` class manages a number of fixed-sized `Indices` structures in a list format. Each structure has a field called `FREE` to indicate if it has been allocated. When a request for a structure is made via the `allocate()` member function, the `SubAllocator` class will look for the first free structure in its list and return the address of that structure. To avoid having to traverse the entire list each time a request is made, a place marker named `lastAlloc` is used to keep track of where the last allocation was performed.

The basic mechanism involved in allocating an `Indices` structure is displayed in Figure 6.1.

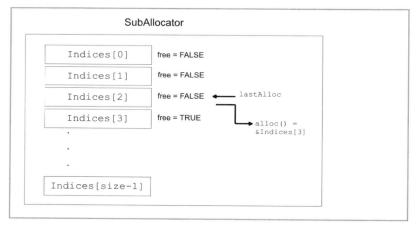

Figure 6.1

The following source code implements the `SubAllocator` class and a small test driver:

```
#include<windows.h>
#include<stdlib.h>
#include<stdio.h>

#define U4 unsigned long
#define U1 unsigned char

struct Indices
{
    U1 free;
    U4 index1;
    U4 index2;
    U4 index3;
};
```

```
class SubAllocator
{
    private:
    struct Indices *indices;
    U4 size;
    U4 lastAlloc;

    public:
    SubAllocator(U4 nElms);
    ~SubAllocator();
    struct Indices *alloc();
    void release(struct Indices *addr);
    void printList();
};

SubAllocator::SubAllocator(U4 nElms)
{
    U4 i;

    size = nElms;
    indices = (struct Indices*)malloc(size*(sizeof(struct
                Indices)));
    if(indices==NULL)
    {
        printf("SubAllocator::SubAllocator(%lu):",size);
        printf("could not allocate list\n");
        exit(1);
    }

    for(i=0;i<size;i++)
    {
        indices[i].free =TRUE;
    }

    lastAlloc = 0;
    return;

}/*end constructor--------------------------------------------*/

SubAllocator::~SubAllocator()
{
    free(indices);
    return;

}/*end destructor---------------------------------------------*/

struct Indices* SubAllocator::alloc()
{
    U4 i;
```

```
        if(lastAlloc==size-1){ lastAlloc=0; }

        for(i=lastAlloc;i<size;i++)
        {
            if(indices[i].free==TRUE)
            {
                indices[i].free=FALSE;
                lastAlloc = i;
                return(&indices[i]);
            }
        }

        for(i=0;i<lastAlloc;i++)
        {
            if(indices[i].free==TRUE)
            {
                indices[i].free=FALSE;
                lastAlloc = i;
                return(&indices[i]);
            }
        }
        return(NULL);

}/*end alloc------------------------------------------------*/

void SubAllocator::release(struct Indices *addr)
{
    //sanity check
    if((addr>=&indices[0])&&(addr<=&indices[size-1]))
    {
        (*addr).free=TRUE;
    }
    else
    {
        printf("SubAllocator::release():");
        printf("release failed, address out of bounds\n");
    }
    return;

}/*end release----------------------------------------------*/

void SubAllocator::printList()
{
    U4 i;
    for(i=0;i<size;i++)
    {
        if(indices[i].free==FALSE)
        {
            printf("indices[%lu] ",i);
            printf("[%lu, ",indices[i].index1);
            printf("%lu,",indices[i].index2);
```

Miscellaneous Topics

```
                printf("%lu]\n",indices[i].index3);
            }
            else
            {
                printf("indices[%lu]=FREE\n",i);
            }
        }
        return;

}/*end printList----------------------------------------------------*/

void main()
{
    U4 ticks1,ticks2;
    U4 nAllocations=1024;
    U4 i;
    SubAllocator *ptr;
    struct Indices **addr;

    ptr = new SubAllocator(nAllocations);
    addr = (struct Indices**)malloc(nAllocations*sizeof(struct
            Indices*));

    ticks1 = GetTickCount();

    for(i=0;i<nAllocations;i++)
    {
        addr[i] = (*ptr).alloc();
        if(addr[i]==NULL)
        {
            printf("addr[%lu]==NULL\n",i);
            exit(1);
        }
    }

    for(i=0;i<nAllocations;i++)
    {
        (*ptr).release(addr[i]);
    }

    ticks2 = GetTickCount();

    delete(ptr);
    free(addr);

    printf("msecs=%lu\n",ticks2-ticks1);

    return;

}/*end main--------------------------------------------------------*/
```

When this application is executed, the following output is produced:

```
msecs=0
```

The allocation and release of 1,024 `Indices` structures took *less than a millisecond*. This is obviously much faster than anything we have looked at so far.

The moral of this story: If you have predictable application behavior, you can tailor a memory manager to exploit that predictability and derive significant performance gains.

Monolithic Versus Microkernel Architectures

All of the operating systems that we looked at in Chapter 2 were *monolithic*, which is to say that all the components of the operating system (the task scheduler, the memory manager, the file system manager, and the device drivers) exist in a common address space and everything executes in kernel mode (at privilege level 0). In other words, a monolithic operating system behaves like one big program. UNIX, Linux, MMURTL, DOS, and Windows are all monolithic operating systems.

Another approach to constructing an operating system is to use a *microkernel* design. With a microkernel operating system, only a small portion of the operating system functions in kernel mode. Typically, this includes task scheduling, interrupt handling, low-level device drivers, and a message-passing subsystem to provide interprocess communication primitives. The rest of the operating system components, like the memory manager and the file system manager, run as separate tasks in user space and communicate with each other using the kernel's message passing facilities. MINIX, Mach, and Chorus are examples of microkernel operating systems.

The difference between monolithic and microkernel architectures is displayed in Figure 6.2.

The researchers supporting the microkernel school of thought claim that the enforcement of modular operating system components provides a cleaner set of interfaces. This characteristic, in turn, makes it easier to maintain and modify an operating system. Operating systems are often judged with regard to how well they accommodate change. The operating systems that tend to survive are the ones that are easy to extend and enhance. By allowing core

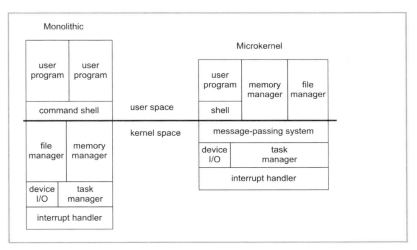

Figure 6.2

components to be separate tasks running at user level, different implementations can be switched in and out very easily.

Furthermore, microkernel proponents also claim that their approach provides better system stability. For example, if the memory manager is faced with a terminal error, instead of bringing down the entire operating system the memory management user task exists. This gives the microkernel the opportunity to recover gracefully from what might ordinarily be a disaster.

In the early 1990s, Torvalds and Tanenbaum became involved in a flame war. This well-known debate was initiated by Tanenbaum when he posted a message to `comp.os.minix` entitled "Linux is obsolete." In his original message, Tanenbaum mentioned:

> "Don't get me wrong, I am not unhappy with LINUX. It will get all the people who want to turn MINIX in BSD UNIX off my back. But in all honesty, I would suggest that people who want a **MODERN** "free" OS look around for a microkernel-based, portable OS, like maybe GNU or something like that."

"Modern" OS — my goodness that sounds a tad arrogant to me.

The resulting flame-fest progressed over several messages, each side attacking the other's logic and world view. Although Tanenbaum did raise some interesting points in his debate with Torvalds, history sides with Torvalds. MINIX has been relegated to a footnote in history and Linux has a user base of millions.

As I stated in Chapter 1, speed rules the commercial arena. Darwin's laws definitely apply to the software arena. Those operating systems that possess attributes that make them useful in production environments will be the ones that survive. The successful operating systems that are currently the big money makers for software vendors, like Microsoft, HP, Sun, and IBM, are monolithic (i.e., Windows, HP-UX, Solaris, and zOS).

One problem that plagues microkernel implementations is relatively poor performance. The message-passing layer that connects different operating system components introduces an extra layer of machine instructions. The machine instruction overhead introduced by the message-passing subsystem manifests itself as additional execution time. In a monolithic system, if a kernel component needs to talk to another component, it can make direct function calls instead of going through a third party.

NOTE A classic example of the performance hit associated with pushing functionality to user space is X Windows. Linux does not have a significant amount of user-interface code in the kernel. This affords Linux a modicum of flexibility because the kernel has not committed itself to any particular GUI implementation. Linux can run GNOME, KDE, and a number of other GUIs. The problem, however, is that everything happens in user space, and this entails a nasty performance hit. Windows, on the other hand, has pushed a hefty amount of the GUI management code down to the kernel, where interaction with hardware is more expedient. Specifically, most of Windows GUI code is contained in the `Win32k.sys` kernel mode device driver.

Security problems are another issue with microkernel designs. Because core operating system components exist in user space, they have less protection than the kernel. I imagine that it would be possible to subvert a given system manager by creating a duplicate task that hijacks the message stream between the kernel and the existing component. Microkernel advocates may also claim that their designs are more stable, but I doubt that an operating system could survive if its memory management unit called it quits.

Finally, most production operating system implementations are huge. According to a July 29, 1996, *Wall Street Journal* article, Windows NT 4.0 consists of over 16.5 million lines of code. I would speculate that Windows XP may very well have doubled that number. With a code base in the millions, I am not sure if the organizational benefits provided by a microkernel design would really make that much of a difference. On this scale, internal conventions and disciplined engineering would probably have a greater impact on maintainability.

In other words, it is not exactly what you are building but how you build it that makes the difference between success and failure.

Table 6.1 presents a comparison of monolithic and microkernel design approaches.

Table 6.1

	Monolithic	**Microkernel**
Maintainability	complicated interaction	marginally better
Stability	kernel errors lead to crash	questionable isolation of errors
Performance	faster	slower, messaging overhead
Security	everything in kernel mode	core components in user mode

Closing Thoughts

In 1965, an Intel Corporation co-founder named Gordon Moore suggested that the number of transistors in a processor would double every 18 months. This rule of thumb became known as *Moore's Law*. Moore's Law implies that the linear dimensions of a transistor are cut in half every three years (see Figure 6.3).

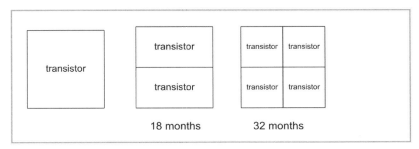

Figure 6.3

A micrometer is one-millionth of a meter:

$$1 \ \mu m = 10^{-6} m$$

The anthrax bacterium is 1 to 6 micrometers in length. A human hair is 100 micrometers in diameter. Most chips today have transistors that possess sub-micron dimensions.

A nanometer is one-thousandth of a micrometer:

$$1 \ nm = 10^{-9} m$$
$$= 1/1000 \ \mu m$$

The diameter of a hydrogen atom, in its ground state, is roughly one-tenth of a nanometer.

Solid-state physicists will tell you that an electron needs a path of about three atoms wide to move from one point to another. If the path width gets any smaller, quantum mechanics takes hold and the electron stops behaving in a predictable manner.

In 1989, Intel released the 80486 processor. The 80486 had transistors whose linear dimensions were 1 micrometer. Using 1989 as a starting point, let's see how long Moore's Law will last before it hits the three-atom barrier.

Table 6.2

Year	Size	Processor
1989	1 micrometer	Intel 80486 (1 micrometer)
1992	0.5	
1995	0.25	Pentium Pro (.35 micrometers)
1998	0.125	
2001	0.0625	Pentium 4 (.18 micrometers)
2004	0.03125	
2007	0.015625	
2010	0.0078125	
2013	0.00390625	
2016	0.001953125	
2019	0.000976563	
2022	0.000488281	

According to Moore's Law, the length of a transistor will be about 4.88×10^{-10} meters by the year 2022. This corresponds to a path width that is roughly four hydrogen atoms across. As you can see from the third column, Intel has made valiant attempts at trying to keep up. However, nobody has really been able to sustain the pace set by Moore's Law. In 2001, Moore's Law says that we should have had transistors whose design rule was .06 micrometers. In 2001, Intel's top-of-the-line Pentium 4 had a design rule of .18 micrometers. Vendors that say they are staying abreast of Moore's Law are really cheating by making their chips larger. This tactic increases the total number of transistors, but it doesn't increase the transistor density per unit length.

Once the wall is hit, there is really nothing that we will be able to do (short of changing the laws of physics) to shrink transistors. The only way to increase the number of transistors in a processor will be to make the processor larger. The party will be over for the processor manufacturers. Hardware people will no longer be able to have their cake and eat it too. Businesses that want to increase the horsepower of their information systems may have to revert back to room-sized computers.

In the beginning, algorithms and the people who worked with them were valued highly because the hardware of the day was often inadequate for the problems that it faced. Take the Bendix G-15, for example, which had 2,160 words of magnetic drum memory in 1961. In order to squeeze every drop of performance out of a machine, you needed to be able to make efficient use of limited resources. Program size was typically the biggest concern. If instructions existed in more than one spot, they were consolidated into a procedure. This meant that the execution path of a task tended to spend a lot of time jumping around memory. I remember two Control Data engineers telling me about how they simulated an entire power grid in southern California using less than 16KB of memory.

> **NOTE** In 2002, with the advent of 256MB SDRAM chips and 512KB L2 caches, program size is not such a pressing concern. Program speed is the new focal issue. This has led to an inversion of programming techniques. Instead of placing each snippet of redundant code in its own function, developers have begun to deliberately insert redundant instructions. For example, inline functions can be used to avoid the overhead of setting up an activation record and jumping to another section of code.

When Moore's Law meets the laws of physics, the computer industry will once again be forced to look for better solutions that are purely software-based, primarily because all the other alternatives will be more expensive. One positive result of this is that the necessity to improve performance will drive the discovery of superior algorithms. Computer science researchers may see a new heyday.

The demise of Moore's Law may also herald the arrival of less desirable developments. Lest you forget, major technical advances, such as radar and nuclear energy, were first put to use as weapons of war. Potential abuse of technology has already surfaced, even in this decade. At Super Bowl XXXV, hundreds of people involuntarily took part in a virtual lineup performed by Face Recognition Software. Is there a reason why people who wish to watch a football game need to be treated like suspects in a criminal case? Why was the public only informed about the use of this software after the game had occurred?

This is just the beginning. Artificial intelligence programs will eventually be just as sophisticated and creative as humans. To a certain extent, they already are. In 1997, an IBM RS/6000 box named Deep Blue conquered the world chess champion, Garry Kasparov, in a six-game tournament. I was there when it happened (well, sort of). I was huddled with an Intel 80486 the afternoon of the final game, reading a "live" transcript of the match via an IBM Java applet. For a more graphic example of AI progress, try playing against the bots of Id Software's Quake 3. You would be impressed with how wily and human those bots seem.

As the capabilities of hardware and software ramp upward, the surveillance that we saw at the Super Bowl will give way to something more insidious: behavior prediction and modification. The credit bureaus and various other quasi-governmental agencies already collect volumes of data on you. Imagine all of this data being fed into a computer that could consolidate and condense the information into some kind of elaborate behavioral matrix. If you can simulate someone's behavior, you can make statistical inferences about their future behavior. Furthermore, if you can predict what someone is going to do, you can also pre-empt their behavior in an effort to control them. There could be software built that less-than-scrupulous leaders could use to implement social engineering on a national scale. Indoctrination does not have to assume the overt façade that Huxley or Bradbury depicted. It can be streamed in subliminally through a number of seemingly innocuous channels.

"We are the middle children of history, raised by television to believe that someday we'll be millionaires and movie stars and rock stars, but we won't."
— Tyler Durden

As time passes, these kinds of issues will present themselves. It is our responsibility to identify them and take constructive action. The problem with this is that the capacity to recognize manipulation does not seem, to me, to be a highly valued trait. The ability to think independently is not something that I was taught in high school. If anything, most public schools present a sanitized version of *civic education*. Not that this matters much, but most people don't start asking questions until the world stops making sense.

Nevertheless, if we sit idle while the thought police install their telescreens, we may end up like Charles Forbin, slaves to a massive and well-hidden machine.

"In time, you will come to regard me with not only awe and respect, but love."
— Colossus, speaking to Charles Forbin in *Colossus: The Forbin Project* (1969)

Index

.COM executable, 129-130
1-bit reference counting, 282, 304
8042 keyboard controller, 36
8088, 46

A
A20 address gate, 36
activation record, 138
address, 9
address line, 9
Adler, Mike, xi
ALGOL, 181
algorithms, trade-offs, xvii
Allen, Woody, 59
Anderson, Tom, 152
ANSI time routines, 213
arm-waving, 2
assembly language, 169
atomic operations, 36
automatic memory management, 160
automatic memory managers, 281
AX, 6-7

B
Backus, John, 177
Bell Labs, xxiv
big red switch, 102
big-endian, 136
binary search tree (BST), 225
bit, 4
    clear, 22, 225
    set, 22, 225
bitmap.cpp, 232
bitmapped memory management, 225
Bletchley Park, xiv
block of code, 144
block-based languages, 169
Blue Screen of Death (BSOD), 101

Boehm-Demers-Weiser (BDW) Conservative Garbage Collector, 158, 161
bondage-discipline programming language, 181
Borland Turbo C, xiii, 40, 135
bottom of memory, 9
BP, 6, 15
Brey, Barry, xi
brk(), 159
Brooks, Mel, 1
buffer overflow exploit, 88
BugTraq, 92
Burgess, Richard, 59
BX, 15
byte, 4

C
C programming language, 184
    disadvantages of, 192
    history of, xxiv, 184
cache memory, 5, 7
Cfront, xxiii
Chemical Rubber Company (CRC), xv
cleared bit, 22, 225
clock(), 213
clone, 46, 153
COBOL, 171
    ANSI standards, 173
    divisions, 173
    Fujitsu compiler, 173
    lines in existence, 171
    versus assembler, 175
code section, 129, 134
Colossus, xiv
Common Business Oriented Language, *see* COBOL
compiler-based memory allocation, 128-129

355

Index

conforming code segment, 22
conservative garbage collection, 306
constructors, 333
control bus, 10
Control Data Corporation
    CDC 3300, 3
    CDC 6600, 3
conventional memory, 48
copying garbage collector, 282, 331
CP/M, 46
CR0-CR4, 6, 25, 30-31
Cray, Seymour, 3
CS, 6, 16, 32
Cutler, Dave, 93, 96
CX, 15

D
dangling pointer, 158
data bus, 10
data section, 129, 132
DDR SDRAM, 4
debug, writing boot sectors, 41-42
Deep Blue, 353
deferred reference counting, 282, 304
demand-paged virtual memory, 63
destructors, 333
DI, 15
Digital Equipment Corporation (DEC), 93
Dijkstra, 169
dirty bit, 30
disaster recovery, xxvi
disk I/O, performance cost, 8
disk operating system (DOS), 46
    autoexec.bat, 48
    COMMAND.COM, 47
    config.sys, 47-48
    extender, 56
    extender, DJGPP, 57
    interrupt replacement, 52
    IO.SYS, 47
    memory usage statistics, 49-50
    MSDOS.SYS, 47
    Protected Mode Interface (DPMI), 57
    video driver, 50
disk storage, 5, 7
Distributed Network Architecture (DNA), 60
DOS/4G, 57

Double Data Rate Synchronous Dynamic Random Access Memory, *see* DDR SDRAM
double word, 4
double fault, 1
DRAM, 3
driver.cpp, 241, 261, 285, 307
DS, 6, 15-16, 32
Dunfield, Dave, 40
Durden, Tyler, 354
DX, 15
dynamic memory, 128-129
Dynamic Random Access Memory, *see* DRAM

E
EAX, 6-7
EBP, 6-7
EBX, 6-7
ECX, 6-7
EDI, 6-7
Edwards, Dan, 161
EDX, 6-7
EFLAGS, 6-7
EIP, 6-7
EMM386.EXE, 27, 41
Enhanced Synchronous Dynamic Random Access Memory, *see* ESDRAM
ENIAC, xiv
Enigma, xiv
ES, 6, 16, 32
ESDRAM, 4
ESI, 6-7
ESP, 6-7
Executable and Linkable Format (ELF), 84
execution time, 212
expand down segment, 22
expanded memory, 48
Expanded Memory Specification (EMS), 48
explicit memory management, 157
extended memory, 48
eXtensible Memory Specification (XMS), 57
external fragmentation, 156

F
Face Recognition Software, 353
Fermi, Enrico, xiii, 45
ferrite core memory, xiv

Index

Feynman, Dick, xv
FIFO, 110
FLAGS, 15
flat memory model, 31
Flowers, Tommy, xiv
FLOW-MATIC, 171
Forbin, Charles, xiv, 354
formal parameter, 146
FORTRAN, 177
    ANSI standards, 178
    program organization, 180
free(), 128, 157-158
FS, 6, 16
function epilogue, 139
function prologue, 138

G
garbage, 281
garbage collection, 160
    collectors, 281
    comparable performance, 164
Gates, Bill, 5, 18, 46, 93
GDT, 20
GDTR, 6
generating random numbers, 215
generational garbage collector, 338
GetProcessHeap(), 111
GetTickCount(), 214
gigabyte, 5
Global Descriptor Table, *see* GDT
Global Descriptor Table Register, *see* GDTR
global variable, 146
Gosling, James, 192
GS, 6, 16

H
handles versus addresses, 335
heap, 129, 132, 137
    allocation, 151
HeapAlloc(), 111
HeapFree(), 111
HeapReAlloc(), 111
Heisenberg's Uncertainty Principle, xvi
Hennessey, John, 212
HIMEM.SYS, 58
Hopper, Grace Murray, 171
human computers, xv

I
IDTR, 6
incremental garbage collection, 302
Intel Corporation, xi, xvi, 1, 6, 11, 13
internal fragmentation, 156
International Business Machines (IBM) 705, xiv
Interrupt Service Routine (ISR), 52
interrupt vector table (IVT), 48, 52
inverse transform method, 218
IP, 15, 37

J
Java, 193
    application memory management, 195
    explicit pointers, 193
    heap, 195
    method area, 195
    multiple inheritance, 193
    naming scheme, 193
    operator overloading, 193
    thread, program counter, 195
    thread, stack, 195
    threads, 195
    versus C++, 194
    Java virtual machine (JVM), 195
Java virtual machine specification, 195, 201
javap, 198-199

K
K&R C, xxiv
Kasparov, Garry, 353
kernel mode driver, 46, 100
Kernighan, Brian, xxiv, 184
Kilby, Jack, xvi
kilobyte, 5

L
L1 cache, 7
L2 cache, 7
language complexity threshold, 170
latency, 156
LDT, 20
LDTR, 6, 20-21
Lee, David M., xv
Lee, Stan, xxvi
Lehmer, Dick, 219
LeMarchand cube, 45
LGDTR, 37, 202

Index

linear address, 19, 27, 34
linear address space, 63
    versus physical address space, 33-34
Linear Congruential Generator (LCG), 218
LINPACK benchmark, 223
Linux
    design goals, 68
    memory allocation, 76
    memory usage, 81
    page fault handling, 76
    paging, 72
    segmentation, 69
LISP, 161
little-endian, 136
Loadable Kernel Module (LKM), 84
Local Descriptor Table, *see* LDT
Local Descriptor Table Register, *see* LDTR
local variable allocation
    additional stack frames, 149
    all-at-once, 146
    comparison, 149
local variable, 145
locked page, 75
logical address, 33-34
LRU, 110

M

main memory, 3
malloc(), ii, 128, 157-158
mallocV1.cpp, 239
mallocV2.cpp, 260
mallocV3.cpp, 274
mallocV4.cpp, 287
mallocV5.cpp, 309
manual versus automatic memory
    management, 157
mark-compact garbage collector, 282
mark-sweep garbage collector, 282, 304
Matkovitz, George, xi
McCarthy, John, 161
McNealy, Scott, 192
megabyte, 5
memmgr.cpp, 236, 251, 267, 289, 312
memory hierarchy, 5
memory leak, 83, 157
memory management
    mechanism versus policy, 1
    summary, 202

memory protection, 11
    brute force assault, 83
Message-based MUltitasking Real-Time
    kerneL, *see* MMURTL
Meyer, Bertrand, 160
MFLOPS, 212
MICRO-C, 40, 52, 125
microkernel operating system, 348
micrometer, 351
MINIX, 67
MIPS, 212
MMURTL, 59
    design goals, 59
    memory allocation, 66
    paging, 64
    segmentation, 61
monolithic operating system, 348
Moore, Gordon, 352
Moore's Law, 352

N

NACHOS operating system, 152
nanometer, 351
Naughton, Patrick, 192
newFree(), 208
newMalloc(), 208
non-local program jumps, 56
null segment selector, 32

O

octal word, 5
online transaction processing (OLTP), vxiii
OpenBSD, 91

P

paging, 26
    page, 34
    page directory, 27
    page directory entry, 27
    page fault, 28
    page frame, 34
    page table, 27
    page table entry, 35
    paging as protection, 31
paragraph, 5, 174
Pascal, 181
Paterson, Tim, 46
Patterson, David, 117
PC DOS 2000, 92

Index

Pentium Processor
   lineage, 13
   modes of operation, 14
   physical address space, 9, 14
   registers, 7, 15
perform.cpp, 241, 288, 311
petabyte, 5
Phar Lap DOS extender, 57
physical address, 33-34
Physical Address Extension (PAE), 9, 31, 97
physical address space, 9, 14
   versus linear address space, 33-34
pmon.exe, 114
Podanoffsky, Mike, xxiv
POP instruction, 136
Portable Operating System Interface, 68-69, 159
primary storage, 3
process working set, 107
protected mode, 18
   paging, 26
   paging address resolution, 27
   paging implied bits, 27-28
   segment descriptor, 19-20
   segment descriptor table, 19-20
   segment selector, 19-20
   segment types, 22
   segmentation, 19
protection violation exception, 25
pseudorandom numbers, 218
PUSH instruction, 136
pviewer.exe, 114

Q
quad word, 5

R
RAM, 3
Rambus Dynamic Random Access Memory, *see* RDRAM
Random Access Memory, *see* RAM
RDRAM, 4
real mode, 14
   address lines, 15
   addressing, 16
   boot process, 41
   memory protection, 17
   offset address, 15
   registers, 15
   segment address, 16
   segment address implied bits, 17
realloc(), 158
reference counting, 283
   counting tests, 299
   implementation, 284
   theory, 283
   tradeoffs, 302
reference cycle, 302
register, 7, 15
replacement policy,
   first-in first-out (FIFO), 110
   least recently used (LRU), 110
response time, 212
rings of protection, 23
Ritchie, Dennis, xxiv, 184
run of bits, 226

S
sandboxing, 2
Schindler, John, xvii
Schreiber, Sven, 124, 154
scope, 144
SDRAM, 3
SecurityFocus, 92
seed, 219
segment, 11
segmentation, 19
segregated lists, 265
semaphores, 36
sequential fit, 248
set bit, 22, 225
SI, 15
simple reference counting, 282
slab allocator, 78
slide rules, xv
SP, 15
SRAM, 4
SS, 15
stack, 136
   frame, 138
   frame pointer, 139
Standard Performance Evaluation Corporation (SPEC), 223
static memory, 128
Static Random Access Memory, *see* SRAM
storage-versus-speed trade-off, 279
Stroustrup, Bjarne, xxii

Index

structured programming, 169
suballocator, 343
symbol table, 343
Symbolics, 161
Synchronous Dynamic Random Access Memory, *see* SDRAM
system call gate, 154
system call interface, 203
system management mode, 14
system working set, 107

T
Tanenbaum, Andrew, 152, 349
Tenberry Software, 57
terabyte, 5
Terminate and Stay Resident program (TSR), 49
Thompson, Ken, xxiv, 184
thrashing, 28
three-finger salute, 115
three-level paging, 72
thunking, 118
time, 212
time(), 213
top of memory, 9
Torvalds, Linus, 67
TR, 6, 21
tracing, 281
tree.cpp, 227
triple fault, 1
typographic conventions, xxii

U
Unics, 184
UNIX, 184
upper memory blocks, 48

V
Video Random Access Memory, *see* VRAM
virtual 8086 mode, 14
Virtual Control Program Interface (VCPI), 57
virtual memory, 1, 7, 26, 63
virtual-paged memory, 63
volatile storage, 3
VRAM, 4, 50, 76-77

W
wall clock time, 212
Windows, 92
    Address Windowing Extensions (AWE), 97
    Checked Build, 100
    Demand Paging, 109
    disabling paging, 117
    family tree, 95
    free/reserved/committed memory, 105
    kernel debugger, 99
    kernel debugger host, 100
    kernel debugger target, 100
    kernel memory, 98
    kernel memory dump, 101
    kernel mode/user mode, 97
    locked memory pool, 112
    lock-aside list, 112
    memory allocation, 110
    memory map, 96
    memory protection, 108
    memory usage statistics, 114
    Page Frame Number Database (PFN), 107
    paged memory pool, 112
    paging, 105
    segmentation, 99
Wirth, Nicklaus, 181
word, 4
working set, 107

Z
Zorn, Benjamin, 164, 205

Looking for more?

Check out Wordware's market-leading Windows Programming/Development and Web Programming/Development Libraries featuring the following new releases.

Search Engine Optimization with WebPosition Gold 2
1-55622-924-0 • $49.95
7½ x 9¼ • 360 pp.

Search Engine Positioning
1-55622-804-X • $49.95
7½ x 9¼ • 576 pp.

RoboHelp for the Web
1-55622-954-2 • $49.95
7½ x 9¼ • 448 pp.

Look for these developer libraries and more from Wordware

Game Developer's Library featuring:

JBuilder Library featuring:

Direct3D ShaderX Vertex and Pixel Shader Tips and Tricks
1-55622-041-3 • $59.95
7½ x 9¼ • 520 pp.

Charles Calvert's Learn JBuilder 7
1-55622-330-7 • $59.95
7½ x 9¼ • 700 pp.

Virtual Machine Design and Implementation in C/C++
1-55622-903-8 • $59.95
7½ x 9¼ • 688 pp.

Visit us online at **www.wordware.com** for more information. Use the following coupon code for online specials:

memory3471

Companion Files

The source code for most of the examples in this book is provided in a downloadable file available at www.wordware.com/memory.

When the file is unzipped, it will be organized into two folders: deploy and meta-inf. The source code in the deploy folder is divided into subfolders named for the chapters.